HUMAN SERVICES COORDINATION

HUMAN SERVICES COORDINATION

A Panel Report and Accompanying Papers

Edited by Harold Orlans

Published in association with
the Council of State Governments
and the National Academy of Public Administration

Pica Special Studies

PICA PRESS

New York

Published in the United States of America in 1982 by
PICA PRESS
Distributed by Universe Books
381 Park Avenue South, New York, N.Y. 10016

82 83 84 85 86/10 9 8 7 6 5 4 3 2 1

Printed in the United States of America

Library of Congress Cataloging in Publication Data
Main entry under title:

Human services coordination.

    Contents: Administrative issues in improving the
provision of human services / David M. Austin—Coordinating services for children / John Mudd—Coordinating
services for the elderly / Robert Morris—[etc.]
    1. Social work administration—United States—Addresses,
essays, lectures. I. Orlans, Harold, 1921-
HV91.H77   1982   361'.0068   82-8357
ISBN 0-87663-734-9 (Universe Books)   AACR2

Contents

Tables

Charts

FOREWORD

In the spring of 1980, the Council of State Governments and the National Academy of Public Administration sponsored a series of four regional meetings at which the practical and professional problems of coordinating human services for children and the elderly were discussed. The Council assumed primary responsibility for the conference arrangements and invitations, while an Academy panel commissioned seven background papers and set the agenda for the meetings.

This report presents the text of those papers and an introduction that reviews the background of the project and summarizes the conclusions drawn by the panel from the conferences and its own discussions.

We are grateful to the Ford Foundation for a grant that enabled this project to be conducted; to William J. Page, Jr., former executive director of the Council, who helped to initiate it; to panel cochairmen Mitchell Ginsberg and William Stewart and the other panel members named in the Introduction for their leadership in planning and conducting the meetings; and to some two hundred public and private officials, scholars, and human service professionals for their participation in the meetings. Thomas Lehner at the Council and Harold Orlans at the Academy served as joint staff directors for this project.

Frank Bailey, Executive Director,
Council of State Governments

George H. Esser, President,
National Academy of Public Administration

INTRODUCTION

The Academy's current interest in the coordination of human services began in 1977 when a panel chaired by Wayne Anderson, executive director of the Advisory Commission on Intergovernmental Relations, evaluated the Florida Department of Health and Rehabilitative Services at the request of its secretary, William J. Page, Jr. The department had been reorganized at the initiative of the legislature in a 1975 statute that put eight independent health, social, and rehabilitative programs under common management in both the capital and eleven districts—the most comprehensive and radical experiment in services integration undertaken by any state government. Despite the resultant turmoil and dislocation, the panel's 1977 report, *Reorganization in Florida: How is Services Integration Working?*, endorsed the reorganization as a pioneering venture promising to improve the quality and accessibility of client services.

However, the panel recognized that few states were likely to copy the Florida model. Many professional and advocacy groups opposed it; the categorical nature of federal funding and of the provision—even the conception—of most services posed additional obstacles. Therefore the panel sought to learn more about the approaches other states had employed to coordinate independent programs, especially at the local level where citizens receive government-funded services from governmental and private agencies.

A grant from the Ford Foundation, which had also supported the Florida study, enabled the Academy to establish a new panel to conduct this broad inquiry. It included three members who had served on the Florida panel: Wayne Anderson and, serving as cochairmen, Mitchell Ginsberg, dean of the School of Social Work,

Columbia University, and William Stewart, acting head, Department of Public Health and Preventive Medicine, Louisiana State University Medical Center. The other members were Robert Ball, scholar-in-residence, Institute of Medicine; Mary Jane England, commissioner of the Massachusetts Department of Social Services; Jean Harris, secretary of the Virginia Department of Human Resources; T. M. (Jim) Parham, professor, School of Social Work, University of Georgia; Harold A. Richman, professor, School of Social Service Administration, University of Chicago; and John H. Romani, professor, Department of Health Planning and Administration, University of Michigan School of Public Health.

In cooperation with the Council of State Government, four regional meetings were held in April and May 1980 in Atlanta, Boston, Chicago, and Seattle. Participants included officials of public and private agencies responsible for state and local human service programs, academic authorities, and representatives of constituency, provider, and advocacy groups. They were asked to discuss issues involved in coordinating health, mental health, and social services for children and the elderly; to review significant developments and examples of coordination; and to suggest how coordination might best be fostered in a period of economic duress. Seven papers were commissioned: one on the status of human services coordination in each of four regions; two on the coordination of services for children and the elderly, respectively; and one on administrative issues confronted by efforts at coordination. The present report contains the text of these papers.

The words "integration" and "coordination" of services are often used interchangeably. However, our panel has assigned a different meaning to each. By "integration," we mean the concerting of two or more services provided by an agency headed by an official with budgetary and administrative authority over all the services. By "coordination," we mean the concerting of services provided by autonomous agencies.

Both "integration" and "coordination" can utilize the same devices; the key distinction is that in "integration," they can be prescribed by higher administrative authority, whereas in "coordination," they are employed voluntarily or by mutual agreement or contract. The devices often employed include the common location of services; identical service districts; common or shared administrative and transportation services; common client intake and referral procedures; common or compatible eligibility rules; a common system of recording and exchanging information about

services to the same client or family; common, collaborative, or mutually informed diagnosis and case management; linked, complementary, or interrelated services; and central or comparable planning, budgeting, financing, evaluation, and accounting for different services. The use of case managers to shepherd clients and monitor their performance through the maze of services received perhaps the widest acceptance at our meetings.

We cite devices which can directly affect the nature of client services, because our main focus in these discussions has been on the client. However, coordination can be pursued in Washington and state capitals as well as in communities and neighborhoods. David Austin notes that coordination can proceed at several levels in the administrative pyramid—the "policy management," "program administration," and "case service" levels—and that these levels are so loosely coupled that client services can be coordinated at the bottom without any notable coordination at the top; vice versa, coordination at the top, as in the formation of the amalgamated federal Department of Health, Education, and Welfare or state departments of human services, may produce no visible change in local service arrangements.

During the 1960s and early 1970s, "umbrella" departments embracing various health, mental health, and social service programs were formed in many states; subsequently, a counter-trend to dismember some departments has developed. In retrospect, the promises and expectations that a single state secretariat could coordinate the local services financed or provided by discrete federal and state programs, each with its own mission and doctrine, budget and regulations, staff, providers, and clients, now seem excessively naive.

No department encompasses all necessary services and, if it did, the problems of interdepartmental coordination would merely become intradepartmental. Many internal committees seek, with varied success, to coordinate the research of the separate National Institutes of Health. It is said that the Office of the HEW Secretary, which was supposed to coordinate the activities of that massive department, grew so large and complex that it was itself in need of coordination.

Specialization is necessary for good service—a podiatrist and a pediatrician, an ophthalmologist and an obstetrician are not interchangeable—and will and should be perpetuated in any administrative reorganization. No matter how far services coordination and integration may go, specialized services and programs must be preserved if there are to be meaningful services to coordinate. As Alfred Kahn and Sheila Kamerman write:

Nobody seriously believes that medical, correctional, income maintenance, and child abuse intake—to pick a few examples—can be unified at the case level and that one generalist can take on continued service and case accountability . . . for all of these. Such an approach runs counter to existing political and professional trends and interests, and would in all likelihood be doomed from the start. Moreover, and no less important, no one worker, faced with the diversity and complexity of individual needs and requests could possibly manage the array of knowledge and technology required across all human services systems.

The concentration on access, case management, co-location of independent units, management information systems, rather than on truly integrated local service delivery is no accident. Integration cannot seriously mean one unspecialized delivery system for all human services.[1]

Specialization can also be overdone; in medicine and social work, in graduate and professional education, we can have too many specialists and not enough generalists. Educating more generalists and educating the members of related professions to understand and work collaboratively with neighboring professions (psychiatrists with psychologists and social workers, doctors with nurses and social workers) is one basic way to coordinate services.

The amalgamation of independent programs into a single department, John Dempsey observes, is only one of many means by which coordination is pursued by state government: Interagency councils and committees, government-wide information, planning, evaluation, and above all budgeting processes play their part. Central government administrative and policy offices such as those of the governor, the budget, revenue, and personnel, are natural promoters of program coordination and policy conformity. Sitting high above the horde of specialized programs and services, each of which proclaims its uniqueness, they see the common features of, and seek comparable information and performance from, disparate programs to fulfill their own responsibilities of monitoring, management, evaluation, and policy direction. Yet their responsibilities are so broad, they must deal with these programs in broad terms, not in terms of the individual transactions between a citizen and a public employee or private professional. The information that filters up to them from the ranks is dated and systematized, drained of life and individuality, and the instructions which they issue, based on that information, can be as irrelevant to events in the field as (in *War and Peace)* are Napoleon's orders to his troops engaged in battle.

We should have a clear and realistic idea of what coordination is possible within and between bureaucracies, be they governmental or private, large or small, distant or local, if we are to attain what is attainable and then recognize and sustain it. Too often, services coordination and especially services integration represent a utopian ideal in which separate bureaucracies, programs, and professions are somehow melded into a smooth-functioning, frictionless whole like a harmonious family or community. That is a splendid ideal, but ideal conditions are hard to attain or sustain. A more realistic (albeit still difficult) goal for coordination is the ability to utilize available community resources, regardless of their geographic or organizational location, to meet a client's needs.

A residential institution—a hospital, nursing home or home for the aged, for orphans, delinquents, retarded, the handicapped, or mentally disturbed—must be relatively self-contained, providing all the services necessary to sustain life. Since it is directed by one administrator, its services are, by our definition, integrated. That integration is expensive, requiring a heavy capital investment in buildings, plant, and equipment, and a large staff, with diverse specialists, to operate it and care for the residents 24 hours a day. However, it is also convenient and efficient, since both patients and services are housed together and one need not bring services to house-bound patients or require clients to visit, and wait at, several locations to receive them.

It might be said that coordinative mechanisms aim to replace, in a normal home and community setting, the more expensive and comprehensive arrangements by which necessary services are provided to residents of an institution. The need for effective coordination has been accentuated by the process of deinstitutionalization which has moved many residents of institutions for the disturbed, handicapped, or retarded back into the community. As Barbara Blum points out, a court may order patients discharged from a mental hospital (administered by a department of mental health) before adequate provision can be made (by a department of social services) for their housing and care.

At our meetings, the emphasis of government programs on institutional care and their relative neglect of services in the home and community was repeatedly deplored. Robert Morris stresses the importance of balancing the government's institutional "bias" with expanded programs to serve the elderly in their homes and neighborhoods. Such programs are less traumatic than institutionalization and cheaper, a clear advantage in a period of austerity. The greater use of volunteers, self-help, "natural" groups

and networks, and reimbursement or tax incentives to family members and neighbors to care for persons who might otherwise be institutionalized were discussed by conferees. However, the difficulties of each course were recognized. Volunteers can threaten the income and authority of professionals; "natural" groups can become formalized and bureaucratized when recognized and financed by the government; and since community care will be added to institutional care, its relative economy will nonetheless increase the total cost of services.

Some management enthusiasts put great reliance on computerized data systems to link clients to services, keep track of available beds in institutions and the community, and provide data necessary to evaluate and improve services. But, as Dempsey observes, such systems are "very time consuming and expensive." So are most, or many other, techniques of coordination. Professional staff often charge that coordination takes money away from direct service. But professional staff must also maintain client information and record systems—"direct" services cannot be provided without them; even doctors or psychologists in private practice must exchange information and coordinate their work with insurers, hospitals, and other institutions and agencies. *Some* information and *some* coordination are inescapable and necessary: The question is how *much* and what *kind,* and *who* shall collect the information and do the coordinating. As Mitchell Ginsberg remarked at our meetings, every profession is prepared to coordinate its activities with those of allied professions if *it* does the coordinating; and no profession wants to *be* coordinated.

Federal block grants have been suggested as a means to consolidate categorical programs and enable state and local governments to allocate funds as local conditions warrant. But categorical programs were often instituted to ensure that neglected groups—the poor, minorities, handicapped persons, children, or the elderly—received more resources than previously, and many groups fear that they will lose ground under a block grant system. Such a system would move the locus of political conflict from Washington to state capitals and city halls, and groups which are well-organized nationally but not in many states and regions could be hurt by it.

Reagan administration proposals would radically alter many human service programs and the relations between the governmental and private agencies which finance, administer, and/or provide them. Many categorical programs would be consolidated into block grants; the level of federal funding, detailed federal reg-

ulations, and direct federal financing of local government programs would be markedly reduced. State governments would have greater discretion to allocate block funds, to set program standards, and to finance or discontinue many services. Though the administration is ideologically committed to the private sector, its budget cuts will reduce the number of private service providers as well as federal program staff.

In 1981, 62 federal categorical programs were eliminated and another 77 consolidated into nine block grants in education, mental health, health, social and community services, and other program areas. In January 1982, the administration proposed that the federal government bear the full cost of Medicaid and that the states bear the full cost of food stamps and Aid to Families of Dependent Children (AFDC). In subsequent years, the administration would turn over to the states responsibility for administering and financing many other programs.

Because they have been accompanied by major funding reductions, these proposals have been strongly opposed by categorical program constituencies and state government representatives who might otherwise favor them. Hinging financing on state, rather than federal, revenues will reduce per capita expenditures in poor or conservative states; the probable influx of clients will place added burdens on states with high per capita expenditures.

Regardless of the funding level, many believe, on both philosophical and practical grounds, that the federal government should be especially responsible for income support programs. If these programs are morally right and socially necessary, then they are right and necessary for all who need them, not just for those who live in certain states.

Whatever may be the fate of the Reagan administration's attempt to shift authority and taxing power from the federal to state governments, the volume of block grants, the discretion of state agencies, and the pressure to economize are likely to grow. These trends will render the fuller coordination of available services more urgent and will give state governments greater freedom, incentive, and power to promote it.

Aside from governmental officials with broad policy or managerial responsibilities, the constituency for coordination is widely dispersed. Many clients would benefit from readier access to multiple services. Nonetheless, client groups, like professional groups, tend to be organized along categorical lines. As taxpayers, citizens may support, whereas as advocates, they may well oppose economizing consequences of coordination. In Florida, there were some

signs that services integration operated to equalize per capita resources devoted to various services, raising those which had previously been below average and reducing those which had been above average. Therefore, services and clients which may benefit from such an effect—broadly speaking, services provided by more lowly-paid staff—should favor integration while those which may lose should oppose it. Doctors, psychologists, and vocational rehabilitators have strongly opposed it.

Can advocates of at least some categorical programs recognize that, in a period of financial stringency, the coordination of local programs can be in their common interests and join forces to promote it? Our meetings explored that possibility, but the results were inconclusive. In the Midwest, there was a positive hostility to the idea; in other regions, it had a more favorable reception. John Mudd of the Children's Defense League spoke forcefully for a selective kind of coordination focused on the specific needs of specific client groups: "efforts to improve coordination must flow from strong policy commitments to deal with specific problems, and their impact must be rigorously assessed. Coordination can be critically important for millions of children, but it must be brought down to earth."

We agree. If there is one conclusion we would draw from our discussions, it is that an ounce of measurable coordination, drawing together two separate staffs and services which should work together—like the discharge service of a mental hospital or nursing home and the community placement service of a social welfare department—is worth a pound of generalized talk about the immeasurable value of coordination. Excessive expectations can produce excessive disappointments; modest but clearly defined measures can produce demonstrable, if modest, gains. Even a demonstrable failure can be more useful than an equivocal outcome, as one then knows what *not* to do.

The persistent appeal of services coordination and integration, despite the failures and limited success of many efforts to achieve it, Janet Weiss suggests, is due to its symbolic value. "The symbol epitomizes widely shared social values of rationality, comprehensiveness, and efficiency, thus reinforcing public confidence in the role of reason in policy making." But, at a more concrete level, coordination can mean so many different and even contradictory things that they cannot all be achieved together:

> Programs billed as coordination or integration of services have attempted to accomplish not only better coordination among service

providers but also comprehensiveness, accountability to clients, accountability to government, accessibility, administrative efficiency, improved participation by clients, communication among providers, and innumerable other worthy objectives. . . . From the public point of view, coordination simplifies the problems in human services by implying that the worst problems are merely administrative and that improvements in service quality will follow automatically once the organizational questions are resolved.[2]

The criticism or warning is sound. If some proponents claim too much for coordination, they will achieve too few of their claims. Better administration and coordination of human services is an important goal, but the best administration cannot overcome the limitations of resources, of professional knowledge and ability, of our social and human condition.

The provision and locus of health, mental health, and social services has changed profoundly during the last two decades, William Stewart points out. Home health, rehabilitation, social, and mental health services have been increasingly included in prepayment schemes, though these remain limited and there is a clear need for broader and improved community-based services. The growing chronicity of illnesses seen in hospitals requires long-term supporting services after their acute episodes are stabilized. Treatment of the mentally ill has shifted from specialized psychiatric units to general hospitals and community facilities—in 1975, one million more patients with a primary psychiatric diagnosis were discharged from general hospitals than from specialized psychiatric units. Reflecting on these trends, Stewart observes that in considering

> the need to coordinate human services we have tended to look at the administrative-managerial axis as the seat of the problem of uncoordination and the place where interventions will solve the problem. It may be that the fundamental changes which have occurred in the content, characteristics and loci of human services may underlie and overshadow the administrative and managerial difficulties in coordinating human services.[3]

Another member of our panel, John Romani, voiced the same concern that focusing on the administrative aspects of services coordination may lead to the neglect of more basic social aspects.

> the problems of service inadequacies, gaps, and duplication may not be amenable to a strategy of administrative reorganization. . . . we may be at a point . . . comparable to that in the 1930s. The system for helping people was inadequate to the situation which

then obtained, and we were required to reorder that system in terms of policy, foci of responsibility, finance and management. The restructuring with its emphasis on categorical programs, federal financing and minimum national standards has contributed to the changes in the "content, characteristics and loci of human services" which, as Bill Stewart has . . . noted, "may underlie and overshadow the managerial difficulties in coordinating human services."[4]

Romani quotes the assessment of the Carnegie Council on Children that

> at the same time that families have been shorn of the many traditional roles with children, new expectations about children's needs have arisen and, along with them, new specialists and institutions to meet the expectations. . . . What has changed is the content and nature of family life. Families . . . are extraordinarily dependent on "outside" forces and influences. . . . All families today need and use support in raising children; to define the "needy" family as the exception is to deny the simplest facts of contemporary family life.[5]

We have no answer, let alone one simple answer, to the question of how to provide more satisfactory and comprehensive services to our citizens. At the present juncture, when there is such widespread disaffection with government institutions, especially those which are distant from the people, more of the answers must be sought in the community. Surely the answers will be found not by administrators or professionals acting alone and apart but by both acting together with the citizens whom they serve. If Stewart and Romani are right, the question that should be asked is even larger than how to coordinate services. It is how to strengthen our society and community so that the needy individual and fractured family will not stand alone, but can find the help they need to persevere.

Notes

1. Alfred J. Kahn and Sheila B. Kamerman, "Services Integration and the Division of Labor," unpublished paper, 1979, pp. 4, 7.
2. Janet Weiss, "Substance vs. Symbol in Administrative Reform: The Case of Human Services Coordination," *Policy Analysis,* Winter 1981, pp. 37, 39.
3. April 29, 1980 letter to Harold Orlans.
4. June 18, 1980 letter to Harold Orlans.
5. Kenneth Kenniston et al., *All Our Children,* Harcourt Brace Jovanovich, New York, 1977, pp. 17, 22.

ADMINISTRATIVE ISSUES IN IMPROVING THE PROVISION OF HUMAN SERVICES

David M. Austin

Background

Problems

Current human services programs reflect contradictory legislative mandates, defective service techniques, weaknesses in evaluation, problems in financing, in the geographic and ethnic distribution of service, and in public understanding and attitudes. Administrative and operational problems present additional barriers to effective service.

> This fragmented and inconsistent array of local programs must surely be seen by clients . . . as a "many splintered thing." Service workers, attempting to deal with the multiple problems of real people, can only experience frustration in arranging referrals through this maze of specialized community agencies, each treating part-problems. Political and administrative decision makers can hardly ignore the realities of duplication, gaps in services, failures in accountability, and unnecessary expense resulting from the conglomeration of separate specialty programs characteristic of human services today. Site visits conducted in several urban centers and rural regions of the country in 1977 and 1978 by staff of the President's Reorganization Project found private citizens expressing strong concern about complex application forms, inconsistent eligibility standards, lack of information on available services, and the fragmentation of services among different agencies in different locations.[1]

The exact form and extent of the problems noted in this quotation have not been studied in detail.[2] Most reports, explicit about the existence of problems, are largely impressionistic about their

extent and relative urgency. Norms or standards defining satisfactory service levels, and comprehensive, comparable data on program achievement or failures in different states and cities are
lacking.

In this situation, each participant in the provision of services
has a distinctive perspective which may result in a different analysis of the most critical issues. The service user is primarily concerned with the procedures and results of service; the service
worker and administrator, with individual and program outcomes
and with maintaining the service organization; and the policy-
maker, with program effectiveness, efficiency, and conformity to
established policy. This paper focuses primarily on the concerns of
administrators and service workers about administrative and programmatic changes designed to improve human services. Concerns about the multiplicity of providers and categorical programs—about the "confusing array of costly duplicative human
services"[3]—have often led to an emphasis on services integration
or coordination as the administrative solution to the problem of
fragmented service.[4] However, the issues are broader than coordination and many of the approaches which need consideration apply to categorical as well as to integrated systems.

Assumptions

This paper assumes as a point of departure that during the 1980s:
• Federal funding, regulations, and monitoring requirements will
continue mainly in categorical program channels.
• There will be little increase in "real" federal dollars for human
services except for Social Security benefits, financial assistance,
and medical programs with open-ended appropriations. Efforts by
states and localities to comply with under-funded federally mandated service coverage in other programs will stretch available
funds even more thinly.
• There will be no decrease in the "demand" for services given
the pattern of demographic changes, economic conditions, and
continuing high levels of individual, family, and community
stress.

Two other assumptions about the nature of human service programs underlie this discussion:
• Most human service programs involve interrelationships between federal, state, county, and municipal governments as well
as administrative, financial, and policy interdependencies among
separate service units and organizations.[5] The achievement of pol-

icy objectives in one program often requires complementary and compatible policies in related programs; the achievement of program objectives and the provision of adequate case services often requires the collaboration of a number of program components in different organizations.

• All public and private programs involve the provision of both public and private goods; that is, they must simultaneously be responsive to the needs and preferences of users and to the "public interest" objectives set forth in enabling legislation or organizational charters.[6] All human service programs may, therefore, be criticized simultaneously for being insufficiently responsive to the needs of individuals and families, and for insufficient attention to specific legislative and policy mandates.

The following sections present a series of administrative and program alternatives involved in designing human service programs. Though the choice of a particular alternative may be explicitly dictated by public policy, policy-makers, administrators, and professional staff usually have significant degrees of freedom in designing programs, especially when agencies are undergoing administrative reorganization.

Empirical, fiscal, and policy analyses can clarify the available choices. However, the choices themselves will reflect the balance of political forces in the policy process. The choices are also affected by the compatibility of particular elements in a service system. The choice of certain alternatives in initial design stages will exclude other alternatives in later stages. Moreover, the process of change may be slow and gradual, following a general blueprint over an extended period of time, or massive and abrupt. Each alternative involves a particular set of financial, political, and personal risks—for service users, staff, and policy-makers. The discussion of program design issues which follows is applicable in either case.

Basic Program Design Issues

The existing pattern of human service programs developed piecemeal with initiatives from many sources and a wide variety of program designs. The decision to intervene deliberately in the existing network of programs to improve its overall performance, in contrast to initiating a new component in a specialized, categorical program, raises many program design issues. Many of the difficulties in working relationships among service agencies are created by differences in program design. Action to improve service

delivery forces decisions about program design. The following section identifies a series of basic program design issues which emerge any time there is an effort to plan deliberately for human service programs. These issues are pertinent if the focus is on improving service delivery in a categorical, a coordinated, or an "integrated" service system. The final section deals with design issues associated with deliberate efforts to establish a coordinated service system.

Alternative Service Models

Existing service systems represent a mixture of approaches. At least three "ideal type" models can be identified: the market, the public administration, and the network model, which may guide the overall development of a service system.

Market Model

The market model emphasizes the role of the client as the primary coordinator of services.[7] It strives to increase freedom of choice by financial aid, vouchers, or prepaid insurance for service users. The relative level of demand for services leads to their supply at different quantities and prices. When the demand is high, clients may have an opportunity to choose among many providers and practitioners. Services are coordinated by the client or by a professional practitioner chosen by the client to perform this function. Direct appropriations to governmental or nonprofit services are reduced. Licensing assures a minimal level of service quality. The provision of services responsive primarily to user preferences is emphasized.

Public Administration Model

The public administration model emphasizes the role of central policy bodies and administrators in service coordination. Independent programs may be consolidated to increase control. Service levels reflect systematic needs assessment, priority determination, and centralized planning. Resource allocation is controlled centrally to avoid duplication and provide equitable access to service by all geographic, income, and ethnic groups. New programs are initiated by administrative decision. Efficiencies of scale in facilities and support services are sought. Internal administrative monitoring and accountability systems serve to enforce standards. Internal conflicts are referred to higher authority. Fee charges set by administrators reflect program objectives and budget needs

rather than demand levels. Services to individuals are coordinated jointly by the user and agency staff. Users have a limited choice of agency and no choice of practitioners. Both public and private goods are provided; but appropriations are justified primarily on the grounds of the benefits to society rather than to individual users.

Networking Model

The networking model emphasizes decentralized, collaborative decision-making processes among service organizations, consumer constituencies, and clients rather than any single administrative structure. The main objective is to increase operational linkages among providers around the needs of service users; responsibility for this process is assigned to a core agency in each program area. The pattern of services and funding priorities is based on needs assessment procedures together with a process of bargaining and negotiation by consumer representatives, public officials, civic leaders, and organizational personnel. A combination of categorical and block grant funds is preferred, allowing for adaptation to local needs and preferences while ensuring that specialized needs are not ignored. Similar services may be provided by several small organizations rather than a single large organization.

Efficiencies of scale are sought by negotiated cost-sharing agreements. New service organizations may be created by community planning or individual initiative. Services are coordinated by users and/or core agency case managers supported by formal interagency agreements on referrals and purchase of service agreements. Information and referral services help clients and staff to find appropriate services. Charges are set by each organization. Conflicts between providers or consumers and providers are handled by negotiation or arbitration; quality control and consumer protection are handled by independent community channels for investigating complaints and recommending corrective action. Users may have choices of service organizations but usually not of specific service personnel. Individual organizations may emphasize either public or private goods.

Elements of each of these models exist in our present melange of health, mental health, and social services, but any deliberate attempt to improve the structure of services requires a choice among these models, since it is impossible to pursue all three simultaneously. In the remainder of this paper, the program design issues addressed are primarily applicable to the public administration or the networking model. Some of the issues are applicable to a mar-

ket model, but that model poses additional issues not dealt with in this paper.

Professional-Administrator Relations

Some professional practitioners function independently of any organization and some service organizations employ nonprofessional personnel who are identified only as organizational employees. Most human service programs, however, involve staffs of professional specialists who are also organizational employees.

In most health, mental health, and social service programs, a core or dominant profession can be identified whose members usually occupy the highest administrative positions. In some instances, they are legally required to do so. The bonds between the core professionals in such programs and the leaders in professional schools and professional associations function to maintain the pattern of categorical service dominated by designated professions.

Professional and administrative imperatives are in constant tension.[8] It is often said that a good professional cannot be a good bureaucrat and that bureaucratic rules and regulations are major barriers to good professional service. And, contrariwise, that a responsible administrator who has a professional background must put the needs of his institution and the public before the self-interest of an organized profession, which may assume too easily that what is good for the profession is automatically good for the public.

Efforts to improve the administration of human service programs must contend with the existing prerogatives or "turf" of each profession, with the dependence of services upon professional knowledge and skills, and with the tension between professionals and administrators. Solutions to these problems often adopt one of the three alternatives:
• putting administrative personnel under the authority of professionals;
• creating a bargaining organization for professionals and resolving conflicts by formal negotiations between administrators and professional representatives; or
• requiring all personnel, including professionals, as a condition of employment, to acknowledge the overriding authority of responsible administrators.

None of these alternatives is fully satisfactory because none takes into account the fact that conflicts between administrators

and professionals serve as a form of organizational "checks and balances." Professionals in direct contact with clients can, and should, function as advocates of clients' interests, whereas administrators must reflect the interests of public policy-makers, taxpayers, and institutional maintenance. The dominance of an organization by professionals can produce a financial crisis if efforts to improve service quality are not tempered by a concern for professional standards.

Administration concerned with the achievement of organizational goals and professional practice concerned with client needs are both essential for effective programs. Both must be maintained by a combination of buffering and linkages. Examples include:

• delegating the maintenance of service standards to relatively self-governing, specialized professional service units headed by a professional who is responsible for reconciling the unit's performance with broader program policies and budgets;
• providing administrative training and experience to professional personnel so that they can understand the requirements of organizational functioning and opportunities for administrators to gain an understanding of the objectives and requirements of professional service so that the two groups can work together effectively;
• contracting with private agencies, groups of professionals, and health maintenance organizations for complex and comprehensive professionalized services;
• providing in union contracts for specific means of resolving policy disputes involving professional practice issues;
• establishing at senior administrative levels multi-professional staff advisor groups representing the principal service professions to help to maintain and evaluate service quality and effectiveness.

Operational Rationales

Different human service programs embody different rationales or conceptions of their mission which have extensive implications for the types of personnel employed and for the organization and administration of services. It can be essential in any effort to coordinate different programs to formulate a rationale that is compatible with existing conceptions of service and yet can unify staff aspirations for a more comprehensive mission. Until such a new rationale replaces existing rationales, programs which are administratively united may remain intellectually fragmented and staff

in one program may not be able to "hear" what those in another
program are saying.

Among the major rationales which underlie human service programs are the following:

The *clinical* or "illness" rationale (important in health and mental health programs) assumes that an individual, family, or group
has an ailment or syndrome which can be diagnosed and treated.
Clients must accept treatment specified by professionals if their
condition is to be remedied or stabilized.

The *environmental* rationale (prominent in employment, housing,
or community action programs) assumes that a social or health
problem arises from deleterious environmental factors which can
be corrected by accurate analysis and intervention. Examples are
the removal of a source of air pollution, the provision of jobs for
unemployed youth, the repair of slum housing, and the formation
of neighborhood associations for social or political purposes.

The *developmental* rationale (significant in educational and mental retardation programs) assumes that a malfunction can be corrected by removing emotional, social, or organic obstacles to
normal development or, failing that, that the individual can be
helped to develop some minimal level of functioning.

The *individual-environment* or *interactive* rationale (important in
programs dealing with such problems as delinquency, illegitimate
births, family conflicts, or multi-problem families) assumes that
individual and community problems arise from unsatisfactory relationships between the individual and the social environment.
The intervention may attempt to modify individual behavior,
change environmental conditions, or change both simultaneously.

Modes of Program Operation

Every human service program has a distinctive operational pattern governing the selection of service personnel and the process of
assigning tasks to them and to the service user. Six operational
modes will be briefly characterized. Attempts to improve or reorganize programs may require an examination of current program modes and possible alternatives.

A *professional* mode assigns to a specialized professional the central role in diagnosing and meeting client needs. Service is organized around "case loads"; administrative functions are regarded
as subordinate to, and supportive of, professional functions.

A *system* mode entails a "delivery system" or "pathway" routing
a client through a sequence of functions such as intake, diagnosis,

planning for provision of service, case management, monitoring, and evaluation. The entire organization, rather than any one professional, is ultimately accountable for the mobilization and quality of service. Monitoring and evaluation help to maintain standards. At several points in the sequence, the client may have opportunities to choose service alternatives. Administrators have the broad responsibility to develop and maintain the entire system; professionals have the responsibility to provide specialized services.

A *social care* mode provides service in the household or other "living" settings for persons who are dependent or in need of care and protection. Key service personnel include foster and house parents, homemakers, ward attendants, home health aides, child care workers, and volunteers such as Big Brothers or Big Sisters. Professionals prepare service plans and train and supervise such aides. The agency employing the aides is largely responsible for quality of service.

A *natural care* mode fosters service by the family or by neighborhood, community, or peer "natural care networks." A relative or family may be given financial assistance to care for an elderly or retarded person; or a peer group of ex-alcoholics or addicts may help and support an addict. Agency staff identify and support care arrangements and monitor quality; professional specialists may advise and assist those who provide the cure.

The *research and development* or *public health* mode stresses research to identify the nature and context of a broad problem, and the development of a wide variety of measures to deal with it. Research may include laboratory studies, surveys, and field investigations. Intervention may include legislation, a new professional service or educational program, application of specialized medical technology, or changes in the physical and social environment.

The *"first aid"* mode provides immediate, short-term service— funds, shelter, referrals to specialized services, or counseling—in response to a crisis: for example, the neighborhood service center, "hot-line" counseling, emergency financial assistance, or travelers' aid. Professional education is seldom required of front-line staff who may be given brief training or may learn on the job. Knowledge about other community resources may be the most important aspect of staff competence. Agency rules and practical realities govern the service provided. Supervisors and reporting forms are used to monitor quality of service.

Each of these modes of operation may be used in any program area. The choice is dependent upon the program's nature, objec-

tives and traditions, the state of the available service technology, and the needs and preferences of policy-makers, staff, and clients. Many programs involve a combination of program modes, but the differences in staff and structural requirements can create administrative stresses.

Operational Auspice Choices

Services in any given program area may be provided directly by governmental staff or by the staff of nonprofit or for-profit organizations under government contract. Nonprofit organizations may be long-standing or newly formed at the initiative of private citizens or government officials. To administer a specific program they may rely entirely upon government funds or also have independent revenue for endowment and private gifts and fees. The for-profit or proprietary organization may be a large hospital, nursing home, day care center, clinic for emotionally disturbed children, or a small group of doctors, psychologists, social workers, or nurses in private practice. Contracts with proprietary groups may provide for a fixed cost per unit, cost reimbursement up to a set ceiling, or cost plus a fee or profit.

It can be argued that the standards of direct service by government staff can be better controlled and accounted for than those of private providers. But direct service operations involve a larger and more permanent investment in facilities and the maintenance of civil service staff. Civil service regulations and union contract provisions can reduce administrative flexibility, particularly the ability to terminate programs that are no longer required.

Service Allocation

In almost every program area there is a substantial gap between the total need for services and the available resources. The allocation of limited services may be determined by such accidental or implicit measures as the deliberate use of unattractive and remote facilities or the employment of poorly qualified staff. Systematic allocation procedures may employ service fees, with or without provision for exceptions for low-income households. Priority service lists may be established based on order of application for service or the severity, urgency, or remediability of individual conditions. Legal eligibility rules utilizing such elements as income, assets, age, sex, place of residence, or household status may serve to limit demand. Without procedures to allocate available ser-

vices, the effect of a severe gap between need and resources may be to reduce the quality of services. Differences in policy on allocating scarce services can be a major barrier to program cooperation, and a major source of disruption in program consolidations.

Consumer Participation

Unlike many business and industrial operations, human service programs are particularly dependent upon interaction with and cooperation from clients. The service program is planned in response to the specific needs of users, who generally must provide personal information about their problem before a service plan can be prepared. The effects of human services are jointly produced; active cooperation is required for success. Moreover, since human service programs are intended to provide benefits to both individuals and the general public, it is essential that user interests be represented in program policy making. Formal provisions for representation include: explicit agreement of users to service plans and provisions for appeal of decisions about service; independent complaint investigation procedures; user evaluations of service; public hearings on program policies and regulations; and representation of users and user constituencies on advisory and policy-making bodies. Program coordination approaches may dilute informal and formal user input and reduce program responsiveness, unless consideration is given to such provisions.

Coordinated Service Operations

As indicated earlier, one approach to the improvement of service which has frequently been advocated is service coordination or "integration." This section summarizes some of the experience with efforts to achieve services integration, identifies a number of program design issues which must be dealt with in efforts to achieve greater coordination of specialized service programs, and concludes with a listing of specific issues involved in establishing a coordinated services delivery system in the community.

Services "Integration" Experience

The "integration" or coordination of services seeks to make them more comprehensive, accessible, effective, and accountable and less duplicative and fragmented. However, the literature contains little information on the extent, and little agreement about the

meaning of, services "fragmentation," "duplication," "gaps," or
"inaccessibility."[9] There is little systematic information about the
number of persons who have not received service because of
"gaps" or conflicting eligibility requirements, as distinguished
from a lack of funds. There is little information on the number of
individuals seeking multiple services or the number of families
classified as "multi-problem." There is, in short, little objective
information about the deficiencies of the categorical service system
with which the operation of a coordinated system can be compared.

Improvement in the accessibility, comprehensiveness, and continuity of service is not, of course, the only reason for instituting
coordination. It may also reflect the wish of public officials or legislatures to increase their control over, to obtain comparable data
from, or to impose better management on compartmentalized
programs.

Despite the lack of base-line data and motivated by disparate
objectives, the search for solutions went on during the 1970s.
They can be divided into those that dealt with: (1) the policy
management or program direction level, (2) the program operation level, and (3) the case service level.

"Umbrella" human service agencies were created in over half of
the states and in nearly all states west of the Mississippi. This was
a significant innovation at the *policy management* level.[10] In several
instances such an agency was created as part of a broad reorganization of state government. The umbrella agencies include such
income maintenance programs as AFDC and food stamps, public
social services (Title XX), and some combination of mental
health, public health, services to the elderly, youth corrections,
and vocational rehabilitation. Umbrella agencies can be classified
as *confederated,* with common top policy management and few
changes below, as in Massachusetts; *integrated,* with a complete
restructuring of prior service components, as in Florida; and
consolidated, with a less radical restructuring, as in Louisiana.[11] In
several states, such as Massachusetts, separate financial assistance
and social service organizations have been established within the
umbrella agency, dividing the traditional "public welfare" agency
services.

Umbrella agencies have not yet produced widespread integration of local services, although Florida and Utah have taken steps
in this direction. In Massachusetts, integrative, sub-state multi-
program planning is being proposed to parallel the policy management process at the state level. The degree to which these

reorganizations have led to significant program innovations, simplification of regulations, or joint planning and program development is inadequately documented.

A substantial number of demonstration projects in the early
1970s sought to integrate local *program administration*. Many were
initiated as Services Integration Targets of Opportunity (SITO)
projects with federal funds.[12] The majority of these projects disap-
peared after the initial demonstration funding period, failing to
withstand the pressures of established federal categorical program
requirements. SITO projects made limited provision for research
and produced little systematic information that would enable
them to be compared with traditional services. Project services
were somewhat more costly because of the addition of coordinating and case monitoring activities.

Some projects did survive (for example, the Human Services
Coordination Alliance, Louisville)[13] and new projects emerged in
the late 1970s, particularly as a result of state efforts to integrate
county services, for example in Wisconsin, Minnesota, and Utah,
and local efforts to coordinate services planning, as in San Diego
County, California. Local projects have included funding from Title XX, mental health, elderly, and developmental disability programs. Innovations have included a single organization for varied
services, a single information and case-tracking system, a single
point of client access to all services, collocation, and common support services.

At the *case service* level much attention is now being given to the
unified case management of multiple-problem cases such as older
persons with functional limitations and individuals with chronic
mental illness, substance addiction, development disabilities, and/
or severe physical handicaps. The trend, and often legal require-
ment, to discharge or divert such patients from institutions has
made it increasingly necessary for community services to deal
with them. The case manager or team is responsible for coordinating and maintaining the continuity of client services. Their work
may be facilitated by interagency agreements on referrals and
payments. Case managers are employed by categorical as well as
integrated programs. The case-management function, which is
being promoted by several federal agencies, is viewed as primarily
facilitative rather than therapeutic.

While the initiatives of the 1970s have not resulted in significant
data on outcomes, they have clarified the fact that coordination
may proceed at several organizational levels. At the policy management level, it can be promoted by common planning and bud-

geting, and designation of a common point of liaison and review
in the executive or legislative branch of government. Such coordination usually occurs at the initiative of the governor or legislature to simplify and strengthen their oversight and control of
programs which have often developed more in response to federal
initiatives than to state initiatives and funds. Control of Title XX
funds can be an important aspect of policy management coordination. Coordination in the state capital need not be accompanied
by similar coordination in local communities.

Program operation coordination in counties or cities can range
from the collocation of services to the common administration of
programs. It may be instituted to gain flexibility in the use of
funds, personnel, and facilities; to facilitate client access; or to
consolidate technical, support, and information services, case
monitoring, budgeting, and planning. Local coordination may
embrace a broader range of programs than those of a state umbrella agency—for example, housing, neighborhood activities, and
collaboration with voluntary agencies. It may function without
corresponding policy management coordination or any change in
direct service procedures.

Services to clients can be coordinated without any program
reorganization at administrative or policy levels by the use of case
managers; designation of core agencies responsible for case management; agreements on referrals, reimbursement, and eligibility;
standardized case records; and consistent case monitoring.

General Design Issues in Coordination

Financial Management Structures

Categorical appropriations and accountability requirements
pose a major obstacle to coordination. Most government appropriations can be used only for designated, highly restricted purposes. Few, if any, human service programs have direct tax
authority, as do some school and hospital districts, though they
may obtain revenue from multiple governmental sources as well
as from gifts, fees, and insurers. Even when federal funds can be
used flexibly, as in Title XX social services, state legislatures
often restrict their use and monitor compliance with statutory prescriptions. Since most federal appropriations for human services
respond at least in part to the pressures of special interest groups,
it is understandable that they usually contain explicit definitions
of the target groups and eligibility conditions. These help auditors
and evaluators to determine if the funds have been used correctly.

Moreover, our intergovernmental system provides no direct chain of administrative command between federal and state or state and local governments. Prior plan approval, contract and grant conditions, program regulations, manuals, and training, and after-the-fact reports, inspections, audits, and evaluations are among the procedures employed by federal and state agencies to bind local programs to legislated designs. Such categorical bonds hamper local flexibility in responding to client needs. Differences in eligibility rules may make it difficult to use funds from different programs to serve a client. Funds may be provided for services but not for the transportation to obtain them or the planning and administrative functions required to supply them.

Variations, delays, and disruptions in funding cycles among federal, state, and local funding bodies make budget and grant preparation, allocation and expenditure a year-round process with great uncertainty at all times about the actual level of program funds. Compliance with comprehensive plans prepared in advance becomes totally improbable under these conditions.

Coordinated services require financial management and accountability procedures which take this uncertainty and the constraints of categorical appropriations into account.[14] Three approaches are:

• The retention of categorical programs with a loosely confederated agency with coordination taking place primarily at the case service level of each individual. Flexible funds are used for case managers and contracts with providers to fill service gaps. Funding proposals and accountability remain each program's responsibility.

• A comprehensive central organization responsible for all funding proposals, financial and program reports, and internal budgeting consistent with categorical program requirements. Categorical funds are assigned to discrete components responsible for accountability. Flexible funds are used for guidance and integrative functions, and for filling "gaps" and interruptions in categorical funds.

• A central pooling of all income and its allocation to functional and geographic units on the basis of needs assessment and priority planning, and to smooth out funding irregularities. Service and time accounting provide categorical program report data. Grant proposals and reports, and relations with all funding sources, are centrally managed.

Each approach represents a different way of adapting categorical funding to local needs, of developing a full service system, and of buffering it against funding disruptions.

Policy and Program Guidance

Coordination at the policy management or program operations level requires broad needs assessment, legislative and policy plans and proposals, budgeting and accounting, management information, program monitoring, and evaluation. More sophisticated management is required for coordinated than for categorical programs to deal with their complex interactions, provide the financial and substantive reports required by categorical programs, and meet the expectations of fuller accountability and responsiveness to client needs which have often contributed to the establishment of coordinated agencies.

The establishment of such technical management functions involves decisions on:

• Appropriate scope and cost. Elaborate technical procedures can substantially increase costs without increasing service. Additional information or reporting requirements for service personnel can reduce the level of service and increase worker "burn-out" and turnover.

• The use of staff and/or outside consultants for technical functions.

• The degree of influence of such functions as program planning and evaluation over program budgeting and management and the weight given to information from such sources in comparison to information from service personnel and political sources.

• The confidential, or public, status of various program and management data, plans, evaluations, and reports.

Linkage Personnel

Effective "horizontal" program linkages require specialized staff in such positions as project leaders, contract negotiators and monitors, program liaison staff, and case managers. Traditional professional or management training offers little preparation for such roles. Attention must be given to the training, experience, and personal characteristics which personnel in these positions need, and to the range of discretionary authority and responsibility for accountability which should be assigned.

Generalists and Specialists

Proposals for coordinated services often emphasize the use of generalist case managers or service workers who deal with several types of clients (for example, mentally retarded persons in a group home or elderly persons requiring protective or homemaker services) or perform several functions (for example, diagnosis, eligibility determination, counseling, mobilization of community re-

sources, or case advocacy).[15] This is in distinction to "specialists" who are viewed as concentrating on one service or function.

The conception of generalists and specialists as radically different roles is not consistent with the reality of most service agencies. Unrealistic also is the assumption that an entry-level generalist can be knowledgeable about a wide variety of services and act as a therapeutic counselor, advocate, and community planner. The role prescribed for service workers in any innovative program will depend on specific local conditions including the need for flexible assignments, the degree of specialization required for effective service, and the complexity of the service network.

Conflict Resolution

In existing categorical programs, conflicts among staff and with clients are usually resolved by the judgment of senior professionals and administrators; client appeal procedures and public review boards may also be provided. In coordinated program networks which lack a common administrative hierarchy, these conflict resolution procedures may be unavailable. Other procedures must be developed to resolve conflicts between programs, providers, and clients. These may include the use of mediation and non-binding arbitration, hearing officers or panels of professionals, public review boards and consumer complaint bureaus, and ombudsmen.[16]

Design Issues in Coordinated Service Delivery

Administrative issues which may be confronted in program administration coordination include:

Collocation

Collocation—the location of different services in the same facility—has been advocated to render services more visible and accessible, reduce facility and administrative costs, and improve program planning and case coordination. These benefits do not occur, however, without careful administrative planning. Moreover, the collocation of programs with diverse clienteles and missions may produce conflict, as can disagreements over facility costs and maintenance services. In rural areas, single facilities adequate to the needs of diverse programs may not be available.

Common Administrator

State and local governments may authorize one local administrator to oversee many separate programs. This may involve direct program control or general oversight. In either instance this

person will necessarily become involved in the relationships of these programs with local education and employment services and with the business community, on the one hand, and with state and perhaps federal agencies on the other. The designation of the accountability and reporting procedures for such a position is of great importance.

Staff Structure

Administrative coordination is compatible with the maintenance of specialized local staffs for child welfare, rehabilitation, alcoholism, mental retardation, and other services. However, it may be desirable to combine staffs such as those providing home services for the elderly and those working in senior citizen centers. More extensive reorganization may result in teams of generalists and/or specialists to provide comprehensive services in given geographic districts.

Common Rules and Procedures

Effective coordination often requires common or simplified regulations and procedures for different programs. Despite the obstacles posed by federal and state requirements, local action can improve the commonality of: different program procedures; eligibility levels; definitions of income and assets, "first dollar in" requirements, and the appropriate "point of entry" for particular services; procedures for sharing case information and protecting confidentiality; diagnostic categories; and service districts.

Common Point of Access

One unit which receives applications and determines eligibility for all public services can facilitate the maintenance of central case records, statistical reports, and the allocation of services in short supply, such as day care and nursing homes. If application can be made directly to individual programs, standardized forms and records can still be maintained at a central location.

Outreach and Facilitating Access [17]

Many programs require special efforts to increase public awareness of their services and help those who need service to obtain it. A combined outreach effort may strengthen several programs. The lack of transportation can be a major obstacle, and the consolidation of fragmented transportation arrangements and funding can foster coordinated services. Service access can also be fostered by providing services at convenient times and locations, by attrac-

tive facilities with adequate arrangements for the care of children, by facilitating access for handicapped persons, and by utilizing bilingual staff or translators.

Client Pathway

A standard "client pathway" to assist citizens in using services may include a complex "systems" structure involving different specialized personnel for eligibility determination, diagnosis and assessment, the preparation of a service plan, service referral, and case management, service monitoring, and evaluation. Alternatively, a generalist case manager may handle all of these functions in a given service situation.

Information and Referral[18]

A community-wide information and referral system to assist the public in effective use of the service network may be developed by the creation of a single system or by a network of separate units, including specialized units within large organizations such as medical centers. The community system may or may not be linked to a statewide system. It may be designed for use by the public and/or by service personnel. It may be manual or computerized with periodic or continual up-dating. A directory of service information may be issued for the use of staff or direct access to the computerized files can be provided for staff via decentralized computer terminals.

Summary

There is widespread concern about administrative and program structures in human service programs. Some problems are a direct consequence of inadequate funding; others are not. These problems require deliberate consideration of a wide range of program design issues.[19] Many of these issues are interrelated; to be effective, the various design decisions must be compatible. Many design issues are essentially technical; others are linked to broader political and ideological issues such as the balance between public and private benefits in a specific service program. Some design issues cut across all types of program structures; others are associated with efforts to improve program coordination.

There is a marked lack of research on the consequences of alternative program designs, particularly as these affect the quality of services. Comparative studies of traditional and innovative program structures using common outcome measures are especially

lacking. Without such research to determine if a given set of problems has, in fact, been resolved, innovations and reorganizations may lead to an almost endless cycle of reorganization and experimentation.

The need for such research will become increasingly acute as financial constraints force decisions on policy-makers and administrators.

Notes

1. Beaumont R. Hagebak, "Local Human Service Delivery: The Integration Imperative," *Public Administration Review*, Vol. 39, No. 6, November/December 1979, p. 595.
2. See Rocco D'Amico and Bill Benton, "Addressing the Problems in Human Service Delivery," unpublished paper, The Urban Institute, Washington, D.C., 1978, for discussion of the gap between the identification of service delivery problems and proposed changes.
3. Hagebak, *op. cit.*
4. An extensive body of reports and articles deals with the issue of "service integration" in the 1970s. The most comprehensive discussion, together with an extensive bibliography, is Robert Agranoff and Alex Pattakos, *Dimensions of Service Integration: Service Delivery, Program Linkages, Policy Management, Organizational Structure*, Human Services Monograph Series, No. 13, Project Share, U.S. Department of Health, Education, and Welfare, April 1979.
5. See Benny Hjern and David O. Porter, "Implementation Structures: A New Unit of Administrative Analysis," International Institute of Management, Berlin, and School of Social Work, University of Texas, Austin, 1979, for an extended discussion of the implication of interdependencies among service organizations in service delivery and the nature of implementation structures.
6. See David M. Austin, "The Political Economy of Social Benefit Organizations: Redistributive Services and Merit Goods," Center for Social Work Research, School of Social Work, University of Texas, Austin, 1979, for discussion of the "public good" aspects of human service organizations.
7. This point of view has been applied to the human services by Professor Milton Friedman of the University of Chicago and other economists who follow his theories.
8. Professional-organization relations have been discussed extensively. Two current analyses are Irwin Epstein and Kayla Conrad, "The Empirical Limits of Social Work Professionalization," in Rosemary C. Sarri and Yeheskel Hasenfeld, editors, *The Management of Human Services*, Columbia University Press, New York, 1978, and David M. Austin, "Social Work and the Social Services: A Scenario for the 1980s," in National Association of Social Workers, *Perspectives for the Future: Social Work in the 1980s*, Washington, D.C., 1980.
9. See Penelope Caragonne, "Services Integration: Where Do We Stand?", *Journal of Health and Human Resources Administration*, Vol. 1, No. 4, May 1979, and Edward Baumhier and John DeWitt, *Issues in Coordinated Administration and Delivery of Human Services: A Policy and Research Agenda*, Center for Social Research and Development, Denver Research Institute, University of Denver, 1977, for a discussion of the difficulties involved in the systematic analysis of problems in service delivery systems.
10. See Chapter 5, "Organizational Structure," in Robert Agranoff and Alex Pattakos, *op. cit.*; David M. Austin, "The Politics and Organization of Services: Consolidation and Integration"; and Harold Hagen and John E. Hansan, "The Politics and Organization of Services: How the States Put the Programs Together," *Public Welfare*, Vol. 3, Summer 1978.
11. See *Human Services Integration: State Functions and Implementation*, Council of State Governments, Lexington, Kentucky, 1974.

12. See Marshall Kaplan, Gans, and Kahn, and The Research Group, *Integration of Human Services in HEW: An Evaluation of Services Integration Projects,* Volume 1, Department of Health, Education, and Welfare, Washington, D.C., 1973; and The Human Ecology Institute, *Human Service Development Programs in Sixteen Allied Services (SITO) Projects,* Wellesley, Mass., 1975, for an analysis of the SITO experience.

13. See *Human Services Coordination Alliance: Partnership to Improve the Delivery of Service,* Human Services Coordination Alliance, Louisville, Kentucky, 1976.

14. See David O. Porter and David C. Warner, "Organizations and Implementation Structures," unpublished paper, School of Social Work, University of Texas, Austin, 1979, for discussion of "multi-pocket budgeting" and "marginal mobilizing" as financial management strategies under conditions of multi-source funding.

15. For one view of the generalist/specialist issue see Alfred J. Kahn and Sheila B. Kamerman, "The Politics and Organization of Services: The Course of 'Personal Social Services,'" *Public Welfare,* Vol. 36, No. 3, Summer 1978.

16. Mediation and conciliation functions in the human services area have not been systematically developed. A current example, however, on the role of W.J. Usery, former Secretary of Labor, as an interorganizational intergovernmental mediator in St. Paul, Minnesota, is described in John Berber, "Labor Mediator Takes on Government Fights," *New York Times Service,* December 1979. This and similar efforts are being supported by the Charles F. Kettering Foundation, Dayton, Ohio.

17. For discussion of a range of issues related to access see David M. Austin, *Improving Access in the Human Services: Decision Issues and Alternatives,* American Public Welfare Association, Washington, D.C., September 1979.

18. David M. Austin, "New Roles for Information and Referral in Social Services Networks," *Information and Referral,* Vol. 1, No. 1, Spring, 1979.

19. This paper is a revision of a more extended discussion of these program design issues prepared as background material for the regional conferences. Persons interested in receiving a copy of the original paper may obtain one from David M. Austin, School of Social Work, University of Texas, Austin, Texas 78712.

COORDINATING SERVICES
FOR CHILDREN

John Mudd

Summary

Services coordination is significant, often critical, for meeting the needs of children and youth. But the fundamental governmental issues affecting children in the 1980s still remain questions of public policy and budgetary resources, not administrative coordination.

In looking at the coordination problem anew, we need to adopt a broad perspective about the services to be considered and not limit our vision by some predetermined conception of what programs could be included in a superagency or a block grant. The new opportunities to deal with the enormous problems of special education for handicapped children, youth unemployment, or housing discrimination against families with children, for example, are too important to be dismissed in a reassessment of "human services" coordination.

The underlying framework of publicly supported assistance for children will remain categorical grants and entitlements. But this creates a special obligation on policy-makers and administrators to encourage techniques to coordinate these programs at the point where they affect children and families in their communities. Superagencies, block grants, collocation, information, and referral may in some cases improve coordination; but they are techniques and not ends. Too often they have produced less than their promise. Perhaps we should now focus less on grandiose, organizational solutions and more on coordination for specific groups and problem areas, like insuring that all day care children do in fact get Early and Periodic Screening, Diagnosis, and Treatment (EPSDT) or Child Health Assessment Projection (CHAP) health screening and treatment.

Advocates, administrators, and academics alike must rigorously assess the impact of past coordination systems and judge proposed options for their actual, not presumed, impact on children or other groups. Federal support for human services is unlikely to increase dramatically in the foreseeable future. Coordination systems can siphon money, or divert attention, from services. We must ensure that the benefits of coordination outweigh the costs.

Basic Facts about Children

Number
In 1979, there were 58.5 million children under 18 in the U.S.; 17 million were under 6; 17.8 million were black; 4.2 million were Hispanic.

Family Status
47.8 million children (82 percent) lived in two-parent families; 10.8 million (18 percent) lived in single-parent families—9.8 million with their mothers and 900,000 with their fathers. From 500,000 to 750,000 children were in foster care, group care, or institutions.

Children in Poverty
In 1977, over 10 million children lived in families with incomes below the poverty level. This was 16 percent of all children compared to 11.6 percent of the whole population.

Over 50 percent of the children in families headed by a woman lived in poverty. 3.9 million or 42 percent of all black children lived below the poverty line.

In March 1979, 7.3 million children were in families receiving Aid to Families with Dependent Children (AFDC) benefits; children are 70 percent of all AFDC recipients.

Children with Working Mothers
In 1979 over 30 million children, including 7.2 million under 6 years old, had mothers in the labor force. In 1970, 39 percent, and in 1979, 51 percent of children had working mothers.

In 1978, over 16 million or 53 percent of all mothers (63 percent of black mothers) worked. 5.8 million working mothers had children under age 6 and 3.1 million, children under age 3.

Day Care

In 1975, there were only 1.6 million licensed day care slots in the country. There are now over 7 million children under 6 whose mothers work. Proportionately less licensed day care is available for children under 3.

Child Health

In 1974, one in seven children, or 9.8 million, had no known regular source of primary health care.

A 1976 study found that 18.2 million children under 17, or one in three, had not seen a dentist.

In 1976, the infant mortality rate in medically underserved counties was 48.8 per 1,000 births, compared to the national rate of 16.1 per 1,000. In 1977, there were 46,975 infant deaths, or 1 in 71 infants (among nonwhites, the rate was 1 in 46).

In 1978, only two-thirds of preschool children were immunized against diphtheria, tetanus, and pertussis; only 61–63 percent were immunized against polio, measles, or rubella, and 51 percent, against mumps.

Education

In 1976, almost one million children between 7 and 17 were not enrolled in school and were not high school graduates. For every 100 graduates, there were 29 dropouts (among black and Hispanic youth there were 52, and among Native Americans 82 dropouts).

Almost 1.8 million students were suspended from school at least once during 1976. Almost 8 percent of the black students, or 1 in 13, were suspended. This was more than twice the rate for white students.

Nutrition

In October 1979, over 10 million children received free and over 16 million others, subsidized lunches. Only 3.5 million children were enrolled in the school breakfast program.

Special Education

In December 1978, 3.8 million students, or 8 percent of all students, received special education in the public schools. In 1976, about 820,000 handicapped children were not being served by public school programs.

In 1978, black children were assigned to programs for the edu-

cable mentally retarded at over three times the rate for white children.

Unemployment

In 1979, the parents of over 6.6 million or 11 percent of all children (2.3 million or 30 percent of all black children) were unemployed or not in the labor force.

In October 1978, 1.4 million or 15.4 percent of teenagers (35 percent of black teenagers) were unemployed.

Housing Discrimination Against Families with Children

There are no national statistics on the numbers of children in substandard housing.

In 1979, the General Accounting Office reported that 10.1 million renter households were living in substandard or overcrowded housing or paying more than 25 percent of their income for rent. The U.S. Department of Housing and Urban Development estimated that 250,000 federally subsidized or insured units would account for 75 percent of all new multifamily construction in 1979.

Housing discrimination against families with children has reached dramatic proportions in large cities. In California metropolitan areas, 70 percent of rental housing excludes children. In Denver, 80–85 percent of existing apartment buildings are for adults only. In Houston, almost 75 percent of all new construction excludes children. This scarcity of family housing, in both publicly subsidized programs and the private rental market, has a disproportionate impact on minority families and families headed by women.

The Coordination Problem in Perspective

What do we mean by coordination?

Certainly there are many complaints about the "lack of coordination" in government. But it is often not clear whether the critics are talking about coordination, inadequate *policies,* inadequate *resources,* uncertain *knowledge,* or some other problem.

Coordination tends to be a public administration term. It implies both a process and a goal. As a goal, it means that the actions of two or more government agents are consistent and mutually reinforcing, without unintended conflict or duplication.[1] It may involve planning, policy-making, budgeting, or operations in

sequential steps over time or simultaneously. Deficiencies can occur vertically among different layers of government or horizontally
within or between agencies or among public and private
organizations.

What do we know about the extent and nature of service co-ordination problems?

We don't know as much as we should, after all the discussion of
the issue over the past two decades. There are many examples but
little systematic data.

In the human services, the lack of coordination can be burden-
some and inefficient. A high proportion of health and welfare clients—some say over 85 percent[2]—have multiple problems requiring varied, simultaneous, and sequential attention. Yet studies estimate the odds that an individual will get to a single service
at four in ten, and the likelihood of a successful referral to a second agency, at one in five.[3] Thus, apart from any questions about
the quality of the services, less than 10 percent of those who need
two services receive them.

The absence of rigorous policy-relevant data is a critical gap in our
ability to understand the problems of services coordination for
children and undercuts our ability to design effective solutions.
Federal, state, and local research collecting precise information on
the dimensions of the problems and the specific issues affecting
different target groups or functions (the handicapped, children out
of their homes, child health, and so forth) should be strongly
encouraged.

What scope, or range, of services should we consider?

The core of our concerns here is with child welfare, health, and
mental health services. Along with some basic entitlement programs like AFDC and Medicaid, these include the major programs that many states and localities have grouped within
superagencies. But people don't come neatly divided in bureaucratic parts, and our consideration of the public services required to meet children's needs should not be limited by present
administrative arrangements.

Human service agencies face critical issues in establishing both
the boundaries of responsibility *and* cooperative relationships with
other organizations in order to deal with the pressing needs of
children and youth. This is particularly true of relations with local
education authorities in developing effective programs for all

handicapped children. Questions about the appropriate coordination of social, health, education, and employment training services are crucial in giving minority youth a chance to achieve economic independence. President Carter's youth employment proposals gave these questions increased public attention. Income support payments provide enormous subsidies for shelter, and the quality of housing is often vital to the physical and social health of children. Yet the lack of coordination between social and housing agencies, the failure of publicly subsidized programs to deal with the housing needs of large families and the growing discrimination against families with children in the private rental market present major problems for children and their families.

Thus, we must look beyond the standard preventive, restorative, or developmental services for children to consider education, special education, employment, job training, and housing to identify the full need for coordination, if not how it can best be met.

What questions about service areas should we consider?

In addition to different eligibility and reporting requirements, one *organizational* consequence of categorical programs is the proliferation of different geographic planning and administrative districts for separate services. More than four thousand sub-state districts have been spawned by federal programs in health, criminal justice, employment training, and so forth.[4] States and localities are themselves experimenting with various regional administrative boundaries embracing more government authorities. The different boundaries of different programs and governmental units inevitably increase the complexity of coordinating services.

Accountability: Citizen Participation and Individualized Plans

Federal requirements have flowered during the last decade. An estimate issued in 1978 found more than three hundred federal programs with participatory requirements.[5] Public involvement processes vary widely with little consistency, coherence, or effectiveness across functional program lines. There are vast differences in the composition and powers of local advisory groups—in Head Start, day care, health planning, Title XX social services, community mental health centers, Title I education, and CETA employment training programs. Department of Agriculture nutrition programs have no requirements at all.

Child advocates are splintered among various categorical pro-

grams. Those concerned with day care rarely know or work with child health groups, which are organized separately from the mental health or mental retardation activists. Each program constituency has a different mix of advocates, client representatives, provider systems, and federal, state, and local administrative interests. This categorical orientation perpetuates fragmented attention to children's needs and prevents the development of programs that can deal with children and families as a functioning whole. It often leads human service constituents to compete for pieces of the budget pie rather than to cooperate to increase the size of the pie.

The development of specific plans for individual children and youth is required by the Education for All Handicapped Children Act (P.L. 94-142) and other programs, sometimes for the same children.

Participatory and planning rights can offer parents multiple ways to attempt to make service providers more accountable in meeting the needs of children. But out of this vast experience, what are the most constructive approaches that can have a positive impact on children and their families? How do we ensure coordinated, individualized planning and effective implementation of the plans?

What do we know about the most common strategies used to achieve coordination?

Not as much as we should. Despite the multiplicity of organizational reforms, research, and demonstration projects, we have little systematic data about their impact on children or families. There is some indication that coordination of service delivery requires decentralized service management. Statewide superagencies, area-wide planning, check-off review procedures, information and referral systems, collocation, coterminality (the creation of common service district lines) and case management all may facilitate coordination, but none ensures it.

Some major organizational reforms of the past decade, like the creation of superagencies, collocation, and coterminality, have had disappointing effects on the coordination of service delivery. It is extremely difficult and rare for superagencies to become more than a new facade for the old bureaucratic systems. Central administrative reforms are unlikely to change the way services are provided without a complementary reorganization of field operations.

Collocation has generally provided a narrow range of additional, rather than coordinated, services. It frequently leads to the

decentralized *delivery* but not *management* of services. Other complementary administrative reforms are necessary if the multi-service center is successfully to attack the coordination problem. The walls that insulate bureaucracies from each other are organizational, not physical.

Coterminality is a response to the usual spaghetti-like patchwork of administrative boundaries. While full coterminality may represent a common-sense ideal, it can be very costly and will bring few improvements in service without parallel changes in the patterns of authority over service planning and operations.

Even when all three strategies have been implemented simultaneously, as in Florida, where a superagency, decentralized management, coterminality, and collocation have all been instituted, the jury is still out in judging the effects. The management traumas of the initial transition period have to some extent been overcome. But will the new statewide structure improve the substantive coordination of services for children and other groups? In theory, it could deal with certain cross-cutting problems, such as detection and prevention services, permanency planning in child welfare, comprehensive state budgeting for children, or the development of appropriate community facilities to accompany deinstitutionalization in the mental health, mental retardation, and juvenile justice systems. But such efforts are just beginning, and their impact remains to be seen.

Where do we go from here? "Sub-system" coordination and target group programming

We will continue to have a federal system dominated by categorical, national purposes. But this compartmentalization in Washington creates a special federal obligation to encourage the development of national, state, and local institutions and devices to coordinate these segmented programs at the point of local service to children and families. We may see no major increases in the proportion of resources devoted to health and social services, although there may be some increases in child health, welfare, handicapped, and youth employment programs. Nonetheless, coordination remains critical for meeting children's needs and effectively implementing existing programs. But how should we proceed?

It may be more useful at this stage to look less at grandiose organizational reforms and more at concrete improvements in coordinating specific services for specific groups of children. How can the millions of Head Start and day care children receive their

EPSDT screens and treatment? How can the hundreds of thousands of children caught in impermanent foster care and institutions be given permanent homes and good community care? How can handicapped children receive the appropriate related services identified in their individual educational plans? What services do dropouts need in order to enable them to complete their education and find jobs? These are the kinds of questions that the next sections will discuss.

This coordination strategy has its problems. The effort to be concrete cannot hope to be comprehensive. Incomplete descriptions of problems, demonstration projects, and possible models presented here are offered as examples of the kinds of analysis and action that may help to improve the lives of children.

We must rigorously assess the impact of proposed measures upon the quality of service. Organizational reform or paper agreements do not necessarily change the behavior or effectiveness of service workers.

New organizational arrangements should reflect substantive policies (not merely managerial requirements) and a commitment to monitor and evaluate their effects on children and families. Too many projects have produced less than their promise, absorbing resources that could have gone to services.

Target Group Planning Dilemmas and Demonstrations

Implementing EPSDT (CHAP)

Broad improvements in child health would require a universal, adequately financed entitlement to basic, primary health services. This demands more than pumping money through a fragmented medical treatment system. Preventive, comprehensive, and continuing care should be stressed. Better implementation of the Medicaid EPSDT program could lay the groundwork for a reoriented child health system.[6]

About 12 million children are eligible for the preventive health screening and treatment mandated under EPSDT. (Proposed CHAP legislation may expand eligibility to another 2 to 5 million children and broaden the services covered.) However, only a fourth are ever screened, and less than half of the conditions detected are ever treated. Professionals predict that 95 percent of children will need dental care, but some states show referral rates as low as 1–3 percent.

EPSDT has been plagued by coordination problems. It is the one Medicaid program which requires states to reach out and en-

sure that a target population is served, but state and federal Medicaid agencies have traditionally acted as passive processors of provider payments. There has been inadequate outreach and followup, difficulty in access and eligibility determination, and a shortage of appropriate providers. It was assumed that parents could find appropriate medical and dental care and that a positive effort to reach children and families was not needed. There was often inadequate coordination between the state and local public welfare departments, which must determine EPSDT eligibility, and state and local health departments, maternal and child health projects financed under Title V, Community Health Centers, or rural health clinics. Medicaid agencies made little or no effort to use Head Start and day care centers or the schools to provide EPSDT information, referrals, or services. Hence, millions of children have been deprived of necessary preventive health care, and they and society will bear the future cost of their untreated problems.

The initial failures of EPSDT have recently provoked an aggressive federal attempt to encourage increased coordination. And some states have developed their own strategies to improve coordination.

The Health Care Financing Agency which houses EPSDT has arranged interagency agreements with the Public Health Service, the Social Security Administration, the Department of Education, and selected programs in the Office of Human Development Services (Title XX social services, Head Start, child welfare, developmental disabilities, and rehabilitation). These agreements are designed to remove impediments (for example, specifying that immunizations at public health centers can be reimbursed by EPSDT) and encourage state and local cooperation. Medicaid will use schools for outreach, referral, and service, and the two agencies will fund ten model demonstration projects.

Federal interagency agreements often promote coordination on paper, rather than in the community. To translate their intent into practice requires significant commitment by administrators. Even with these efforts, major unresolved issues remain. For example, federal Social Security Administration officials assert that the AFDC program has no legal obligation to inform Medicaid-eligible families about EPSDT. Yet the vast majority of the 12 million eligible children qualify because they and their families are AFDC recipients. They will certainly contact the welfare center, where they could be informed of EPSDT. Even this would not ensure their participation. In contrast to AFDC, Head Start has made a vigorous effort to cooperate with EPSDT, and the Federal

Interagency Day Care Requirements will mandate receipt of EPSDT or equivalent child health services.

Demonstration: State of Pennsylvania

In 1975, the Pennsylvania Governor's Office for Human Resources formed an Interagency Task Force on Early Health Screening,[7] which included state agency representatives, local program operators, and professional experts. It focused on the provision of technical assistance and training in day care, Head Start, maternal and child health programs, and school health services. Detailed negotiations brought about changes in state regulations, for example to make the periodicity of health examinations in Head Start and day care conform to EPSDT standards. Aggressive efforts were made to use Head Start programs for outreach and referrals. In 1975–76, only 39 percent of those eligible among the 12,000 children enrolled in Head Start received EPSDT screening; by 1977–78, 90 percent of eligible children were screened. The rate of screening for those eligible among the 20,000 children in day care programs rose from about 25 percent to 75 percent. Demonstration programs are now being implemented in Philadelphia public schools.

Approximately 12,000 Pennsylvania children are in some placement outside their homes. Prior to the enactment of a new state law and work by the Task Force, few participated in EPSDT though all are eligible. Generally, the adolescent, teenage, and over school-age populations are least likely to obtain EPSDT health care. In 1977, less than 50 percent of the eligible 16–21 year-olds and only 10 percent of the 19–21 year-olds were screened. The Task Force has developed cooperative agreements with family planning programs to supplement their health care with EPSDT services. In many cases, substantial cost savings have resulted for private agencies, education authorities, and local and state governments.

The Pennsylvania program staff stress that whatever successes the Task Force has had came less from interagency agreements than from the nitty-gritty work of changing regulations and providing adequate technical assistance and training to state and local program operators.

Other states have adopted different strategies. Some, like Michigan, have developed strong links to the state health department combined with computerized management information tracking systems.

Child Welfare: Children Without Homes

Public child care systems annually place between five hundred thousand and seven hundred and fifty thousand children in foster homes or institutions away from their families. Incredibly, we don't know precisely how many.
• A recent study estimated that in March 1977 approximately 502,000 children were in foster care and the responsibility of public socal service departments.[8]
• A 1975 study reported 47,000 youth in public juvenile detention centers, training schools, and other correctional facilities; another 27,000 were in private custodial facilities.[9]
• In the summer of 1976, 27,000 children under 18 were in psychiatric institutions and 55,840 in facilities for the mentally retarded.[10]

We deem ourselves a pro-family society, yet children at risk of placement are subject to an anti-family bias at all points in the placement process. They may be unnecessarily separated from their families, cut off from their families when placed, and may linger in care indefinitely, neither returned to their families nor adopted.

Federal funding patterns actually encourage out-of-home placement and discourage services which might prevent unnecessary placement or reunite children with their families. We pay the most to institutionalize a child; the next highest amount to place a child in a foster home; and only a pittance for services to prevent family breakup. The cost per child may be over $14,000 a year in institutions, $5,000 in foster homes, and $2,300 in intact families.[11] New York State, for example, spends $376 million on children in foster care and only $21 million for preventive services to keep children in their homes.[12]

In addition, *federal policies* do not ensure adequate preventive services, placement in least restrictive settings, periodic case reviews, and dispositional hearings so that children are returned home or freed for adoption. Current policy and funding priorities should be reversed to provide preventive services for children in their families, quality care in alternative settings, and permanent placements for all children.

Our programs are not organized to deal with children and their families in a coordinated, holistic way.

In the traditional child welfare system, several case workers from different administrative offices are often involved in a single case of child abuse. A protective services staff member works with

the family; one foster care worker is responsible for placement and
another for group homes; yet another case worker is responsible
for adoption. And these functions often involve, and the case
workers may be attached to, different levels of government—city,
county, regional, or state.

A continuum of care is important, but almost impossible to
provide, for children and families. The organization of child welfare does not support children in their families. Split responsibility
frustrates prevention and reunification services. Agencies working
with children do not communicate with those working with the
family. Alcoholism treatment services and other family services
are usually separated from child protective services. The actions
of social service agencies are not coordinated with those of health
or housing agencies.

Similarly, bureaucratic fragmentation blocks necessary entitlement or supportive services for the out-of-home child. For example, foster parents caring for AFDC children often do not know
that they are eligible for EPSDT health screening and treatment.
There is confusion about who has the right to obtain necessary
supportive services for the child. School authorities may tell the
foster parents of a handicapped child that they have no say about
special education because the welfare department, as the legal
custodian, must request it. Obtaining special education for institutionalized children is even more problematic. The Education
of All Handicapped Children Act, P.L. 94-142, specifies that
states establish "surrogate parent" programs for children whose
parents are unknown or unavailable, but few have done so.

Relations between the juvenile justice and social service systems
are often uncoordinated and confused, handicapping effective service for offenders and dependent or neglected children.

The notable effort to remove children inappropriately placed in
largely custodial institutions for delinquents, the mentally disturbed, or the retarded has, unfortunately, been poorly coordinated with agencies responsible for subsequent services to these
children in community settings.

To piece together the splintered services and untangle the knot-
ted regulations, case management for the whole child and family
is essential.

A Demonstration Model: Lower East Side Family Union

The Family Union is an independent agency originally sponsored by five settlement houses in New York's Lower East Side. It
set out to counteract the traditions of child welfare services which

stressed out-of-home placement rather than family welfare, so that children could remain with their parents.[13]

Beginning operation in 1974, the Family Union focused on work with "high risk" families and developed a number of unusual approaches to prevent undesirable foster care. The Union staff is organized into teams of social workers and homemakers who work with the family service agencies. After an extensive assessment, a written contract between the family, the agencies, and the Union is prepared. A Family Union worker is responsible for enforcing this agreement as case manager and advocate.

One key to supporting children in their families is the extensive use of homemakers, drawn from the neighborhood and trained on the job, who live with the family to substitute for or supplement the parents when the family is threatened with disintegration. The homemakers are viewed as role models and teachers for the parents. If it proves necessary to remove children from their homes, the goal is to use neighbors or nearby relatives for short-term placements. Only as a last resort does the Union turn to formal foster care, and then every effort is made to find a home in the neighborhood.

In an average year, the Family Union has been approached by four hundred families; about half qualify for intensive work as high risk. Only 5 percent of the most troubled cases require foster care, in many cases for brief periods. Thus, instead of waiting for families to fall apart and having to remove their children, the Family Union has demonstrated that adequate support can keep families together. It has integrated the various services troubled families need in their home and neighborhood. It has found that public and private agencies, although sensitive about their own prerogatives and autonomy, will work cooperatively with an independent organization dealing with specific high-risk families.

Child Development

There are twelve major sources of federal funds for children's day care and preschool programs: Title XX; Head Start; the Work Incentive Program; Comprehensive Employment and Training Act (CETA); Community Development Block Grants; Community Action Programs; Appalachian Regional Commission; Title IV-B, Child Welfare Services; Title I, Elementary and Secondary Education Act; P.L. 94-142, preschool incentive; AFDC income disregard; and income tax credits.

The data on these programs are poor. Most cannot estimate the

number of children served; a few cannot even estimate the money spent for day care. The Congressional Budget Office produced a table which indicates the variety and scale of federal support for day care, but the statistics should be viewed with some skepticism (Table 1).

With increasing numbers of poor, minority, and working or single-parent families using full-day child care arrangements, the role of these providers becomes crucial for millions of young children and their families. Day care should link children to needed health, nutrition, dental, and other services and families to food stamps, Supplementary Security Income (SSI), welfare, and so forth. But the multiple federal programs, eligibility rules, and financial arrangements compound the difficulty of doing so. The lack of comprehensive federal day care legislation complicates the allocation of day care resources, the provision of information about available services, the improvement of service, and the coordination of day care and other services. In some programs, like Head Start, the coordinating connections are written into performance standards. On March 12, 1979, HEW Secretary Patricia Harris signed the final HEW Day Care Regulations, awaited for more than a decade, that will apply to Title XX, WIN, and IV-B child care programs. Unfortunately, the new social services block grant approved in 1981 specifies that only state and local standards need apply, so the potential for this federal stimulation of services coordination has evaporated.

The new regulations present an important opportunity for major child care providers to improve their coordinating role with human service agencies. For example, the day care facility must now ensure that children have had health assessment equivalent to that of EPSTD. It then must inform parents about and assist them to obtain community health services. Simultaneously, the state day care agency must see that day care centers have the necessary information about child health services and that children eligible for government health services receive them.

The day care facility must also provide parents with information about social services and help them to obtain them. The state must ensure that eligible children receive necessary government-financed services. However, the methods of effecting this coordination between state and local health and social service agencies have yet to be developed.

Information and Referral: The California Experience

Parents need information about the child care arrangements in their communities. This is no small task, but it is important in

Table I
Federal Obligations for Children, FY 1977

Agency and Program	Obligations (millions)	Children served (thous.)	Obligations per child
Agriculture			
Child Care Food Service	$ 120	580	$ 207
Appalachian Regional Commission	9	47	197
Community Services Administration, Community Action Agency	3	N/A	N/A
Health, Education, and Welfare, Social Security Act			
Title XX, Social Services	809	799	1,013
Title IV-A, AFDC Child Care	84	145	582
Title IV-A, Work Incentive	57	85	672
Title IV-B, Child Welfare	5	19	247
Health, Education, and Welfare, Head Start	448	349	1,283
Health, Education, and Welfare, Elementary and Secondary Education Act			
Title I, Preschool and Kindergarten	136	367	371
Title I-A, Migrants	14	38	382
Title VI-B, Education for the Handicapped State Grants	8	260	30
Title VI-C, Early Education for the Handicapped	14	14	1,000
Housing and Urban Development			
Community Development Block Grant	43	85	500
Interior, Bureau of Indian Affairs			
Kindergarten	3	2	1,125
Parent-child development	1	N/A	2,222
Treasury, Tax expenditures	500	4,000	125
Total	$ 2,252	6,790*	$ 332

Source: See text. *May be inflated due to overestimates and double-counting.

helping parents to make adequate choices between center and family day care. Some organizations provide much more than the traditional information and referrals (I&R), technical assistance to programs: data on the need for child care, support groups for single parents, and clearinghouses for day care jobs.

There is no explicit federal policy on I&R although Title XX encourages such systems for all human services without regard to income or eligibility limitations. Over the past few years, California has funded over thirty broad "resource and referral" centers. Although rigorous evaluations have not been completed, the approach appears to be a success in helping families gain needed child care.[14]

Child care I&R systems face some difficult policy questions. What is the role of I&R in licensing or evaluating the quality of day care programs? Who should sponsor and deliver the service? Should I&R cover a wide range of human services or focus on specific concerns like child care? The contribution of I&R to the accessibility, coordination, and improvement of children's services needs further analysis before the advantages and drawbacks of alternative models are better understood.

The Handicapped Child: Special Education and Related Services

For the millions of handicapped youngsters, service coordination is critical. They have multiple needs, often from birth throughout their lives. They require a sequence of simultaneous support services adapted to their stage of development, involving health therapy, developmental training, the use of physical equipment, training in braille or sign language, and so forth. Day care or Head Start provide the pre-school child education and training, respite for parents, and advocacy for other services. At the elementary and secondary school levels, education and related services must be tailored to each youngster's needs with a gamut of assistance from transportation to health, psychological, hearing or speech therapy. For older youth, vocational education and occupational therapy may become crucial. The strains on some families may make homemaker assistance, respite care, or even out-of-home placements vital. With support, most handicapped persons can usually become productive members of society. Coordination of multiple agencies and services is crucial—and rare. Without it, millions of our young will lead unnecessarily constrained and dependent lives.

The Education of All Handicapped Children Act of 1975 makes state and local education authorities responsible for providing every handicapped child a "free appropriate public education" including necessary "related" special services.[15] A written Individualized Education Program (IEP) prepared by a team of professionals, school officials, and parents must specify the services and goals required for each child. In theory, the IEP is a contract for individualized coordinated services. In fact, parental involvement is pro forma, too many plans are standardized, and their implementation can be feeble, particularly when they involve the cooperation of health and social service agencies.

The exact number of handicapped children is unknown. Schools currently serve almost four million handicapped children 5–17 years old, and have identified almost one million more whom they cannot serve; among the latter are many poor children, Hispanics, and those in rural areas. Contrariwise, too many blacks (proportionately three times as many as whites) are labeled as educable mentally retarded. Many children under 5 and over 17 (on some estimates, one million or more) are unidentified and unserved. Children in foster care or in mental and correctional institutions may be particularly neglected.

P.L. 94-142 places immense new responsibilities on state education departments to meet the needs of the handicapped and develop interagency coordination arrangements. Although legal accountability has been placed on school systems, handicapped persons will not be adequately served unless other human service systems aggressively accept their shared responsibility for them. Historically, education agencies have operated independently. They now must develop working relationships with other agencies. Too often this process has produced squabbling over which dollar should be used first, or who is responsible for particular kinds of children.

Where do P.L. 94-142, Title I, Title XX, Medicaid and EPSDT, Community Mental Health, SSI Disabled Children, and so forth begin and end? Educators argue that children are being unfairly dumped into their laps. Others argue that the schools are trying to raid their funds. These are critical policy questions. But while the disputes rage, the coordinated services intended by the law are not being delivered.

Federal leadership in promoting effective coordination has been at most facilitative. The Bureau of Education for the Handicapped (BEH) has negotiated with nine federal education and human service agencies to clarify some of the major policy and

coordination issues involved in ten major programs. Many agency rules, joint policy statements, and interagency agreements have resulted.[16] They stipulate, for example, that education agencies can be EPSDT providers or that Title XX funds can be used for contract services without violating the prohibition against paying for "generally available" services.

How such agreements will help handicapped children has yet to be seen. The record of federal interagency agreements in producing significant changes in state and local services has been unimpressive. BEH has sought to persuade agencies to accept joint responsibility and undertake cooperative activities for handicapped children. It has not adopted an aggressive or consistent program to require the kinds of coordination called for in the law. Such leadership, combining pressure and technical assistance, will be necessary to overcome bureaucratic inertia and resistance.

Under the law, "surrogate parents" must be appointed to ensure that children in institutions or in foster care receive the benefits and protections to which they are entitled. BEH has been satisfied with paper assurances. Not one state has a surrogate parent program in operation, and many children are still being placed in inappropriate, restrictive settings.

Despite the legal mandate for extensive interagency agreements within the states, many services are not being provided because of interagency territorial disputes. A classic example is set forth by Judge Harold Green of the U.S. District Court for the District of Columbia in *North* v. *District of Columbia Board of Education* (1979). Authorities who agreed that a child needed multiple services in a residential setting twice let him be assigned to parents who could not provide proper care. The cognizant agency instituted neglect proceedings, when the parents were providing insurance payments and fighting for their child's rights. The court ordered the Board of Education to pay for residential treatment.

Education and human services agencies must develop means to resolve such issues short of the courts, which can be effective only in individual cases. The federal government should give technical assistance to, and if necessary put pressure on, the states to adopt and implement effective interagency agreements. Without these agreements, as the *North* case indicates, no single agency will take responsibility for funding and the services—vocational rehabilitation, occupational therapy, counseling, residential placement, and physical therapy—that everyone acknowledges are necessary will not be provided.

Different State Responses

State agencies have adopted three different strategies to meet their
coordination responsibilities under P.L. 94-142.
• The state education agency has attempted to become the
provider for the full range of services, as in the Dakotas and
Nebraska.
• A number of states, such as Louisiana and Massachusetts,
have attempted to develop comprehensive planning for the handicapped from the top down. Six states—Connecticut, Idaho, Iowa,
Hawaii, Louisiana, and Oregon—have model project funding
from the Bureau of Community Health Services and assistance
from BEH.
• Most states are concentrating on improving coordination in
specific areas. Michigan has focused on a detailed agreement between vocational and special education. A number of states and
such cities as Hartford and New Orleans have stressed closer ties
between schools and EPSDT.[17]

Policies for the Future

State Offices for Children

Children's problems cut across many agency responsibilities.
Comprehensive and coordinated planning, budgeting, and administration cannot, therefore, be carried out by individual operating
agencies. Thirty-one states now have some form of high-level office, council, committee, or commission specifically designated to
review the needs of children and often their families.[18]
The number of children's offices is increasing; twenty were
formed in the last decade, eight of these since 1977. Seventeen are
lodged in the governor's office; ten (the number has grown), in
state social service agencies; and four, in state legislatures. The
majority of these offices have small budgets and staff. Many have
recently concentrated on planning for the White House Conference on Families. But eleven state offices have budgets of over
$100,000 and substantial agendas for action and analysis in pro-
moting legislation and coordinating the planning and implementation of children's services.
Examples from the two largest offices, New York funded at
$740,000 and Massachusetts with $5.5 million, illustrate these
varied efforts. As creatures of the governors, many children's of-

fices have high level access to state governments, but they are also
more visible and vulnerable to changes in political administra-
tions. The struggle over the Massachusetts Office for Children is a
case in point. The office was established by statute in 1972. In a
unique approach, it soon established over forty area "Help for
Children" offices to provide information, referral, follow-up and
advocacy services throughout the state.[19] The offices directed parents to needed services and helped children who were rebuffed or
fell between the gaps of different programs. When cases could not
be resolved locally, they were referred to one of seven regional
Help for Children units where interdepartmental teams reviewed
them and assigned responsibility for the child to a specific agency.
If the agency refused, the case went to the state department commissioner for resolution.

Such a system prevents the file drawer burial or round-robin
buck-passing that may occur in difficult cases. It focuses on the
individual child, not on abstract organization or planning. The
Help for Children offices process about 30,000 annual requests for
help, about 95 percent have been handled at the local level, with 5
percent referred to the regional teams. Over two-thirds of the
cases have involved special education problems.

The New York State Council on Children and Families, formed
in 1979, has concentrated on a number of difficult groups where
coordination is particularly important: hard-to-place children;
out-of-state placement; interagency agreements to encourage joint
review, inspection, and supervision of providers serving similar
children in different programs; the overlapping fiscal responsibilities for special education students, and so forth.[20] As a special project, the Council developed and published a state *Children's
Budget: 1980–1981,* which attempts to identify and analyze the
nearly $12 billion spent on children's services by function (over
two-thirds went for education), agency, and source of funds. Several other states, such as California and North Carolina, have prepared similar budgets. They provide a wealth of data for administrators and advocates, highlight the relationship between public
policy and funding priorities (such as treatment versus prevention), encourage interagency planning, and identify service gaps.

One-stop Eligibility Determination

Under a presidential directive, the Office of Management and
Budget and the Department of Health, Education, and Welfare
established an interagency study team, in January 1979, to sim-

plify and streamline the eligibility policies of the major, basic federal assistance programs. The group concentrated its analysis on the inconsistent and duplicative information requirements of seven programs with over $45 billion in federal funding for FY 1979: AFDC, SSI, Medicaid, Title XX, Food Stamps, Section 8 Housing, and CETA.

A glossary of definitions was compiled for the elements of income and assets covered by all seven programs, and recommendations to achieve conformity were made. These definitions would make it easier for states to use one application form in determining financial eligibility for all seven programs.

Eligibility simplification would facilitate the creation of one-stop eligibility determination centers. Under present practice, an individual or family must go to four locations to receive support under the seven programs: (1) local welfare offices, for AFDC, Medicaid, food stamps, and Title XX; (2) public housing authorities for Section 8; (3) prime sponsors for CETA; and (4) local SSA district offices for SSI. A single center would reduce travel and encourage people to learn about and utilize complementary assistance programs. This might be particularly beneficial to handicapped and elderly persons. It could also reduce administrative costs and free workers to concentrate on program services.

How can the one-stop eligibility center best improve the coordination of children's services? Should eligibility determination be tied to case assessment, management, or advocacy, to information and referral, or to transportation? Who should sponsor and house the center? The study team suggests local welfare offices or private contractors. Can eligibility determination be delegated to nonprofit or advocacy organizations? Do public agencies with budgetary responsibilities have the necessary incentive to ensure that eligible populations enroll and participate?

The relationship between improved accessibility and one-stop centers is unclear, especially if the centers replace the many independent access points to agency services. Centralization could increase travel costs for some. Many, particularly elderly persons, interested in selected services such as food stamps or Medicaid are reluctant to go to a "welfare" center. Computer consoles might combine the benefits of one-stop eligibility determination with decentralized access to the system in a variety of local facilities.

Final Note

Major issues, like the coordination of human service and youth employment programs or the conscious use of welfare housing subsidies to improve living conditions for the poor, have not been dealt with.

The examples of coordinated, target-group services we have cited could be greatly multiplied. North Carolina has passed a "New Generation" law that sets up a working cabinet for children chaired by the governor and authorizes county managers to do the same. Minnesota recently instituted a social service block grant that increases the flexibility of county administrators in implementing multiple services for children.

This paper has stressed that organizational efforts to improve coordination must flow from strong policy commitments to deal with specific problems, and their impact must be rigorously assessed. Coordination can be critically important for millions of children, but it must be brought down to earth. As one city councilman who lived through a major reorganization put it: Those who have their eyes on the stars are likely to trip over the cracks in the sidewalks. I, for one, would be satisfied with getting the cracks in the sidewalks fixed.

Notes

1. With some modification, this definition essentially follows the one suggested in James L. Sundquist, *Making Federalism Work,* The Brookings Institution, Washington, D.C., 1969.

2. Sheila B. Kamerman and Alfred J. Kahn, *Social Services in the United States,* Temple University Press, Philadelphia, 1976, p. 44.

3. A summary of the studies in Lancaster, Los Angeles, Boston, and Macon County, Illinois is found in the "Interim Report of the FY 1973 Services Integration R&D Task Force," U.S. Department of Health, Education, and Welfare, Washington, D.C., mimeod, no date, p. 3.

4. See *Sub-State Regionalism and the Federal System,* Advisory Commission on Intergovernmental Relations, Washington, D.C., 1973.

5. *Citizen Participation,* Community Services Administration, Washington, D.C., 1978. For an attempt to sort out the multiple participatory policies in one department, see *Ties that bind . . .,* U.S. Department of Health, Education, and Welfare, Region X, Seattle, 1976, pp. 48–52.

6. See "Early and Periodic Screening, Diagnosis and Treatment Program," Section 1905 (A) (4) (B) of the Social Security Act, P.L. 90-248, Title III, 1967.

7. See *Annual Report: Interagency Task Force on Early Health Screening,* March 1977–November 1978, Commonwealth Child Development Committee, Governor's Office for Human Resources, Harrisburg, Pennsylvania, November 1978.

8. A. Shyne and A. Schroeder, *National Study of Social Services to Children and Their Families—Overview,* Children's Bureau, Office of Human Development Services, U.S. Department of Health, Education, and Welfare, Washington, D.C., 1978, pp. 8–9.

9. See *Children in Custody,* Information and Statistics Service, U.S. Department of Justice, Washington, D.C., 1977, pp. 18–19.

10. See *1976 Survey of Institutionalized Persons,* Current Population Reports, Series P-23, No. 69, Bureau of the Census, June 1978, p. 73.

11. Assistance Commissioner Beverly Sanders, New York City Department of Social Services, testimony before the Subcommittee on Public Assistance and Unemployment Compensation, Committee on Ways and Means, House of Representatives, March 27, 1979.

12. See *State of New York Children's Budget, 1980–81*, Office of the Governor, Albany, 1980, pp. 29, 60, 80, 82.

13. See Bertram M. Beck, *The Lower East Side Family Union: A Social Invention*, Foundation for Child Development, New York, 1979.

14. See James A. Levine, *Breaking the Day Care Stalemate: The Prospects and Dilemmas of I&R*, Center for Research on Women, Wellesley College, Wellesley, Mass. [n.d., 197?].

15. Children aged 5–18 were eligible by September 1, 1978 under P.L. 94-142; those 3–4 and 19–21 were to be eligible by September 1, 1980, unless state law or practice prohibited serving either age group. There is no provision for 0–2 year-olds.

16. See Lisa Walker, *A Status Report on Federal Interagency Agreements*, Institute for Educational Leadership, George Washington University, Washington, D.C., November 16, 1979, draft.

17. See *State and Local Models*, Institute for Educational Leadership, George Washington University, draft, Washington, D.C., no date (1979?).

18. The information on state offices for children was gathered by Children's Defense Fund Staff in a January–February 1980 telephone survey.

19. *Help for Children Policy Manual*, Office for Children, Commonwealth of Massachusetts, Boston, October 1978.

20. *Annual Report*, New York State Council on Children and Families, Albany, October 1979.

COORDINATING SERVICES FOR THE ELDERLY: THE PROMISE AND LIMITS OF COORDINATING HEALTH, MENTAL HEALTH, AND SOCIAL SERVICES

Robert Morris

American society has sought to help the elderly and their families to adapt to aging: to survive, in many cases, to very old age with decreased income, reduced mobility, increased illness and disability, and a lack of useful purpose. To provide this help, programs have been created, administered, or funded by many federal and many more state agencies and conducted by thousands of governmental and private bodies. Federal and state programs are directed by independently authorized departments and agencies. The Wisconsin Department of Health and Social Services sums up the complex situation for home services alone:

> The whole subject of long-term support is fraught with complexity. . . . There exists a wide range of services involving several professional disciplines, provided under a variety of authorizations and having a number of eligibility requirements. Individuals with substantial needs, but not requiring institutional care, face the interrelated problems of having plans of care developed, locating services that fit their needs, financing those services, organizing the services and coordinating the flow of necessary information among themselves, their service providers and third party payors.

Coordination: Context and Objectives

The modest administrative changes which coordination promises are better realized with a full understanding of the larger context in which they are embedded. This includes: a serious under-funding of some sectors (non-medical home care, family care, mutual aid, and stimulation for the institution- and house-bound) and

relative over-funding of others (episodic acute medical care, drugs, and custodial institutions); the lack of clear policies about coordination and the objective of public services; rigid service structures; and public and professional attitudes and practices. Most basic of all, perhaps, are public attitudes.

Coordination is not simply a technical matter of imposing an efficient, logical structure on heterogenous programs. The American ideal is an independent, self-sustaining individual and family. For the elderly, the issue is how to maintain independence during a succession of adjustments and accommodations to declining capacity imposed by age, the economy, or the way younger people build cities. The need for help increases at a different pace and for different reasons for each individual. Each categorical service seeks to handle a single symptom of malfunction, which is inherent in aging or man-made.

Families are smaller and move farther and more often; science helps more people survive to old age to encounter unfamiliar debility. But attitudes and basic social organizations such as the family and church change slowly. Our culture encourages the belief that every "problem" has a solution that can be quickly found if we work at it. If one is not found, our energy and thoughts turn to problems we can solve. But aging is not "solved." King Lear seeks "to shake all cares and business from our age, conferring them on younger strengths, while we unburdened crawl toward death," but the "crawl" is long and not "unburdened." We hope, like Isaiah, that "No child shall ever die an infant, no old man fail to live out his life; every boy shall live out his hundred years before he dies," but the final decades of those hundred years are discomforting and can be tragic.

Coordination is no substitute for money, clear policy, wisdom, and humanity. But it is worth struggling for. The effort calls for patience and satisfaction with limited goals.

Coordination is complicated by a shift in the provision of services from large, hierarchical organizations to complex networks of smaller, relatively autonomous agencies. At least in principle, the activities of a large pyramidal bureaucracy can be planned and controlled at the summit. But in a dispersed service network, decisions are more decentralized and the qualification of staff are more critical. Accounting is complex; administration is loose, not tight. As the configuration of autonomous agencies can change rapidly, prior experience can provide unreliable evidence of future performance.

For this paper, coordination is defined as lying somewhere be-

tween the undirected, accidental interaction of independent organizations and completely controlled planning—the consolidation
of all services into a single hierarchical organization. Coordination
seems to need four major components: (a) an administrative linkage of related health, mental health, and personal social services
used by many clients; (b) the delegation of authority to a local
administrator to supervise these services; (c) a common intake
and assessment system; and (d) case management to provide simultaneous or linked sequential services.

A reasonable goal of coordination is to improve the balance and
equity of the allocation of separate programmatic resources and
services to the elderly. Coordination is unlikely to improve everyone's quality of life or to create a more ideal society, especially
when public resources are severely husbanded.

The foregoing goal requires a level of funding for community
and personal services at home comparable to that for services at
hospitals and clinics. This would help the elderly to live useful
and satisfying lives in the most normal environment compatible
with their physical and psychological condition. This goal is to be
distinguished from such narrower purposes as improving the
quality or increasing the quantity of existing services, or concentrating resources on the poorest or oldest persons.

These purposes are important not only to husband resources,
but to prepare for the demographic changes of the next twenty
years when the proportion of older persons will increase and that
of persons over 75, with the severest disabilities, will increase still
more. The proportion of severely disabled infants, children, and
young adults who survive for long years will also rise.

Several long-term considerations lie beyond the scope of this
paper. Improving the quality of life for all older citizens is not
considered, nor is the relation between service and basic income
maintenance programs, the proper borderline between family and
public responsibility, or the respective roles of proprietary, nonprofit, and governmental providers. Coordination of services for
"the elderly" is only part of the story since most of the problems
to be dealt with arise at all ages. The transition from decade to
decade is not abrupt and clear. At all ages, functional impairment
can intrude. But we concentrate on the elderly, for their physical
decline is almost inevitable, although its rate and duration varies.
It may persist for many years or a few weeks. Independence may
erode slowly or suddenly, owing to illness or injury. As life is pro-
longed, the need for care increases. Our success in prolonging life
has not been matched by equal success in coping with the
consequences.

For the elderly, as for other groups, the state of dependence is interwoven with activity to retain or restore independence, which can engage medical, mental health, and social services. The aged individual requires all these services simultaneously or sequentially; but they are not organized and administered so that they can easily and efficiently be provided at one time or in a smooth sequence, without interruption. Each system of medical, mental health, and social services has evolved its own pattern of organization, staffing, funding, and methods of operation.

The elderly may be divided into two groups: the "young aged" below 75, and the "old aged" over 75. The younger elderly are more likely to be physically active, better educated, and economically independent. They are interested in new housing, in maintaining or reestablishing health and transportation, social and community links, and finding a new purpose in life with retirement.

Significantly more of the "old old" are less mobile; their income has been further eroded by inflation; they have increasing medical and physical needs. They become progressively dependent upon others, but their network of peers, friends, and family diminishes as they outlive many age mates.

Coordination must handle both groups in addition to the special problems presented by an estimated 20 percent of the elderly who have no close relative. The capacity of the elderly to maintain themselves without recourse to public or private services is heavily dependent on help from their family. Lacking that, organized services face additional complexities. But the lack of a family is seldom considered a condition which may require progressively more attention, extra coordination, or different priorities in allocating scarce resources. Most service agencies and categorical programs assume a family is present.

Coordination, within this context, is confronted with a variety of discrete and practical problems in each provider system. The following summarizes some of these problems.

The Health System

The comprehensive coordination of health services must embrace various types of services: acute and chronic hospitals, nursing homes, congregate residences with medical support, home health agencies, food services, ambulatory medical care, physical or vocational rehabilitation, respite services, and adult day centers for the disabled.

Coordination is necessary to deal with the following problems:

Medical service seldom monitors slow changes in health status between episodes of acute hospital care or visits to a doctor.

The acute medical system lacks specialized or geriatric personnel familiar with the distinctive physiological and psychological reactions of the elderly to cardiac disease, arthritis or stroke.

General hospitals are under financial and professional pressure to rapidly discharge elderly patients with substantial persisting disability, with no assurance that their subsequent care is satisfactory. Medical and financial records are scattered among institutions and programs, not maintained by the patient whom they concern, and are not easily accessible as patients move from one provider to another.

Suitable beds in nursing homes may be lacking, and third-party reimbursement policies make certain classes of patients unacceptable to proprietary nursing homes. Hospital medical treatment stops at the door of the nursing home, which usually lacks meaningful medical service.

Legal entitlement to medical assistance under Titles XVIII (Medicare) or XIX (Medicaid) of the Social Security Act is often unclear. Upon being discharged from a hospital, some persons can secure care at home, while others with the same condition cannot. Medicare is limited in duration; when it expires, a sick person must apply for Medicaid, but can qualify only by meeting a stringent means test which varies from state to state. Those above the margin of poverty can get professional home health care for a short time, but cannot receive personal services under Medicare; while a poor Medicaid patient may (depending on the state) receive either home health or personal care. Elderly persons qualifying for Supplemental Security Income and moving into shared family quarters lose some income.

Most public medical care expenditures go for nursing homes or hospitals and only 1–5 percent for care at home. This is due in part to federal Medicare eligibility requirements and in part to the difficulty of arranging immediate service for hospital discharges by many small home-support agencies. And it is difficult to distinguish between patients who need no help, who can remain at home with help, and who need a nursing home.

The elderly need proper nutrition and prompt treatment of visual, hearing, and dental conditions. When such basic preventive services are neglected, as they often are, more serious conditions such as glaucoma or malnutrition can arise.

Arduous public and costly private transportation can make visits to health facilities difficult. But medical providers are reluctant to furnish home care.

Health can be damaged by the synergistic or conflicting effects of uncoordinated medication and treatment for separate conditions.

The Mental Health System

The mental health services include mental health centers, special nursing homes, outpatient and ambulatory psychiatric care, halfway houses, group homes for the mentally ill, mental hospitals, family counseling, hospices, adult day centers, and hospitals. Comparable services are often offered separately to retarded or developmentally disabled adults.

Mental health services may be viewed as part of the medical care system, but they have special characteristics reflecting the nature of mental illness and the professions which deal with it. Here are some problems of coordination in mental health:

• An effective, standardized, and widely usable method for diagnosing senility or chronic brain syndrome is lacking; hence patients are often misdiagnosed and sent to nursing homes and mental hospitals.

• Drug prescriptions and monitoring by medical and mental health personnel are inadequately coordinated. Multiple medication can produce a blurring of attention, confusion, and a general reduction of intellectual capacity.

• The transfer of a patient to group living in institutions, nursing homes, or group residences can be traumatic. Interpersonal clashes result from resistance to the accompanying loss of identity and routinization of care. When staffs are inadequate to handle such clashes, patients are labelled "difficult" and special services, which disregard the basic problem of depersonalization, are developed for them.

• Psychological, mental health, personal, and family counseling all have difficulty dealing with family conflicts which do not respond to verbal therapy or drugs. Such conflicts are deep seated and intractable in short-term treatment, which is all that is now available.

• There is an inadequate synthesis of either diagnosis or care for patients with a combination of physical and behavioral or emotional difficulties; and, when they are ill, most elderly persons are likely to suffer from several conditions.

Personal Social Services

Personal social services include homemaker and home helps, chore services, information, counseling, foster or group homes, home repair and maintenance, transportation, protective services for the mentally confused, day centers for socializing and leisure time, housing, and informal family support activities. Eligibility for income maintenance programs is often a condition of eligibility for other services.

Here are some major problems of coordinating personal social services:

• There is an absence of stable federal, state, or local policy about the purposes, directions, or intent of these services. Should they improve the quality of life for all aged, keep people out of institutions, or deal only with the poorest or most disabled?

• Stable budgets to enable in-home and community-based services to take their place beside medical, institutional, and hospital services are lacking.

• Most personal social service providers are small, often voluntary or proprietary. Coordinating many very small units is difficult.

• Financial eligibility and support are often determined by reimbursement policies of income maintenance programs (like Supplemental Security Income, local general relief, or Title XX of the Social Security Act). Such payments are routinized, tied to inflexible regulations, and generally restrict providers to defined tasks for which they can be reimbursed.

• The constant, almost annual, change in the priorities and budgets of public third parties keeps social support services in substantial turmoil and hampers efforts at coordination.

• Lacking stable policy or budgets, provider agencies survive by emphasizing a high volume of easy cases. Professionals prefer to work with hopeful and younger clients and neglect those with severe disabilities which require more—perhaps a permanent commitment of—time and energy.

• Few support services are linked to the major health reimbursement systems such as Medicare, Medicaid, or private insurance.

Multi-System Coordination

Attempts to improve the coordination within separate health, mental health, and social programs are of marginal value without improved coordination among these three service areas. However, the latter type of coordination confronts inherent dilemmas.

The current distribution of resources is supported by strong constituencies, each of which demands maintenance of its own services, budget, and identity.

Organizations and professions have evolved to give special attention to selected problems. They can perform their tasks well, but may resist new tasks. Thus, hospitals cannot provide long-term care outside the hospital; mental health centers cannot cope with senility; social agencies have difficulty providing continuing care for dependent persons.

Agencies prosper by providing quick service for many clients. The aged require laborious, continuing, and expensive service. The penniless are welcomed by few agencies.

The dominance of professional, especially medical, models involves control over how problems are defined and dealt with. Each professional agency therefore resists pressure to modify its intake, treatment, and referral pattern. For example, hospitals which refer patients to designated nursing homes may resist referrals to a new home support system.

The provision of adequate, stable home support services requires a reallocation of current resources or the addition of new resources. With the rising cost of existing services, neither alternative is welcomed although both may be necessary.

The different policies and practices of each level of government hamper coordination and foster administrative rigidity and fragmentation. Each program may be financed under a different federal-state-local cost-sharing formula. Hospital care is financed mainly by federal sources; nursing home and home health services, mainly by 50–50 or 60–40 federal–state matching; most social home support services, by 75–25 federal–state funding. In many states, local appropriations must be factored into such ratios.

Each jurisdiction prefers to underwrite those services likely to benefit its treasury and to ignore those whose costs can be shifted to other jurisdictions. Home health and support services reduce hospital costs borne by the federal government while they increase the burden on state and local budgets. Proposals to reduce the use of nursing homes may increase federal or local costs while they reduce those of the states.

The final pattern of services reflects parochial economic calculations more than the needs of the elderly or a broader economic rationality. The Office of Management and Budget or the General Accounting Office may be able to calculate the costs and benefits of a rational service system, but the jurisdictions which fund and provide services make a more parochial calculation.

Achievements and Limitations

During the past decade, numerous experiments have been undertaken in the search for improved methods of coordinating service
delivery for the aged. Many were dependent on federal waivers for
research purposes; others have been local initiatives. Thumbnail
sketches of some major experiments are given below. They are of
three types:

• Attempts to orchestrate services from above, by umbrella
agencies, ongoing as well as *ad hoc* interdepartmental task forces,
multi-service centers, and altering resource allocation by state
budget controls.

• Meshing from below by citizen groups which may combine
into new associations and create new service patterns.

• The self-linking of professional personnel in countless
provider agencies. Hospitals refer patients to nursing homes, and
sometimes to home care agencies, which, in turn, secure acute
medical care from hospitals. More rarely, nursing homes and
home support agencies collaborate.

The following conclusions may be drawn from past efforts to
coordinate services:

The distribution of services utilized can be altered by central
case assessment when it carries authority to pay for the designated
services or is a prerequisite for third party reimbursement. The
authority to pay for alternative service modes has altered the proportion of the elderly diverted from hospitals to nursing homes or
to home care. Where Medicaid reimbursement of nursing home
care is contingent upon a prior finding that no alternative mode of
care is available, nursing home admissions can be reduced or de-
ferred. Medical or social service personnel with some financial resources at their disposal have been able to increase the amount of
home care and to reduce institutional admission rates for experimental populations.

Shifts in use and expenditure patterns have not yet been shown
to contain *total* expenditures for the elderly. The total costs and
benefits of any program to all federal, state, and local governments, not to mention private patients, have yet to be tallied. Savings in the use of nursing homes or hospitals by public cases may
be offset by their increased use by private patients—who become
dependent upon public funds when their own are exhausted. Narrow methods of accounting may be at fault rather than weak expenditure controls.

Coordination is severely hampered by inconsistent funding and
policies for service to the elderly and the relative position of medi-

cal and social programs. Thus far, public policy has been mainly confined to medical care, although the needs of the elderly are mainly to live, not to be treated.

At each level of government, planning, resource allocation, and the coordination of services should be coherent—and consistent with that at other levels. When it is not, state and local agencies may try to circumvent federal requirements and vice versa.

Case assessment with resource control is much more effective than case management alone.

Coordination is not a satisfactory substitute for money and staff.

Services are sometimes made more accessible for some clients, but most clients remain unfamiliar with available services.

Case management has worked primarily within, rather than between, social and health services.

Alternative Courses

Major reconstruction of the entire system of health, mental health, and social services in the next few years seems infeasible and perhaps unnecessary. An incremental approach would encourage each level of government and type of service to devote some proportion of its discretionary resources:

• To develop stable community-based social care or support to parallel established medical institutions. This should yield some economies and meet the wishes of the elderly. It may encounter resistance from health institutions facing rising costs.

Alternatively, the dominant role of institutions, especially medical ones, can be accepted and continued and home support downplayed.

• To help providers broaden their services. Decentralized case and program planning would give each agency greater flexibility in using public funds than is possible under centralized control. For example, medical agencies could take more responsibility for giving or buying social support services, and vice versa.

Such flexibility could improve the quality or quantity of service if economies were not eaten up by staff benefits. Agencies might diversify and offer varied health and social services, perhaps introducing an element of competition into care for the elderly. Agencies might develop more efficient and useful patterns of cooperation. Some areas might end up with many institutions and little home support; others, with the reverse; but this lack of uniformity can be justified by the accompanying flexibility in each system. A maintenance of effort provision for current clients would probably be necessary.

Alternatively, centralized decisions about how money shall be used can, and probably will, continue. In this event, the capacity of central planning bodies to monitor provider conduct, and the cost of planning and control, should grow.

• To increase client choice of services. While this might please consumers, it could increase costs. Clients are unlikely, for example, to choose home help and then forego a hospital or nursing home if their condition deteriorates. At present, such alternatives are subject to some queuing or channeling. To leave coordination largely to clients is an untried course of action. Some research indicates that client choices for service are less costly than professional choices.

Promising Examples

The following examples illustrate some of the major kinds of coordination which have been attempted. They may be classified by the degree of control exercised by the coordinating unit over resource allocation, the scope of coordination across categorical services, and whether coordination is imposed by government or introduced voluntarily by service providers.

Triage, Plainfield, Connecticut, is a nonprofit corporation created by state initiative and funded as a Medicare experiment with waivers. It serves about 1,800 people a year with a budget of about $5 million. Coordination is achieved indirectly by case assessment and planning by teams of nurses and social workers who use social security trust funds to reimburse providers for social and medical services believed necessary to attain client and project objectives. Only persons eligible for Medicare may utilize the central assessment, but they need not do so. Triage staff do not initiate or administer services. The plan depends upon existing service providers to introduce services that have been lacking or in short supply, for which they can now be reimbursed.

Community Care Organization (CCO), Wisconsin, is a state-initiated program similar to Triage, but funded by Medicaid waivers and limited to income-eligible persons of any age. CCO stimulates the establishment of independent local community care agencies, which are allocated funds on a capitation basis against which reimbursement to providers can be authorized for services to severely disabled persons. The community agency contracts with providers for case finding, assessments, and community support services. CCO also makes its own assessments and operates a case management service. In either case, the designated case planners

receive applications from agencies or individuals, determine needs, and recommend services intended to provide satisfactory care with reduced institutionalization. Recommended services can be financed even if not customarily reimbursed by Medicaid, if Medicaid purposes and eligibility rules are respected. Payments are authorized by the case management unit which tries to direct community attention to unmet needs.

Massachusetts Home Care Corporation is a statewide, publicly mandated body consisting of a network of independent district community care corporations funded primarily by the State Office on Aging. The district corporation boards, which also serve as the Area Agencies on Aging authorized by the Older Americans Act (OAA), receive OAA funds, additional state appropriations, and Title XX funds assigned by agreement with the state's Department of Welfare. Medical care is administered and funded by the state Medicaid program, but fund allocations for the elderly are negotiated with the Office on Aging as part of a broader state health plan. The area corporations fund social services provided mainly by existing agencies according to priorities established by each corporation within state guidelines. The corporations administer intake, case management, and reimbursement of homemaker, chore, and transportation services authorized by individual case plans. Clients are served by agencies with which the corporation contracts. They can apply directly to the agencies, but reimbursement will be made only for cases managed by the corporation. The home care corporations also allocate annual grants from Titles III and VII of the Older Americans Act for needed services (excluding hospital, institutional or ambulatory medical care) initiated by other agencies and conforming to district plans.

Project Access, the Long-Term Care Project, Rochester, N.Y., an experiment relying upon Medicaid waivers, seeks to diminish unnecessary hospital and nursing home use and to strengthen home care. By agreement with state and local regulatory and funding agencies, Access has authority to authorize or disapprove payments to nursing homes for patients, eligible for public funds, who do not require institutional care and for whom living arrangements can be devised by project staff. Central assessment is made by a team with medical, nursing, and social work members. The staff authorize payment for community support services. The program does not affect individuals able to pay for nursing home service, although those who cannot guarantee payment for six months are subject to the program on the premise that they will shortly become eligible for Medicaid.

The State of Florida has sought to integrate a broad variety of services under a consolidated health and human service agency. The Department of Health and Rehabilitative Services (HRS) includes programs for the elderly, delinquent and dependent youth, and the retarded, and social and economic, health, mental health, children's medical, and vocational rehabilitation services. Eleven district offices, with substantial collocation of personnel, provide all departmental services. At the state level, one assistant secretary is responsible for program planning, training, and evaluation, and another for provision of service. A district administrator, appointed by the secretary, has direct *line* authority over all programs and services. Each program is conducted within the legal restrictions and entitlements of its original federal and state authorization, but the district administrator has substantial flexibility in utilizing personnel, assigning tasks, and developing priorities. He is the principal representative for all services in the local communities.

In each district, program supervisors serve as senior staff advisers but not as responsible, line administrators for each major service area. In addition, each district has created informal service networks to facilitate cooperation between direct departmental services and those conducted by contracts and grants to private agencies. The network seeks to simplify and expedite communication, admission, case management planning, and service among the associated agencies.

Multi-service centers have emerged primarily through collocation of services in one site. Complex multi-problem cases are monitored by a social worker who may assign cases to service personnel and who seeks to foster cooperation between different services. However, there is no central or common intake system. Service personnel are governed by the civil service and program obligations set by categorical funding sources, but the district administrator has some freedom to transfer staff between programs and positions.

Urban Medical Group, Boston, is a unique example of coordination achieved by the voluntary agreement of service organizations which rely upon a group of physicians and nurses committed to comprehensive community-based care for the aged. Several neighborhood health centers, proprietary nursing homes, and a large teaching hospital contract with the Urban Medical Group (UMG) for physician services which may be provided at any site. Backup medical service is assured by the hospital on whose staff the UMG physicians serve. Some neighborhood centers operate

clinics and employ homemakers; others contract for these services. Patients or clients who enter the network at any point can be referred by physicians or nurses to any other. Funding is by fee-for-service reimbursement under state Medicare, Medicaid, and Title XX policies, without waiver. The program functions in inner Boston with a population composed largely of the elderly, minority persons, and young families who have low incomes.

Integrated Campus Programs. In comprehensive provider agencies, coordination becomes an internal management problem. Comprehensive services have been developed by many homes for the aged, which may offer apartment housing, nursing and social service, ambulatory medical care, chronic hospital care, and some social, leisure, and recreation services, all of which can be extended to those not living on campus. Such programs are funded by fees, third-party reimbursements, and special program grants. In theory, all services might be offered; in reality, most are centered around housing, a nursing home, or a home for the aged, offering some services to non-residents either on the premises or in their own homes. Thus, many medical, mental health, and social services have been integrated for limited populations.

An alternative to the campus arrangement is the multi-service center, which usually provides varied recreational, socialization, counseling, information, and educational services to aged persons who are relatively well. A few centers have provided day care for the very disabled (the crippled, the very feeble, the blind, the mildly confused or senile, etc.), but they have not mixed well with the able bodied. Recently, some hospitals have used Medicare funds for experimental day center programs for the sick aged.

A Community Program of Social Support. The Council of Jewish Elders in Chicago, originally a sectarian community program, now offers non-sectarian service for a defined district. It has a case load of 7,500 and an annual budget of $4 million. Funded by private philanthropy as well as public grants, it administers or guides a network of services, including apartment house units, sheltered living, homemaker and home health services, transportation, drop-in centers, legal advice, employment, health checkup, counseling, information, and referral. Hospitalization or admission to nursing homes is arranged by referral and case negotiation. Applicants can enter the system at any point but are ultimately reviewed by case managers who serve as case planners in complex cases. This is a completely integrated, rather than a coordinated, system, primarily for community social support service.

HMOs and the Social/Health Maintenance Organization. Health
Maintenance Organizations, such as the Kaiser Plan in Portland,
Oregon, not only accept retired persons for medical benefits, but
manage the use of nursing homes and administer home health
services to reduce hospital utilization. An extension of this concept
has been proposed by the University Health Policy Center, Brandeis University, in the form of a Social/Health Maintenance Organization (S/HMO) with the following components: A new
corporate entity enrolls healthy and independent elderly persons
who require only occasional preventive service and also those who
are severely disabled or require home care. The corporation guar-
antees hospitalization or nursing home admission, when necessary; home health, help, and homemaker services and a variety of
social support services are to be offered initially to Medicaid and
Medicare populations funded by state and federal capitation
agreements fixing a maximum sum per enrollee based upon the
expected use of all services. The provider must operate within the
capitated sum, calculated not to exceed Medicare and Medicaid
expenditures for a similar group. Management of all services by
one agency should reduce administrative costs and fee-for-service
billing and enable some economical services to replace expensive
ones without reducing the quality of care.

Conclusions

The results of efforts to coordinate diverse agencies serving the
elderly have been murky at best, despite positive achievements,
especially for defined groups who select certain services or live in
a given area. Premature institutionalization can be reduced and
the period of living at home lengthened. Because of inadequate
accounting for both costs and benefits, it is unclear if coordination
reduces overall costs. However, in some experiments, cheaper services have been satisfactorily substituted for more expensive ones.

Although the comprehensive coordination of all services has no-
where been achieved, the coordination of some has worked well.

Many coordination mechanisms are being tested, and some are
sufficiently successful to warrant wider adoption. Central assessment of the sick and disabled seems to work best if accompanied
by the power to authorize public expenditures for services which
are recommended and to bar expenditures for those which are
not.

Case management, usually coupled with assessment, involves
responsibility for seeing that planned services are received. With-

out the authority to authorize or contract for necessary services, case management is ineffective. It works best for a few complex cases requiring multiple services or protective attention. What other types of clients would benefit from such case management is still unclear.

The line consolidation of medical, mental health, and social services in one government department is rare. The consolidation of either medical or social programs alone works best when it includes both staff functions and line authority over the programs.

Local agencies with an established record of voluntary cooperation should be helped and not hampered by central government controls. Coordination is better encouraged by the wider adoption of the varied models we have noted than by the promotion of any one model. However, additional experience with these models should be carefully evaluated. Progress will depend on consistent public support for such models, extended over several years and including (1) financial incentives in the form of initial capitalization or relaxed regulation; (2) comparative evaluation; and (3) information dissemination.

SERVICES AND COORDINATION
IN THE SOUTH

T. M. Jim Parham

At both the state and local government level, the South has been very involved in the "service integration" activities of the past decade. Several states have created comprehensive human service agencies combining several programs; many local governments have developed demonstrations of various service coordination strategies.

In 1978, ten of the seventeen jurisdictions had some form of comprehensive agency including major programs in addition to public assistance and social services. Several included vocational rehabilitation, mental health and mental retardation, public health, aging, and services for delinquent youth. Maryland and Kentucky were among the six states in the nation which combined the State Employment Service in such a configuration.[1]

The state human resource agencies represent a variety of approaches to the goal of trying to increase the coherence of public planning and organization for the development and delivery of human services. Virginia, at one end of the spectrum, has developed a human services secretariat, appointed by the governor, with substantial responsibility and authority to coordinate budget planning and resource allocation among several departments—but without direct responsibility to administer those departments. Florida, which might be considered the opposite extreme, has concentrated direct administrative power over major programs in a state secretary and eleven district administrators. North Carolina, Georgia, Arkansas, Kentucky, Maryland, and Oklahoma each represents distinctive variations and histories in the development of state super-agencies.

Most structural changes occurring in the 1970s were initiated by executive branches as part of a broad government reorganization. The Florida reorganization, however, was legislatively ini-

tiated and makes the greatest effort to establish ideal public administration models with clearly identified decision-makers and unimpeded lines of authority. Some states, Tennessee and Texas for example, have changed the names of their basic public welfare agency to reflect a more modern "human service" perspective without adding major new program responsibilities.

Paralleling recent state organizational developments, the region has also been active in coordination efforts at the local delivery level. Four notable, well documented programs were among 45 SITO (Services Integration Targets of Opportunity) projects supported by the U.S. Department of Health, Education, and Welfare (HEW) in the early 1970s. Not part of SITO but also supported by HEW and outstanding in its scope of effort was the comprehensive Services Delivery System established in Palm Beach County, Florida, during the same period.[2]

The SITO projects were:

• The Urban Management Information System in Chattanooga, Tennessee, which expanded a computerized information system developed originally with a U.S. Department of Housing and Urban Development (HUD) grant. Eventually, the program was operated by the City Human Services Department, formed by combining the Community Action Agency, Model Cities, and the Concentrated Employment Program. It provided information, referral, transportation, and follow-up services.

• The Arkansas Service Center Regional Integrated Services System in Jonesboro, Arkansas, involved the collocation of several units of the state umbrella agency in a new service center. It explored a case manager model and the development of a common intake form.

• The Human Services Coordination Alliance, Inc., in Louisville, Kentucky, brought together a consortium of major service providers and political groups. By using common intake and referral forms, participants created a human services information system which provided data for multi-agency planning. The Alliance, which remains intact, spawned an array of interagency linkages and a governance mechanism.

• The North Central Alabama Human Service Delivery System sponsored by the North Central Alabama Council of Governments headquartered in Decatur, Alabama.

The Comprehensive Services Delivery System in West Palm Beach, Florida, tested concepts of regional coordination and one-stop service. It included collocation, joint transportation services,

shared diagnostic resources, multi-program case planning, and a prototype client information system. The findings of this project were extensively analyzed and helped in the design of the 1975 reorganization of the Florida umbrella agency originally created in 1969.

An extensive amount of information on these state and local efforts is available in the literature, synthesized in a very helpful way by the material produced by the HEW Project Share.[3]

Countless other projects related to service coordination have been sponsored by federal, state, and/or local governments, foundations, and other organizations. A full-scale review of their purposes and findings, however, would be far beyond the reach of this paper. An accurate summary would be that the region has been keenly aware of these issues and has devoted considerable attention—time and money, both professional and political—to them. The region has been in tune with the times.

With this brief background, we shall now focus on the current status of such efforts and the outlook for the future, especially in regard to our two most dependent groups, children and youth and the elderly. The papers by David Austin, John Mudd, and Robert Morris have provided substantial food for thought about the problems of administrators seeking improved coordination and the specific problems of the two target groups.

To obtain some current data, I distributed a brief and simple opinion survey to 180 administrators or managers of programs for children and youth and the elderly in the region. The programs included social services, child welfare, mental health, mental retardation, physical health, aging, juvenile corrections, and some broad umbrella-type agencies. A total of 120 responses was received (67 percent), some incomplete.

The survey sought informed opinion on:
- the relative availability of various forms of service for the two target groups;
- the relative awareness and utilization of selected organizational mechanisms for facilitating coordination;
- the degree of agreement with frequently heard assertions on issues of coordination;
- examples of coordinative devices; and
- the importance of coordination as a continuing focus for professional attention.

The survey form and a tabulation of responses are included as an appendix to this paper; the highlights will be summarized here:

The Relative Availability of Services to the Elderly (Table 2)

• Of 24 itemized forms of service, the one said to be most generally available was "information and referral"; however, over 10
percent of respondents rated even this most basic form as relatively unavailable.
• The service least likely to be available was "respite care"; 93
percent cited it as very rare.
• Also rated high in availability were intermediate and skilled
nursing home care, senior citizens centers, congregated meals, and
in-patient mental health care. This order reflects the emphasis
which the Older Americans Act has placed on social services and
nutrition in recent years.
• Rated very low, along with respite care, was hospice care, geriatric medical specialists, group homes/halfway houses, and special
public housing. The unavailability of special public housing may
surprise legislators and the public but is unlikely to surprise
professionals.
• Several services viewed as fundamental to a balanced basic community system, such as home-delivered meals, homemaker chore
help, transportation and escort service, telephone reassurance,
and hospital day care, were still relatively unavailable in the opinion of a large proportion of respondents.

The Relative Availability of Services to Children and Youth (Table 3)

• Of the 24 common forms of service listed, protective child welfare service was rated most generally available.
• The service rated least likely to be available was "adolescent
day care."
• Rated generally high in availability were EPSDT, juvenile probation, family planning, and adoption service. Even some of these
fundamental services were rated as low in availability by up to 14
percent of respondents.
• Rated as most unavailable, along with adolescent day care, were
respite care, extended school day care, adolescent mental health
inpatient service, and sheltered employment. Surprisingly, school
social service was rated low in availability by over half of the
respondents.
• As in the case of services to the elderly, some fundamental services apparently seem to be in short supply—that is, prenatal

Table 2

Relative Availability of Services for Elderly

| Service | Number Responding 1 (Low) to 5 (High) Availability | | | | | | Mean Response |
	1	2	3	4	5	Total	
Information & referral	1	11	17	34	32	95	3.89
Intermediate nursing home care	4	10	20	29	31	94	3.78
Skilled nursing home care	4	14	23	29	22	92	3.55
Senior citizens' center	1	17	35	22	17	92	3.40
Congregate meals	3	20	34	22	14	93	3.26
Inpatient mental health	5	16	33	25	11	90	3.23
Home health/visting nurse	6	18	34	21	13	92	3.18
Out-patient mental health	4	27	26	27	11	95	3.15
Adult protection service	9	22	23	24	13	91	3.11
Home-delivered meals	2	31	44	10	6	93	2.86
Homemaker/chore help	11	28	34	16	5	94	2.74
Transportation/escort	8	36	35	10	3	92	2.61
Day hospital care	33	25	15	10	12	95	2.45
Telephone reassurance	16	36	29	7	3	91	2.40
Home repair/weatherization	20	38	23	7	3	91	2.29
Day care	24	34	22	8	4	92	2.28
Stroke rehabilitation outpatient	21	33	20	10	0	84	2.23
Senior employment service	28	32	22	7	3	92	2.18
Family foster care homes	33	30	15	10	4	92	2.15
Special public housing	14	37	28	9	0	88	2.14
Group homes/halfway houses	40	35	9	3	4	91	1.86
Geriatric medical specialists	37	36	16	3	0	92	1.73
Hospice	54	27	8	2	0	91	1.54
Respite care	54	30	6	0	1	91	1.51

Table 3

Relative Availability of Services for Children and Youth

Service	Number Responding 1 (Low) to 5 (High) Availability					Total	Mean Response
	1	2	3	4	5		
Protective child welfare	0	5	25	33	37	100	4.02
E.P.S.D.T.	1	11	16	34	29	91	3.87
Family planning	4	9	21	32	36	102	3.85
Juvenile probation service	1	11	21	37	31	101	3.85
Adoption	2	12	25	35	25	99	3.70
Crippled children's service	2	15	20	41	21	99	3.65
Child day care	2	9	36	29	24	100	3.64
Well-baby clinic	2	13	36	27	20	101	3.51
Family foster homes	3	17	28	31	21	100	3.50
Prenatal care	2	16	37	32	14	101	3.40
Family counseling	5	22	38	22	13	100	3.16
Vocational assessment	5	23	41	18	9	96	3.03
Neo-natological care	9	25	32	22	9	97	2.97
Service for unwed parents	7	29	44	14	5	99	2.91
Day training for developmentally disabled	10	27	35	23	6	101	2.88
Adolescent mental health outpatient	12	27	32	24	7	102	2.87
Group homes/halfway houses	14	26	38	17	6	101	2.75
Neurological clinic	7	38	35	11	6	97	2.70
School social service	11	41	34	10	3	99	2.53
Sheltered employment	13	36	41	4	2	96	2.44
Adolescent mental health inpatient	20	27	24	14	1	86	2.41
Extended school day care	24	38	26	7	2	97	2.23
Respite care	34	40	24	6	0	104	2.02
Adolescent day care	43	34	17	2	3	99	1.87

care, family counseling, vocational assessment, neo-natalogical care, and services for unwed parents; 20 percent of respondents rated even family foster homes as relatively unavailable.

Utilization of Service Coordination Mechanisms (Table 4)

• Purchase of service contracts and interagency working agreements were much more frequently utilized than the other 22 mechanisms listed.
• Unified intake and interagency case managers were the two least utilized mechanisms for service coordination.
• Relatively high utilization ratings were given to councils of provider agencies, intra-agency case managers, and interagency policy committees.
• Very low utilization ratings were shared by diagnostic assessments, common information and referral units, and the old historical social service exchange.
• All mechanisms but purchase of service contracts and interagency working agreements were rated relatively low in utilization (less than 3 on a 5-point scale) by a majority of respondents. This seems to confirm the impression that, even if there is awareness of the need for service coordination and knowledge of the means exists, the means have been developed only to a very limited extent.

Assertions on Service Coordination Issues (Table 5)

• Opinion was closely divided on eight of the fifteen assertions, indicating a large degree of uncertainty or disagreement.
• 80 percent of respondents agreed that "the best approach to service coordination is voluntary cooperation . . . encouraged by strong top level policy . . ."
• 73 percent agreed that "we will never achieve resource adequacy until we develop more effective and efficient services."
• 95 percent disagreed with the statement that "we should forget service coordination and integration until we achieve greater resource adequacy."
• 48 percent agreed, 52 percent disagreed with the assertion that "the best approach to service coordination is a comprehensive human service agency."

Table 6 indicates the opinion on assertions according to respondents' programs: mental health, general health, aging, youth, social services, and managerial responsibility for more than one program.

Table 4

Uses of Various Coordination Methods

Service	Number Responding that Use is Rare (1) to Frequent (5)						Mean Response
	1	2	3	4	5	Total	
Purchase of service contracts	5	13	32	42	17	109	3.49
Interagency working agreements	10	21	47	21	13	112	3.05
Council of provider agencies	24	34	34	12	6	110	2.47
Intra-agency case managers	28	35	28	20	2	113	2.41
Interagency policy committees	32	33	24	17	5	111	2.37
Multidisciplinary appraisal teams	29	33	30	14	3	109	2.35
Interagency case conferences	22	45	30	12	2	111	2.34
Educational	28	24	22	13	3	90	2.32
Ombudsman/advocacy	30	39	23	15	4	111	2.32
Psychological	28	26	26	10	4	94	2.32
Vocational	29	23	23	13	3	91	2.32
Psychiatric	29	19	34	7	3	92	2.30
Collocation of services	33	38	21	13	6	111	2.29
General medical	29	21	30	8	3	91	2.29
Guardianship	30	34	25	9	5	103	2.27
Multidisciplinary treatment teams	33	34	33	10	1	111	2.21
Neurological	35	19	26	6	4	90	2.17
Social service exchange	34	27	19	11	2	93	2.14
Common information & referral unit	39	37	21	12	3	112	2.13
Shared diagnostic/assessment service	27	19	11	2	2	61	1.90
Interagency case managers	56	34	16	3	1	110	1.72
Unified intake unit	66	20	12	6	4	108	1.72

Table 5

Opinions About Services Coordination

Assertion	Number of Respondents Who					Mean*
	Strongly Agree	Generally Agree	Dis-agree	Strongly Disagree	Total	
1. peers cannot coordinate each other	4	27	47	17	95	-.48
2. service networks exist and providers usually cooperate without being pushed	2	56	50	6	114	-.02
3. the best approach to service coordination is voluntary cooperation encouraged by strong top-level policy	18	72	15	7	112	+.71
4. the best approach to service coordination is a comprehensive state human service agency	16	39	35	25	115	-.12
5. the best approach is to build services for specific client groups and equip those services comprehensively to do the full job	11	44	48	9	112	.00
6. services are hopelessly fragmented among special interest groups	8	41	55	9	113	-.14
7. duplication in current services results in tremendous waste	20	41	48	4	113	+.22
8. increasing competition for resources means the most needy and vulnerable are likely to get left out	16	47	47	3	113	+.23

Table 5 (Continued)

| Assertion | Number of Respondents Who | | | | | Mean* |
	Strongly Agree	Generally Agree	Dis-Agree	Strongly Disagree	Total	
9. competition is the best assurance of vigorous, progressive programs	2	32	65	15	114	-.52
10. vigorous advocacy only occurs around special, narrow interests where clients or their families have a personal stake	12	60	36	6	114	+.32
11. the first priority for Title XX funds should be to support a basic set of public, government administered services	14	46	34	16	110	+.07
12. purchase of service from non-profit voluntary providers is the best use of Title XX funds	9	37	55	9	110	-.16
13. services targeted only for the poor will inevitably be poor services	6	21	63	24	114	-.68
14. we should forget service coordination and integration until we achieve greater resource adequacy	0	5	51	59	115	-1.43
15. we will never achieve resource adequacy until we develop more effective and efficient services	13	71	26	5	115	+.53

* Calculated by assigning the following values: strongly agree, 2; generally agree, 1; generally disagree, -1; strongly disagree, -2.

Table 6

Opinions About Services Coordination by Program Affiliation

| | Mean Response* of Respondents in Program of | | | | | |
Assertion**	Mental Health	Health	Aging	Youth	Social Services	Management
1	-.78	-.22	-.08	-.55	-1.00	-.50
2	.00	.00	-.25	-.17	.00	-.13
3	1.10	.69	.69	.92	.48	.75
4	.89	-.29	-.50	.50	.58	-.13
5	-.22	.14	.53	.08	-.22	-.43
6	-.56	.07	.13	.00	.00	-.42
7	.44	.71	.00	.08	.09	.08
8	-.33	-.43	.13	.33	1.00	.00
9	-.56	-.93	-.19	.00	-1.04	-.42
10	.44	.79	.31	.00	-.08	.46
11	-.56	.00	-.14	-.25	.63	-.22
12	.11	-.36	.75	.17	-.57	.17
13	-1.00	-.71	-.50	-.50	-.92	-.87
14	-1.78	-1.36	-1.31	-1.33	-1.42	-1.46
15	.44	.64	1.00	.58	.13	.50

* Calculated by assigning the following values: strongly agree, 2; generally agree, 1; generally disagree, -1; strongly disagree, -2. The number of respondents in each category was: mental health, 9; health, 14; aging, 16; children and youth, 12; social services, 24; management responsibility for more than one program, 24.

** See Table 4.

• Comprehensive state human service agencies were viewed more favorably by respondents in mental health programs than by those in programs for the aged.
• Respondents in aging programs agreed while those in social services disagreed with the assertion that the best use of Title XX funds was the purchase of service from nonprofit voluntary providers.
• Those in social service programs favored while those in mental health programs opposed using Title XX funds to support a basic set of government administered services.
• Respondents with general managerial responsibilities agreed with fewer assertions than other respondents.

Coordination Mechanisms

Many examples and some interesting commentary were produced by the questions asking respondents to identify existing coordination mechanisms at the policy-making and/or direct service level in their states.

Several Texans mentioned a "Lieutenant Governor's Special Committee on Human Service Delivery System," a study committee of the legislature examining these questions. Another Texan in a health agency wrote, "The Governor has the authority to create Interagency Councils for the purpose of coordinating programs and services . . . but they have not been operative since 1975 or so."

An Arkansas official described a "State Administrative Review Committee composed of a representative from each Human Service Agency . . . plus advocates from the Department of Local Services." An Arkansas mental health practitioner stated, "Title XX here does nothing but administer contracts and reorganize; 85% of our budget in XX is purchase-of-service and private providers—no coordination efforts."

Oklahoma respondents cited the governor's "mini-cabinet for Human Services" and "a new Office of Handicapped Concerns."

A Florida respondent in a program of services for the elderly said, "Coordination Committees . . . have become a revitalized means of discovering overlapping services . . . in the eleven districts."

A Mississippi professional in the children's field said there were no coordination mechanisms "at this time" and added that "top level officials have not seen the need to give support."

A South Carolina worker in the alcohol and drug field wrote enthusiastically, "The State Human Services Coordinating Coun-

cil is made up of agency heads and commission chairmen who
have organized and meet informally with the Governor's office
and legislative groups to coordinate Health and Human Service
activities. Local equivalents exist in most counties. They are
working bodies—not paper bodies."

A long-time Virginia official described an "Interagency Licensure and Certification Team . . . an interagency agreement to facilitate the IEP [Individual Education Plan] for educationally
handicapped children . . . an interagency Prescription Team for
children in need of mental health services" and several others.

A Virginia health official lamented that "multiple eligibility
procedures . . . are confusing even to the professional who is supposed to know. . . . The case manager type is increasingly required if to do nothing else but to help the client cope with the
many and different systems."

A planner from Georgia named "The Interagency Troubled
Children's Committee—5 State Agencies" as one of several interagency groups seeking to focus services on multi-problem cases.

A worker with the Children's Foster Care Review Board System
of the Office of Child Advocacy in South Carolina wrote, "it
seems to us from the advocacy role . . . that these [working]
agreements are usually complex and do not result in improvement
on the direct service level."

Finally, a Washington, D.C. professional identified a key problem. She observed that an interagency committee on child abuse
"is dominated by voluntary interest groups whose main activity is
to demonstrate inadequacies in public agencies" but acknowl-
edged that "they have been effective in securing resources for
child abuse and neglect programs at the expense of residential
care and preventive front line family services."

Should Service Coordination Continue to be a Priority?

To those who try to promote service coordination, it often seems
impossible to mobilize a substantial group of supporting constituents. One often feels like a "voice in the wilderness" whose pleas
go unheeded in the cacophony of urgent demands from cate-
gorically oriented interests. The responses of the leaders in the
field whom we contacted, however, with few exceptions, indicate a
strong feeling that this issue must remain a high priority. Perhaps
the potential support is stronger than we have imagined, and perhaps successful mobilization can be accomplished by better pack-
aging of the concepts.

Thus, a Florida health administrator said, "Yes. Diminishing

resources and inflationary trends require maximum service impact from every available dollar."

An Arkansas youth service leader stated, "The ultimate test of human service delivery from a management standpoint will be the ability to provide services with a high degree of individualized and non-categorical service provision decisions (program decentralization) and an equally high degree of sophistication in centralized administrative accountability and cost allocation ability. It is achievable and a worthwhile goal."

A Virginia aging agency official said that coordination should remain a priority because "clients have a hopeless hassle/tangle of agencies/services to deal with—which both clients and taxpayers perceive as wasteful and inefficient."

A Washington, D.C., children's worker said, "Efforts at service coordination must continue although it is an uphill battle against vested interests." She adds that "service integrity is [not] the opposite of service coordination."

Endorsing strong efforts at service coordination, an official with the South Carolina Office of Child Advocacy wrote: "It is apparent that many professionals appear threatened by having to integrate their case planning and work with others, and . . . are not accustomed to having decisions questioned or evaluated."

A Virginia mental health office wrote: "our fragmented delivery system . . . foments competition of the least constructive sort and discourages cooperative efforts . . . [It is] harmful to those served."

A Kentucky worker stressed coordination because "the client is bewildered; the taxpayer is shafted."

A mental health director in Texas commented: "mental health cannot be separated from social and general health issues. The environment, social status, socio-economic picture and physical health are paramount to the mental health picture."

And an Arkansas respondent wrote: "if we cannot talk to each other for the good of the clients—we are working against systems development, frustrating ourselves by building walls to development of creative, functional, productive services system."

But there were some doubters.

A very thoughtful veteran worker in West Virginia observed: "there is perhaps too much concern about service integration/coordination. Certainly the subject needs attention—but alone it will not solve many of our serious problems. Resources are limited—but we will not receive more until we deliver better quality and effective services. That should be our major goal—not simply integration and coordination."

A North Carolina official was "not sure" of the priority of coordination; "the political, organizational, and attitudinal costs involved in designing, setting, and implementing such a system may be much higher than the resulting benefits."

A Florida respondent cautioned: "We should keep tuned to the issue and try and understand the management dynamics. . . . It may have nothing to do with clients and only serve some system maintenance issue or some 'higher value' of what is an improved social order." This had been preceded by comments which indicated a belief that service integration/coordination efforts favored expansion of program and administrative staff over direct service staff, tending to reduce the quality of service.

". . . it is very comfortable to sit on a . . . committee and . . . talk . . . about how a . . . program should work," an Alabama respondent observed. "The sad . . . fact [is] that only the individual program can effect its own efficient deployment."

"Service integration/coordination should continue to be a priority—but in programmatic and not political terms," a South Carolina respondent wrote.

And a North Carolina respondent: "I have seen a great deal of time and energy expended (particularly at the State level) on efforts described as 'coordination of services' with only negligible results."

Summary

Probably the most striking finding of our survey is the frequent close division between respondents who agree and disagree with various assertions about service coordination issues. In the aggregate, the respondents represent a fair cross-section of administrators in social service, health, and mental health settings. Such divisions seem to indicate a large potential for conflict and tension as further service coordination is attempted.

Very limited use is now being made of many service coordination mechanisms. Only purchase of service and interagency working agreements seem to be widely used, and this can be readily attributed to the recent history of Title XX and program emphases in other federal programs such as the Older Americans Act. With relatively simple methods such as common information and referral, collocation, and interagency case conferences in little use, it will probably be a long time before more complex, computerized methods such as shared management information systems and joint planning are widely adopted.

Opinions about the relative availability of services confirm the assumptions of our authors. John Mudd observes that "the fundamental governmental issues affecting children in the 1980s still remain questions of public policy and budgetary resources, not administrative coordination." Robert Morris remarks that "coordination is worth struggling for," but it "is no substitute for money, or clear policy, or wise manpower." And David Austin writes that "In almost every human service program area there is, and will continue to be, a gap between all possible requests for service, and available service resources."

Obviously, nonexistent services cannot be coordinated. However, as our respondents point out, the limitations of resources make it even more important that we strive for improved effectiveness in the use of what we have. Respondents overwhelmingly endorsed the view that service coordination should remain a high priority.

Notes

1. Harold Hagen and John E. Hansen, "How the States Put the Programs Together," *Public Welfare*, Summer 1978.

2. John Dewitt, "Managing the Human Service 'System': What Have We Learned from Services Integration?" Project Share, *Human Services Monograph Series*, No. 4, August 1977.

3. *Dimensions of Services Integration*, Human Services Monograph Series, Number 13, Project Share, U.S. Department of Health, Education, and Welfare, April 1979.

COORDINATED SERVICE:
THE STATE EXPERIENCE

Barbara B. Blum

Few would deny the desirability of developing a coordinated human service system which would facilitate access, eliminate gaps and duplication, and, by optional use of available resources, lower costs while increasing effectiveness. Even fewer would claim that efforts currently being made to coordinate the planning, administration, and delivery of human services are adequate.

Coordination is lacking between and within agencies and programs, and between and within the various levels of government involved in the provision of services. The absence of effective coordination has its most profound impact on persons with limited mobility, changing needs, and multiple problems. Children and the elderly are particularly vulnerable.

Service fragmentation, though a problem for the entire population, is especially troublesome to those least capable of piecing the fragments together. The elderly are among those most adversely affected by coordination failures. Often in need of a variety of assistance ranging from health services to counseling to economic aid, older people must negotiate a complex system which often cannot help them within their communities.

Children have also been affected profoundly by fragmented services. This impact has been seen most dramatically in their unnecessary placement in foster care. Failure to provide coordinated services can damage children, their families, and society.

The fragmentation of current social services must be addressed if families, children, and the elderly are to be served effectively. This effort will require new approaches to program organization and design and new perceptions by social service professionals.

These complex efforts will be further complicated by changing social policies and changing populations competing for scarce re-

sources. Competition between the young and old is particularly distressing.

In July 1975, an estimated 66.3 million persons or 31 percent of the national population of 213.6 million were 17 years old or under while 22.4 million or 10 percent were 65 percent or over. Three years later, the figures were 63.4 million young people or 29 percent of a population of 218 million, and 24.1 million or 11 percent oldsters. In other words, while the number under 18 dropped about 2.9 million, the number over 64 rose by 1.6 million. Thus services must be provided for an increased number of elderly and a reduced number of children.

This paper will discuss the major barriers to service coordination within the existing system of services, the social policies dependent upon the successful coordination of services, and some significant efforts that have been made to address these concerns.

Barriers to Coordination

Throughout the 19th and during the early 20th century philanthropic and voluntary agencies were the sole providers of social services. The public sector became involved only in the 1930s. Subsequently, human services have been increasingly viewed as a government responsibility. However, government intervention has been neither systematic nor coordinated. The role or roles of governments evolved gradually or, as happened often when they assumed new responsibilities in a crisis, suddenly. The result has been a fragmentation of programs, organizations, and funds, and a generic bias, in government programs and appropriations, toward institutional or residential care.

Programmatic and Funding Fragmentation

The organizational and financial barriers to service coordination can be intimated merely by listing the major government health and social service programs, each with its distinctive history, clientele, and objectives, eligibility requirements, budget, and administrative and professional idiosyncrasies. In New York State, services to children and the aged are funded through the following major programs:

Program   *Primary Funding Source*

Children and Families

Income Maintenance

Aid to families with dependent   Title IVA of the Social
  children   Security Act
Emergency family assistance   Title IVA
General family assistance   State and local
Food stamps   Food Stamp Act

Medical Care
Medicaid   Title XIX
Medical assistance   State and local

Social Services
Family planning   Title XX of the Social
                                   Security Act
Day care   Title XX
Homemaker   Title XX
Housekeeper   Title XX
Information referral   Title XX
Health related services   Title XX

Foster Care
Children eligible for AFDC   Title IVA
Other children   State and local
Adoption subsidies   State and local
Preventive and other services   Title IVB of the Social
                                   Security Act
Family services   State and local
Protective services   Title XX
Mental health services   Title XIX

Adults and the Elderly

Income Maintenance
General assistance   State and local
Emergency assistance   State and local
Social Security   Title II of the Social Security
                                   Act
Supplemental Security Income   Title XVI
Food stamps   Food Stamp Act

Program   *Primary Funding Source*

Medicare Care

Medicare	Title XVIII
Medicaid	Title XIX
Medical assistance	State and local

Social Services

Housekeeper/homemaker	Title XX
Protective	Title XX
Day care	Title XX
Foster care	Title XX
Health related services	Title XX or XIX
Nutrition centers	Older Americans Act
Senior citizens centers	Older Americans Act and Title XX

Mental Health Services	Title XX State and local

A similar list could be presented for each state in the Northeast.

The income maintenance, medical, homemaker, and counseling services required by a troubled family will each be funded and administered separately.

Home care for the elderly must draw upon Supplemental Security Income, Medicaid, Medicare, Title XX of the Social Security Act, and Title III of the Older Americans Act. In such situations, the individual skill and commitment of the social service worker becomes essential to overcome programmatic and organizational barriers. Thus, the shortage of well trained and properly situated professionals aggravates service fragmentation.

Organizational Structure

The organization of social services has, to a large extent, reflected their categorical origin and appropriations. Typically, separate government units have been established to administer separate federal appropriations. Federal mandates, such as that requiring the separation of income maintenance and social services in 1971, have also affected the organization of service.

Inter- and intra-agency organization can make coordination difficult. Divisions may compete for funds, personnel, and authority over program development or administration. Funds for adult protective services, for example, must compete for scarce Title XX funds with home care, senior citizens centers, and a wide range of services for children and their families.

Efforts at program coordination, such as proposals to consolidate cash and food stamp benefits or to put related functions in a single administrative structure, may face resistance by program staff, providers, and advocacy groups accustomed or committed to existing arrangements.

Chart 1, which sets forth the social service administrative structures in Northeast states, indicates the presence of significant functional divisions even in "umbrella agencies." The existence of additional agencies for health, mental health, and the aging suggests that efforts to include all human services in one comprehensive department must confront issues of scale and a pervasive categorical infrastructure, including categorical advocacy groups and resource competition. There are few advocates for organizational consolidation other than general managers, legislatures, and unorganized citizens.

Some recent organizational changes have served to fragment rather than to consolidate services. In Connecticut, for example, the Department of Social Services now administers only income support functions, whereas social services, including day care and employment support, which it formerly administered, are handled by the Department of Human Resources and children's services are handled by the Department of Children and Youth. A new housing agency has also recently been created.

In 1979, Connecticut enacted legislation designed to promote the local collocation of services. Human service agencies must prepare a collocation statement indicating how any new program will promote the accessibility and integration of services.

Policy Bias toward Institutional Care

Service coordination within and between agencies is of particular importance in light of changing policies toward residential and institutional care.

The traditional emphasis of health and social programs on institutional care has reflected the widely held belief that serious medical problems are best treated in hospitals and nursing homes;

frail elderly persons are best cared for in homes for the aged; and afflicted children are best treated in homes for the handicapped, retarded, or disturbed. As self-contained communities, such large institutions face few problems of services coordination, and those can readily be dealt with by the institution director in consultation with the heads of nursing, catering, purchasing, and other services. However, large institutions are impersonal, their residents are isolated from the community, and comprehensive, round-the-clock care is expensive. Hence efforts are being made to provide a range of integrated services in the home and community. Deinstitutionalization policies, spurred by court orders requiring the release of residents, now confront New York, Pennsylvania, and other states with the need to establish in the community services as comprehensive and well integrated as those of residential institutions.

The problems which New York State has faced in implementing the Willowbrook consent decree reflect the difficulties associated with deinstitutionalization. The Willowbrook decree, which the governor signed in April 1975, calls for the care, in the least restrictive and most normal setting possible, of all who were residents of The Willowbrook Developmental Center when the suit was filed in March 1972. The decree also required that the number of Willowbrook residents be reduced from 5,200 to 250 by April 1981.

To implement the decree, it was necessary to expand significantly the number of community placements available for the mentally retarded. A Metropolitan Placement Unit was created by the State Department of Mental Health to place Willowbrook residents in existing or new family-type homes, hotels, group homes, and small intermediate care facilities.

Serious deficiencies in the service system were encountered. Funding was scarce or unavailable, and the number of existing community residences was extremely limited.

By careful analysis of client needs, existing placement options, and the procedures necessary to make successful placements and develop new facilities, the state was able, in the first year, to more than double the number of placements made in the ten previous months.

If adequate long-term community care is to be provided, a series of issues reflected in the Willowbrook experience must be addressed. In 1976, less than 10 percent of public funds utilized for long-term care went for home-based services. Most states do not

Chart 1

Human Service Departments in Northeast States

State and Agency	Services			Administrative Features
	Income Maintenance	Family, Adult	Children	
Connecticut	Department of Income Maintenance	Department of Human Resources	Purchase of service with Department of Children and Youth	The Departments of Human Resources and Income Maintenance are collocated in six district offices. The Department of Children and Youth operates separately in five regional offices.
Delaware Department of Health and Social Services	Division of Social Services			All programs are state administered through three regional offices.
Maine Department of Human Services				Income maintenance and services are administered by bureaus of the Department of Human Services directly or via five regional offices
Massachusetts Executive Office of Human Services	Department of Public Welfare	Department of Social Services		Income maintenance and services are administered by the Office of Human Services' Departments of Public Welfare and Social Services, which operate through Community Service Area Offices.
New Hampshire Department of Health & Welfare	Division of Welfare			Income maintenance and services are administered through the Division of Welfare's 12 district offices.

Chart 1

Human Service Departments in Northeast States

State and Agency	Services			Administrative Features
	Income Maintenance	Family, Adult	Children'	
New Jersey Department of Human Services	Division of Public Welfare		Division of Youth and Family Services	Division of Public Welfare supervises 21 county welfare agencies. Division of Youth and Family operates through a system of 23 state district offices and county welfare agencies, under the supervision of four regional offices. The Division of Medical and Health Services administers medical programs.
New York Department of Social Services	Division of Income Maintenance / Division of Medical Assistance	Division of Adult Residential care	Division of Services	The Department of Social Services' four major divisions (Income Maintenance, Services, Adult Residential Care, Medical Assistance) supervise the provision of services and income maintenance by 58 local social services departments.
Pennsylvania Department of Public Welfare	Division of Income Maintenance / Division of Medical Assistance	Divisions of: Children, Youth & Families, Mental Health, Mental Retardation		Institutions, medicaid, income maintenance, and social programs administered by the state; community-based mental health and retardation, children, youth, and family services are run in concert with the counties.
Rhode Island Department of Social and Rehabilitative Services	Division of Management Services / Division of Medical Assistance	Division of Community Services		Programs are administered by the Department of Social and Rehabilitative Services' Divisions of Management, Community, and Medical Services.
Vermont Agency of Human Services	Department of Social Welfare	Department of Social and Rehabilitative Services		Income maintenance and social services are provided by 12 district offices of the Department of Social Welfare and the Division of Vocational Rehabilitation.

In addition, Connecticut, Massachusetts, New Hampshire, New York, and Rhode Island have separate agencies for the elderly.

even have clear standards and regulatory or licensure provisions governing day care, foster home, or homemaker services.

Government policies have not encouraged family participation in social services. Tax policies, welfare programs, and eligibility policies for government-subsidized health care effectively penalize family members who help to care for aged parents or relatives. Hence government policies have served to reduce or limit the role of the family in providing long-term care.

Available resources are insufficient to meet the demand for long-term care in the community and home. Government categorical programs either prohibit or limit the funding of home care (for example, Medicare coverage of home care is limited to cases involving prior hospitalization). But if they did not, their budgets would have to be greatly increased, or budgets for institutional services be greatly reduced, to meet the resultant demand.

It seems clear that the need for long-term care will grow as the number of elderly and disabled persons grows. Services for this population must be designed to maximize and redirect limited resources. New levels of service coordination, including flexible funding that is responsive to the changing mix of service needs, can help to achieve this. Greater flexibility in the use of funds under Titles XIX and XX and the Older Americans Act would be helpful. Program standards, needs assessment, and utilization reviews should be developed cooperatively by social service, health, and mental health agencies. Finally, public policy should encourage families to care for disabled or aged relatives and provide services to facilitate such care.

Similar issues arise in programs for children. Virtually unlimited federal funds have been available for foster care under Title IVA of the Social Security Act, while very limited funds have been available for preventive and family support services, under Titles IVB or XX.

Alternatives to residential care have been inhibited by traditional service delivery patterns and service worker roles. Accepted standards for determining the need for and type of child placement must also be developed—as well as new professional roles and methods to provide coordinated services in the home and community.

Recent federal mandates such as those of the Education of all Handicapped Children Act (P.L. 94-142) will create added demands for service and make the coordination of health, mental health, and social programs more imperative. The free public edu-

cation of all handicapped children prescribed by P.L. 94-142 will require an extraordinary degree of coordination. Departments of health, mental health, mental retardation, developmental disabilities, social services, and education will have to cooperate at the state and local levels and work closely with federal agencies. The coordination of available services and resources will be essential.

This legislation does not assign clear financial responsibility for operating programs for the handicapped in the public schools, and little federal aid has been given to modify programs and buildings. In FY 1980, federal agencies provided less than $3 million dollars compared to $71 million provided by New York State agencies to implement the act.

First steps are being taken to define agency responsibilities for various services. The Office of Mental Health will provide psychiatric counseling, the Education Department will hire special education teachers, and the Office of Mental Retardation will finance the expansion of community facilities for the developmentally disabled. It is hoped that through such coordinated efforts, successful implementation can be achieved.

Efforts to Coordinate Service Delivery

In New York State, initial efforts to achieve an integrated service system have occurred through planning, new agency organizational structures, and specific program development. Each effort has implications for service delivery.

Planning

There are currently several separate annual planning processes for programs affecting family and children's services in New York State. These include the Title XX plan, the Child Protective Services Plan, and the child welfare services plan mandated by the State Child Welfare Reform Act of 1979.

Formerly under federal law, each local district had to prepare an annual plan for utilizing Title XX funds, and state social service departments in turn had to prepare a comprehensive statewide plan. However, in 1980, the law was revised to permit states to adopt one-, two-, or three-year planning cycles. These plans must include a description of the state and local organizational structure, district demographic profiles, assessments of needs and resources, and identification of unmet service needs.

Child Protective Services

State law requires each local social services district to submit for the Department of Social Services' approval an annual plan demonstrating its compliance with various state mandates for preventing or addressing child neglect or abuse. Plans are currently submitted on a staggered basis between March 1 and April 30.

Child Welfare Reform Act

The Child Welfare Reform Act of 1979 requires local districts to submit an annual child welfare services plan which must incorporate, but is not limited to, preventive, foster care, and adoption services. According to the legislation, the plan should be consistent with and prepared in conjunction with the Title XX, Child Protective Services, and other state and federal plans.

The law further requires that such plans be developed by local districts in consultation with other government agencies, authorized agencies, and concerned individuals and organizations. Planning was to be initiated on April 1, 1980, and annually thereafter.

The plethora, complexity, duplication, and annual nature of plans has resulted in little meaningful planning for family and children's services in the state. The Department of Social Services is, therefore, striving to consolidate and integrate all state planning for family and children's services into a three-year plan with annual updates.

It is hoped that the elimination of duplication and the consideration of problems and solutions within a more realistic time frame will permit the development of suitable and measurable goals, an inventory of resources, appropriate needs assessment procedures and reports, and methods for monitoring and evaluating the achievement of goals and objectives. Finally, consolidated multi-year planning should allow a meaningful integration of plans and budgets.

Much work must be undertaken to establish coordinated planning for adult services. The Community Services Act of New York State encourages the development of community services and comprehensive planning for the elderly. The act, which is administered by local agencies on aging, provides counties with 100 percent state funding to prepare comprehensive plans for community service projects for high-risk elderly. The plans should be coordinated with the planning and program development for Title XX and adult protective services.

Organizational Initiatives

Efforts to address the problem of fragmented or overlapping responsibility for children and adult services have led to the creation of organizations to coordinate and facilitate services.

In New York State, for example, where responsibility for children's services is divided among the Departments of Social Services, Health, and Mental Health and the Division for Youth, problems may occur when interagency cooperation is necessary in an area such as the foster care placement of court-related youth.

To improve communication and cooperation between agencies and mediate their disputes, the state legislature created a Council on Children and Families in 1977. The commissioners of all state agencies which provide services to children are members of the Council, which provides no direct services but is both an advocacy group and a channel for communication. Located in the executive office, the Council works closely with staff of the Division of the Budget in preparing a children's budget, a compilation of all state expenditures for children's services. This interagency budget, which clearly depicts how money for children's services is being spent, will permit more rational and comprehensive decisions on future expenditures. The budget can also serve as a first step in the development of a comprehensive five-year plan for state children's services, which should help to overcome the obstacles to coordinated service planning and delivery caused by fragmented funding.

Services for the elderly may be even more fragmented than those for children. Elderly people needing mental and physical health care in addition to financial assistance and supportive services must meet with the standards and regulations of several agencies such as the Office of Health Systems Management, the Office of Mental Health, the Department of Social Services, and the Office for the Aging. Few programs have offered a comprehensive range of services.

In 1965, the Older Americans Act sought to promote increased attention to the problems of the elderly by the establishment of state agencies on aging. New York established the Office of Aging, which serves as an advocate for the elderly and administers services under the Older Americans and Community Services Acts.

Despite difficulties in securing adequate funding and the sustained interest of other agencies, the Office of the Aging has established more than four hundred nutrition sites and more than four

hundred senior centers. The governor has ordered state agencies serving the elderly to submit all program proposals and other documents to the Office for review and comment. The Office has also worked successfully with the Departments of Social Services and Transportation and other state agencies to expand and improve services for the elderly.

As the Office for the Aging and other agencies have concentrated primarily on the expansion, rather than the coordination of services, a competition for program resources has ensued. The creation of new agencies to facilitate service coordination may add another organizational layer upon those entailed in service delivery.

Local Level Restructuring

In Luzerne and Wyoming Counties in Pennsylvania's Wyoming Valley, the United Services Agency (USA), a local umbrella agency, has been trying since 1972 to develop a coordinated service system. USA was formed after tropical storm Agnes as a demonstration project to reduce service duplication and to help residents obtain federal and state emergency aid. By joint agreement, the state assumed fiscal and managerial responsibility for county social services, including mental health, mental retardation, child care, juvenile probation and detention, aging, and child welfare. In addition, USA administered the state public assistance program. County costs were assumed by the state for the three-year demonstration period.

Although federal and state demonstration funds have been discontinued, the state and counties continue to operate the project with the cooperation of public and voluntary agencies. Its primary objectives are to: (1) allow individuals to obtain services through single entry service centers in major population areas; (2) provide a single service entry point through the use of case managers; ongoing services are provided by generic caseworkers; (3) establish a consumer-oriented program that could also serve as a consumer advocate; (4) implement a system of fiscal and program accountability.

Despite financial difficulties and some conflict with middle management staff of the state Public Welfare Department, the project has achieved a high degree of coordination in its service area and has been able to adapt to the changing needs and moods of the previous eight years.

Program Initiatives

Efforts to coordinate services may be most feasible and successful, and are certainly most tangible, on a small scale and in the local community.

Enriched Housing

In New York State, the Enriched Housing Program, which currently serves some seventy frail elderly persons, is an excellent example. Modeled on a Westchester Jewish Community Services project, it uses SSI grants to support group living arrangements for no more than sixteen people. Through strict eligibility rules, the program selects residents who do not need constant supervision and have similar or complementary needs. They live in existing community housing, use existing community services, and receive assistance with housekeeping, cooking, homemaking, shopping, and other daily activities by purchase-of-service agreements with public and private agencies.

The Enriched Housing project demonstrates that state and local providers, public and private agencies, service agencies, and the community can cooperatively respond to the needs of the frail elderly. This project has recently become a permanent program of the Department of Social Services.

Monroe County Long-Term Care

In New York State, the Monroe County Long-Term Care Access Project, begun in 1977, seeks to limit the number of people unnecessarily placed in skilled nursing facilities. Under a memorandum of understanding with the state Health Department and contracts with the state and county Departments of Social Services, it offers free case assessment to all Monroe County adult residents and case management and services to those eligible for Medicaid. As of June 1979, approximately 2,500 clients had received case assessments funded under Title XI of the Social Security Act; case management services are reimbursed by Title XIX. Some 57 percent of clients are receiving care at home while 43 percent have been admitted to a facility.

Despite continuing problems in ensuring that placements are determined by the type of care needed, not the source of payment, the program has reduced unnecessary placements in institutions and increased the number cared for in the community.

Long-Term Home Health Care Program (LTHHCP)

The Long-Term Home Health Care Program (LTHHCP), or "Nursing Homes Without Walls," was established in New York in 1978 to reduce the unnecessary placement of Medicaid recipients in nursing homes and the cost of long-term care by providing only those services essential to each individual. It also strives to improve the quality of participants' lives by allowing them to remain in their homes.

The Department of Social Services and the Office of Health Systems Management share responsibilities for the program; policies are developed by four interagency committees coordinated by the two lead agencies.

Eligibility is limited to Medicaid-eligible persons at risk of nursing home placement. Each must be evaluated by a physician and judged able to benefit from home care costing no more than 75 percent of a nursing home. Participation is voluntary, but the state requires that all Medicaid recipients at risk of placement who live near a LTHHCP coordinator be notified of this alternative.

These coordinators are located in the certified home health agency, public or voluntary hospital, skilled nursing or health related facility authorized to operate a LTHHCP. There are currently nine such authorized agencies: Montefiore and St. Vincent's hospitals, the Visiting Nurse Service and Metropolitan Jewish Geriatric in New York City, the Rhode Island Street Nursing Home Company and Health Department in Erie County, the Visiting Nurse Association of central New York, and the Onondaga County and the Cattaraugus Departments of Health.

A local Department of Social Services case worker, in cooperation with the LTHHCP coordinator, assesses client needs and designs an appropriate set of services. The coordinator arranges for an array of Title XIX services either directly or by contract. In addition, a waiver has been obtained for the provision of nutritional counseling and education, respiratory therapy, respite care, home maintenance, social day care, transportation, congregate and home-delivered meals, moving assistance, housing improvement, and medical and social services.

LTHHCP will be evaluated by an independent agency over a three-year period to determine its cost effectiveness.

The Enriched Housing Program, the Monroe County Long-Term Care Project, and the Long-Term Home Health Care Program use case management to coordinate community services.

Each is relatively small, utilizes community resources, and relies on a detailed assessment of client needs to determine the appropriate type and level of care. Each requires staff with the information and skills necessary to arrange for comprehensive community services.

Families and Children

Out-of-State Placement

New York State has cooperative interagency efforts to resolve the problems of out-of-state placement of multi-problem children. The foster care system, designed to provide short-term placement for children awaiting adoption or return to their homes, was unprepared to deal with children needing special long-term services. The lack of appropriate foster-care facilities for handicapped children resulted in the placement of large numbers of children in facilities and schools in other states.

As concern about the quality and appropriateness of this care grew, the governor formed an interagency task force on out-of-state placement in 1978. It consists of representatives of the Office of Mental Health, the Office of Mental Retardation and Developmental Disabilities, the Division for Youth, the Department of Education, and the Department of Social Services and is coordinated by the Council on Children and Families. Because of the complex behavioral and physical problems of these children, the involvement of all these agencies is essential to determine the appropriateness of placement and compliance with standards, and to develop an adequate system of care within the state.

To date, the task force has evaluated all out-of-state facilities which house New York children. Children in facilities not in compliance with New York standards have been relocated. Evaluations of the appropriateness of placement of more than three hundred children in out-of-state foster care have been completed and acted upon. The task force is currently working on the development of state facilities.

Family Centers

Perhaps the most striking examples of service coordination are in programs operated by voluntary agencies.

At the Family Reception Center in Brooklyn, services are provided to the entire family. The program encompasses a relatively small area, but within that area its services are extremely

comprehensive. The Center operates on the neighborhood concept, maintaining contact with all potential sources of assistance
and funding for care in the home and community. It offers counseling, case management, leisure time, and temporary shelter activities to children and adults. The project is presently trying to
improve the quality of the local school.

An example of the Center's approach may be seen in the story
of the Conors family who needed a great deal of help to prevent
the placement of eleven children in foster care. At the time of the
Center's intervention, neighborhood schools were pursuing a neglect petition against the Conorses. Management of a public assistance budget, relocation in suitable housing, provision of needed
furniture, help from a homemaker reinforced by regular weekly
guidance and counseling by a center worker helped to ease the
family's situation. One boy received group therapy and four children were admitted to the Center's Mini School. The Center has
had much success in improving family functioning and preventing
the placement of children in foster care.

The Lower East-Side Family Union also strives to prevent the
unnecessary breakup of families. Like the Family Reception Center, it has limited its geographic scope and focuses on the families
of its ethnically mixed neighborhood. The Union assembles teams
to serve as case workers and service coordinators and contracts
with local providers for most services.

The Union's unique approach is well illustrated by the story of
Joan and her six children, who were living in a one-bedroom
apartment that was often without heat and hot water. Separated
from her alcoholic husband, Joan was dependent on public assistance. She suffered from asthma and came to the Union when she
decided that she was too ill and poor to care for her four-year-old
handicapped child.

A Union social work associate talked with Joan and decided
that the first step was to find the family adequate housing. After a
series of setbacks which forced the family to remain in their apartment throughout the winter, a six-room apartment was secured.
The Union also began providing occasional homemaker services,
which allowed Joan to keep doctor's appointments and helped her
manage her limited resources. Bellevue Hospital staff helped to
place the handicapped child in a special school. Four children received scholarships to a Catholic school and an after-school tutor-
ing and recreational program. The family unit was preserved.

Both the Lower East Side Family Union and the Family Reception Center are staffed by involved and well-trained staff. Both

have limited their efforts to a community of manageable size and have thereby been able to make maximum use of existing services. Each is familiar with the special problems and resources of its community. Both seek to prevent unnecessary foster care by working with the family as a whole.

Conclusions

Service coordination is essential for any family at risk of disintegration, for persons needing varied community services and for persons at risk of institutional placement. Children and the elderly are special victims of fragmented services.

Existing funding patterns discourage the development of preventive, family, long-term community services and make coordination of services difficult. Funding mechanisms must be modified if supportive services for children and the aged are to be increased and strengthened.

State governments should continue to experiment with varying organizational and local arrangements to facilitate the provision of coordinated services in communities with different needs. Coordinated interagency and program planning should also be encouraged.

Ultimately, it is at the local level, with and for the recipient, that services must be coordinated. Perhaps the single most effective way to do so is to recruit and train a sufficient number of informed and sensitive staff who are determined to coordinate services. An experienced worker acting on a case by case basis can bend the system until it works for his client. Modifications in state and federal programs and regulations can facilitate but not replace such a worker's efforts.

COORDINATION OF HUMAN SERVICES
FOR THE 1980s

John T. Dempsey

Introduction

The three principal objectives outlined for these regional workshops are:
• to redefine the need for coordinating services to meet the requirements of multi-problem clients;
• to assemble and transmit to policy-makers and administrators the state of the art of services coordination; and
• to outline possible approaches toward more effective coordination of human services.

My specific assignment is to outline some of the services coordination experiences of twelve midwestern states—Illinois, Indiana, Ohio, Iowa, Kansas, Minnesota, Missouri, Nebraska, North Dakota, South Dakota, Wisconsin, and Michigan—with particular reference to services for children and the aged. My efforts to address this task have been frustrating and have caused me to appreciate better the need, indeed the urgent need, for such coordination. In fact, I found little *awareness* of the need and even less success in addressing it, except on a pro forma or ad hoc basis.

In preparing for this discussion, we called the governor's office in each of the foregoing states and asked for information on human services coordination mechanisms. The response was peculiar. No one asked to have coordination defined; each office immediately began providing material on how coordination is accomplished in its state. From this instant response one can assume either that coordination is in an advanced stage everywhere or that no one has really thought much about what it really means. I believe the latter is the more accurate conclusion. (However, as we were not exactly sure of what we were requesting, any "fault" must be mutually shared.)

Coordination means many different things to different people. It is one of those rare political concepts which has survived well the test of time, because (like democracy, limited government, "sunshine" laws, or public accountability) it connotes only positive images. As such, it has obvious advantages:
• It appeals to almost all administrators because it is "good management" practice: elimination of duplication, closing gaps, better awareness of all available resources for appropriate referral, more efficient utilization of service resources, less costly provision of services, etc.
• It has different meanings which are seldom made explicit. Everyone can perceive benefits to his organization without ever clarifying the meaning. Opposing service coordination is almost as rare as opposing services—who would dare?
• It rarely suggests negative consequences. What possible harm can be found in it? It might even do some good; at least it won't hurt; and citizens and legislators will applaud the coordinators, at least for a time.

It seems appropriate to define coordination in order to bring the concept into focus, as well as to assess some of its promises and limitations. Coordination is a process, or series of mechanisms, for exchanging, co-directing, and/or pooling resources (by referrals, information, physical space, personnel, funds, etc.) for more efficient or effective goal achievement. Implicit is the necessity to defend goals and more limited objectives. But goals are rarely defined, except in terms of process. The result of the process of coordination is usually described in terms of efficiency; rarely is effectiveness mentioned.

From a conceptual point of view, the various types of potential coordinating mechanisms fall into six categories:
• organizational realignment;
• inter-organizational decision-making;
• ad hoc response to crisis;
• allocation of resources (that is, budgeting);
• efforts to assure information sharing between involved agencies; and
• efforts to enhance client convenience by service delivery improvements, "one-stop centers," etc.

All of these are employed, to one degree or another, in all Midwestern states.

I shall draw most extensively upon the Michigan experience, since I have first-hand knowledge and understanding of our attempts at coordination at several levels of government. Such expe-

Chart 2

Coordination Measures In Midwest States

State	Interorganizational Decisions	Information Sharing	Convenience of Clients
Illinois	Governor's Subcabinet Directors of major state human service agencies	Illinois human service plans Title XX Common regions for major agencies	
Indiana	Inter-departmental Board for the Coordination of Human Services Programs Includes eight departments and agencies and staff from budget and governor's office	Title XX plan	
Iowa		Title XX plan	
Kansas		State Planning Coordination Committee, Title XX plan	
Michigan	Human Services Cabinet Established in governor's office to coordinate the inter-organizational decisions of the Departments of Social Services, Mental Health, and Public Health	Livingston County Local agency consortium meets regularly to share information on their programs and pool resources for projects needs assessment from which all agencies may benefit. Kalamazoo County Similar to Livingston and also focused on needs assessment. Lenawee County The human services project is an independent department which has focused on such practical goals as a standarized release of information form.	United Way collocation United Way has one location for funded agencies in Adrian and Muskegon Counties; in Wayne County, they share a location with the Department of Social Services district office CHASS Community Health and Social Services in Wayne County share a renovated supermarket with the Departments of Public Health, Social Services, and Spanish Affairs.

State	Interorganizational Decisions	Information Sharing	Convenience of Clients
Michigan		State and Regional Plans These attempts to provide broad descriptions of how agencies may coordinate. They seldom have much impact on agencies which pursue objectives that conflict with a plan.	WIN Work Incentive Program staffs of the Departments of Labor and Social Services are collocated. Other Methods Common eligibility application forms.
Minnesota	Governor: Guidelines for coordination	Data exchange with Social Security Administration and Department of Social Services	
Missouri	Task Forces State Advisory Council on Developmental Disabilities, Governor's Committee on Services to the Handicapped, Interagency Council for Drug and Alcohol Abuse Prevention, Governor's Committee on Children and Youth.	Title XX plan	
Nebraska	Governor's task force: Child Welfare 1977	Title XX plan	Coordinated services for abused and neglected clients
North Dakota		Title XX plan	
Ohio	Task force: Ohio Youth Commission	Data exchange with Social Security Administration Title XX plan	Demonstration: One stop service centers
South Dakota	Interagency task forces Child Abuse & Neglect Adult Services	Title XX plan	Collocation of several services Common needs assessment form for child welfare, older Americans, mental health, and developmental disabilities
Wisconsin		Title XX plan	

riences are merely illustrative and not necessarily exemplary. Many other states have had similar projects; to the extent practicable, I shall cite them.

Coordination: Some Dilemmas

Although virtually everyone agrees on the beneficent character of "coordination," in theory at least, severe problems exist in discussing it, which must be recognized.

Artificial Distinctions

It is impossible and inappropriate artificially to restrict our consideration to agencies that provide services only to children and the aged. Such agencies rarely exist and, when they do, they are never responsible for the entire range of services. Most large state human service agencies and many small public and private agencies provide services to children, families, single adults, and the aged. These agencies make up the network of service providers for clients. Although I shall emphasize services to children and the aged, the limits and possibilities of coordination are applicable to all network relationships regardless of the type of clients.

Expectations for Coordination

Coordination as an integral part of good human service management has led to a set of expectations which may be unrealistically high. Some of the more common expectations include: reduction in duplication, and elimination of gaps; cost savings; reduction in burdens to the client; more client and provider awareness of available services; more efficient use of resources; redirection of inflationary pressures; most appropriate referral for service needed; and most appropriate assessment of need. Some of these expectations appear reasonable; some *are* experienced as a result of increased coordination. However, there are limits to what such efforts can achieve.

Limits of Coordination

In 1972, Sheldon Gans and Gerald Horton did case studies of thirty human service integration projects, including the following five in Midwestern states: Cleveland Mental Health Retardation Project; HUB Neighborhood Service Center, Cincinnati; Voca-

tional Incentives Program, Peoria; Yeatman Neighborhood Service Center, St. Louis; and Youth Advocacy Program, South Bend. Their conclusions highlight some of the factors limiting coordination:

The services integration projects studied were operating in extremely diffuse social service environments made up of a variety of public and private agencies with competing claims to funds and authority. Developing the structure into a unitary system, even if it were desirable, could probably not be done for several reasons:

• There are various approaches to designing systems according to problem or age group, geographic areas or functions—each of which has some defensible rationale.

• There are various funding sources, and they are not likely to agree on a single system.

• Organized constituencies with congressional supporters lobby for services organized around a lead function, such as vocational rehabilitation or mental health, as the prime service with other services as auxiliary.

• There is no consumer group pressuring for a unitary system.

Gans and Horton did not find that various federal funding sources ever agreed on a single system. This appears to be the single largest factor forestalling extensive coordination.

Still, a persistent interest in coordination does exist at the federal level and, in fact, is as alive today as ever. Two examples can highlight this interest. Each is small in comparison to the need, but each is significant in its potential contribution to a more unified human services delivery system.

First is the common application form for Aid to Families with Dependent Children (AFDC), Medicaid, and food programs. This has been piloted and is now being implemented in Wisconsin. Michigan is also moving in this direction. As long as each service program has its own unique application process, resource definitions, and assets tests, the limits of coordination are clear.

Second is the common sampling plan for drawing quality control samples in AFDC, Medicaid, and food programs. The Office of Management and Budget (OMB) has promoted such coordination within the U.S. Department of Health and Human Services (formerly HEW) and is endeavoring to include the Department of Agriculture in future plans. Separate evaluation mechanisms limit effective service or program coordination.

OMB is the focal federal agency from which the greatest amount of coordination could be initiated and maintained. Without common definitions of eligibility, services, and costs and with-

out compulsions for coordination, the possibility of coordination is limited to sporadic collaboration by major departments at the state, county, and community levels. If coordination is to be increased, someone, some agency must take the lead. Since coordination among equals is chancy, the management and budget system appears the most fruitful coordinative tool.

Coordination for What Purpose?

The different coordination mechanisms available to Midwestern states fall into six broad categories based on the purpose of coordination or the situation in which it is attempted. These are: organizational realignment; interorganizational decision-making; response to a crisis; distribution of state resources (budgeting); sharing information for a mutual goal; and coordination for the client's convenience.

Organizational Realignment

In the past two decades, substantial concern and frustration have appeared about the problems of human services delivery. The tax-paying public, legislators, special interest groups, as well as officials who administer service programs have grown increasingly concerned about rising costs, gaps in service eligibility, overlap and duplication of services, and conflicting and confusing administrative processes.

A frequent response has been administrative reorganization— the realignment of human service programs through the creation of an "umbrella" agency, most commonly called a Department of Human Resources or Human Services, which includes a majority of the previously autonomous welfare, public health, mental health and/or mental retardation, corrections, and juvenile programs.

The purpose of reorganization has been clear: to make human service programs more accountable by establishing clear lines of authority to a single administrator appointed by the governor; to assure a coordinated approach to the identification and treatment or service of clients; and to centralize certain administrative activities such as planning, budgeting, and procurement.

Of the twelve Midwestern states, six—Iowa, Kansas, Minnesota, Missouri, South Dakota, and Wisconsin—have established "umbrella" departments.

The consequences of reorganization are less clear. It does not

automatically lead to improved coordination of service delivery, but it does, in part, remove a major barrier thereto, namely turf. Subjective comments do indicate that improved coordination of at least some programs has resulted in the foregoing six states.

However, the trend toward umbrella agencies seems to have ended. No such reorganization has occurred since 1973. Counter pressures have appeared recently. In Michigan, an effort has been made to establish an autonomous youth service agency.

Interorganizational Decision-Making

Where umbrella agencies do not exist, states often employ collective or collegial approaches to secure coordination for decision-making by agencies or departments which share responsibility for services to specific client groups. This type of coordination takes place at all levels of government—state, county, and local—and is often effective in resolving disputes over "domain" or delegating authority and/or responsibility for specific issues or problems. While it does not assure success, it appears to minimize sabotage. It is less effective in developing new initiatives, since it tends to lapse into formalism.

At the state level, governors regularly involve themselves in interagency mechanisms and make decisions based on information provided by the agencies. Examples of this type of coordination include Michigan's Human Services Cabinet, Indiana's Interdepartmental Board for the Coordination of Human Services Program, and the Illinois Human Services Sub-Cabinet. Other states have similar units.

Indiana Interdepartmental Board

In 1977, Indiana passed a law (P.L. 46) creating the Interdepartmental Board for the Coordination of Human Services Programs with a modest budget of $75,000. The twelve-member board is comprised of the commissioners or directors of mental health, health, manpower development, public instruction, rehabilitation, welfare, community services, employment security, the budget, aging, and representatives of the governor's staff.

The board meets monthly and is charged by law with the "effective and efficient delivery of basic human services. . . . Special emphasis should be placed by the board on coordinating the activities of the departments and agencies represented by its membership."

Illinois Human Services Sub-Cabinet

Illinois has a Governor's Human Services Sub-Cabinet, meeting monthly, comprised of the directors of Public Aid, Mental Health and Developmental Disabilities, Public Health, Aging, Children and Family Services, and Rehabilitation Services. Their experience has been similar to that in Michigan.

Michigan Human Services Cabinet

In 1976, the Michigan governor set up five cabinets to resolve issues between major state departments. One was the Human Services Cabinet with a governor's staff member plus representatives (usually the director) of the Departments of Social Services, Public Health, Labor, Mental Health, and Education. The interdepartmental issues which have been presented include: surveillance and utilization of Medicaid providers, which required coordination between the Departments of Public Health and Social Services; adult community placement coordination of homes for the aged (Public Health) and adult foster care homes (Social Services); youth employment programs; and programs for pregnant high school students.

The cabinet is not a decision-making body but rather serves to inform the governor of interdepartmental coordination issues. The meetings are called by the governor, and depend upon the number and nature of interdepartmental concerns.

The governor has found that most issues could have been resolved by independent lateral coordination. And the cabinet has had no budget or staff—governors' staffs do not usually understand or appreciate the long-term programmatic need for interdepartmental coordination. Governors' offices tend to operate from election to election, with relatively little incentive to adopt a longer view.

The minimal investment of the Governor's Office has been aggravated by the fact that each department generally sends a representative who is most knowledgeable about the issue under dispute, with a resultant lack of continuity. Nonetheless, the cabinet is one vehicle for resolving problems between agencies at the state level. The solution is often a clearer statement of expected coordination responsibilities and mandates from the governor.

Advisory Councils

Similar to cabinets are the advisory councils, which are usually more limited in scope than cabinet bodies. Examples include Mis-

souri's State Advisory Council on Developmental Disabilities and Governor's Committee on Services to the Handicapped. A host of advisory committees exists in most Midwestern states.

Interdepartmental Agreements

All states make frequent use of interagency agreements whereby agency units agree in writing on which will do what to achieve cooperation in specified program areas.

Response to a Crisis

The public institutional coordination effort is very much influenced in these times by judicial and legislative responses to our failures. Our inability to emphasize coordination in normal, regulatory, and provider planning processes has resulted in human services failures. Witness some scandal in your own state which involved the failure of separate administrative entities to develop, deliver, and regulate a given human service. We have seen our coordination failures litigated so much that efficient program administration is hampered. State legislatures tend to view our failures as requiring a statutory "package" arraying the full range of administration, regulation, delivery, and planning around each discrete service.

Cabinets, task forces, and advisory councils are best used for normal coordination. Responses to crises are often handled by other means to resolve particular problems quickly. A crisis arises, an agency task force is named and quickly given high visibility to assure the public that the causes are thoroughly investigated and concerted action will be forthcoming. Every state reported some such mechanisms, similar to the permanent councils, cabinets, and task forces but with a more immediate instruction to *resolve* a particular program. Resolution is not always achieved, but crises do recede and attention is diverted.

Appropriation Process

The appropriation process is potentially the best possible means for clarifying coordination functions and expectations. The provision or denial of resources conveys a clear directive. Boiler-plate language attached to an appropriation bill and negotiations during budget hearings often designate the relationships between agencies. This process was rarely mentioned by states as a coordi-

nation mechanism but, in fact, aside from gubernatorial pressure, it is the most powerful force requiring agencies to share resources and formalize such exchanges in contracts or agreements.

Certain other methods of enhancing human services coordination are often associated with the appropriation process.

For example: The State of Ohio has a Service Identification System which tracks all human services by funding source, program, location, provider, eligibility requirements, number of staff providing service, and application and appointment procedure. This system provides a comprehensive indexing of all services.

Wisconsin has a similar Human Services Classification Project in Milwaukee County.

The Illinois Bureau of the Budget integrates all state agency plans into an annual Illinois Human Services Plan. Illinois has also established common planning regions for the Departments of Public Aid, Children and Family Services, Public Health, and Mental Health and Developmental Disabilities.

In Michigan, as in other states, the governor's State of the State address (SOS) integrates the major developments in each state agency and informs other agencies of such plans. In part, the SOS (which is assembled from departmental inputs) represents the culmination of agency attempts to secure a gubernatorial blessing for agency initiatives.

Although the foregoing methods do not themselves result in the coordination of independent state programs, they create an atmosphere which fosters such coordination.

Efforts to Assure Information Sharing

Sharing information generally takes place by methods such as referral directories, regional plans, or a common needs assessment collection process (as in South Dakota). Such mechanisms survive only if all participating agencies derive some benefit from them.

Michigan recently demonstrated (to a degree) the effectiveness of a shared information and referral system with a demonstration project called the Human Services Network, an on-line automated file of human service providers which was linked to computer terminals in delivery sites across the state. Network was designed to:
• improve information and referral by the widespread use and rapid updating of a comprehensive human services resource file with a refined scanning capability (geocoding) to find the combination of needed services in the closest location for the client;

- improve planning, needs assessment, and evaluation by the automatic recording of all requests and answers concerning the availability of and demand for specified services; and
- save money by reducing inappropriate referrals and rapidly locating suitable, available lower-cost facilities and services for clients awaiting placement.

Network was implemented in Detroit and the Upper Peninsula in 1978. We learned several important lessons about trying to coordinate the information and referral processes of all human service agencies.

Agencies use different terms for similar services. A comprehensive taxonomy of services took two years to develop and was never totally acceptable to all agencies.

Human service agencies are numerous, often small, and constantly changing their services and/or providers. Consequently, it was difficult to maintain accurate and complete information of the availability of bed space, licensing status, etc. It is a demanding task to keep all agencies accurately, fully, and currently informed.

Intake workers and information and referral sources conceive of themselves as the experts in community resources. They make decisions based on their experiences, relationships with peers from other agencies, prior referrals, and personal knowledge of specific agencies.

This expertise is a basis of their self-esteem. Rather than utilize and trust a computer, they relied mainly on their own experience. Only 10 percent of the agencies used their computer terminals for referrals during the test period. We have much to learn about implementing coordination mechanisms. *The psychology of the service delivery worker may be the most important and least understood dimension of coordination.*

Agencies were much more willing to assist Network development as long as their resource commitment was minimal. As the necessary commitment increased, their level of involvement decreased. It became increasingly difficult to get active involvement as the Network moved through stages of taxonomy development, an agreement to locate a terminal in an agency (which required convenient floor space), training agency staff to use the terminal (which required staff time), and emphasis on utilization of the terminal (which required supervisory time). Hospital staff were most resistant to the Network; of twenty-four hospitals asked to participate, only five agreed to place a terminal on their premises and only one made full use of it. Lip service was common; full commitment was almost nonexistent.

The development of an information and referral network is very time consuming and expensive. The Network demonstration took four years to develop at a cost of several million (mostly federal) dollars. In the end, the legislature killed it as an "expensive toy." In its absence, the problems it was designed to solve have been exacerbated.

Out of eighty-three counties in Michigan, three, Lenawee, Kalamazoo, and Livingston, are extensively involved in coordination efforts. Both Kalamazoo and Livingston are gathering needs assessment data to be shared by many agencies. Some of the same problems of negotiating a common definition of services have occurred as in the Network project. Nonetheless, county agencies have combined their resources for a common goal. Ironically, such a cooperative venture may result in competition for meeting the needs which are identified.

The Lenawee County human services project was an independent group directly responsible to the Board of Commissioners. At the outset, the establishment of a new department helped to alleviate a number of potential barriers to coordination, because the project staff was viewed as neutral in specific interagency disputes and potential conflicts of interest were minimized. As part of the county government, the project staff gained readier acceptance and legitimacy than they might have as a private or state agency. The staff also had the active support and potential influence of the Board of Commissioners.

The voluntary coordination of human service agencies has been a very slow process. Many barriers had to be overcome before the personnel of one agency were willing to cooperate with those of another. Most administrators had to be assured that their turf would not be encroached upon. Sadly, though understandably, each administrator appeared concerned primarily with the security of his own agency and the welfare of its clients.

During the first two years of the Lenawee project, an atmosphere was fostered in which the human service providers began to cooperate with each other. Rather than approach problems in an isolated manner, they began to address human service issues in a coordinated and comprehensive way. However, this cooperation was limited to non-threatening activities. Providers were hesitant about activities with unknown outcomes and unwilling to participate in those which might jeopardize their autonomy. As the human service system began to function more coherently and efficiently, they grew more cooperative. Furthermore, as the project staff and cooperating agency personnel began to overcome

barriers, providers grew more optimistic about the potential benefits of coordinating services.

In a voluntary project such as that in Lenawee County, the
coordinator has limited leverage, since he has no formal authority
over any department or agency. He cannot require an agency to
participate or give a directive to an agency administrator. He
must rely on persuasion and the influence of the county commissioners and state officials.

Initially, project staff had to rely on altruistic arguments and
refer to the achievements of similar efforts in other communities.
However, when the benefits of coordination began to materialize,
they could stress the project's accomplishments. Skeptical
providers could no longer summarily dismiss the idea of cooperation and coordination. Each successful step increased the project's
potential to improve service delivery.

Two examples of Lenawee County activities which have either
reduced duplication or improved service are transportation and
the standardized release of information. Transportation services
for the mentally handicapped and elderly are now coordinated
and have led to the provision of more service, a reduction in duplication, and a reduction of individual agency transportation
costs. The release of information process is now uniform due to a
format developed by the Human Services Council, which incorpo-
rated the legalities and requirements of all participating agencies.

The coordination of transportation vehicles led indirectly to the
development of a common billing system in a six-state demonstration project managed by the Michigan Department of Social
Services.

Lenawee County's success has been further enhanced by recommendations of the Governor's Committee on Unification of the
Public Mental Health System for the creation of county human
services councils to coordinate mental health services.

In Minnesota, the 1979 Community Social Services Act has established human services boards similar to the foregoing councils.
Among the functions of the boards are to:
• manage the public resources devoted to human services
  provided or purchased by the counties and subsidized or regu-
  lated by the Departments of Corrections, Health, and Public
  Welfare;
• employ staff to manage these resources;
• provide services directly or by contract with private or public
  agencies;
• plan the provision of human services, including corrections,

public and mental health, public assistance, mental retardation, and other social services;
• receive and expend funds; and
• rent and purchase property and equipment.

In short, each major state agency provides a grant to this local county planning agency, which expends the funds. The act states explicitly that "The departments of corrections, health and public welfare shall provide funds from any grant or subsidy program or other authorized source to the human services board, based upon an approved plan. The grant or subsidy shall represent *all* money for human services which each agency commits to programs within counties comprising the human services board."

This exciting development is one of the most significant attempts to coordinate resources systematically at the local community level. There will be considerable variation in various counties' ability to distribute such monies among local providers, but Minnesota's history of strong county government makes it likely that the necessary local leadership and talent will be developed. This experiment will be widely watched.

Coordination for Client Convenience

"One-stop shopping" for human services is a great convenience for the client. The most frequent example of this is the joint location of Department of Labor WIN teams and social service staff of county welfare offices engaged in employment placement. Other examples include Community Health and Social Services (CHASS) in Detroit, which combines staff of the Departments of Public Health, Social Services, and Spanish Affairs and agencies funded by United Way in the same facilities.

However, such collocation does not necessarily mean that the staff know more about each other, make more appropriate referrals, or provide other benefits to the client than physical convenience.

Common intake is another attempt to make service more convenient. In the Comprehensive Community Care project in Michigan, a number of pilot counties are sharing a common intake assessment form for all adult services of the Department of Social Services to minimize the duplication of effort for the elderly who may have a difficult time in being shuffled from agency to agency.

Getting agreement on the items of a common intake form is not

easy. When thirteen Lenawee County agencies listed the intake information they needed, the resultant form was longer than that of any one agency. Moreover, all agency staff needed training to complete accurately items with which they were unfamiliar. When the cost of the client's convenience was recognized, the common intake form was dropped.

This example reinforces the need to assess more critically the meaning of coordination and to weigh seriously both the costs and the benefits which can realistically be expected from specific measures of coordination.

Conclusions and Recommendations

Midwestern states have fostered coordination by five main methods:
• In state governments, relatively common approaches include the amalgamation of human services agencies in umbrella departments, special task forces, advisory councils, and cabinets. In different circumstances, these approaches have been more, or less, effective in resolving interdepartmental problems and making decisions at the governor's level.
• In some counties and communities, resources have been combined for such shared purposes as needs assessment, client transportation, and information and referral data.
• At the client level there are some attempts at the collocation of services and the use of a common application or intake form.
• In all states, a crisis usually leads to an ad hoc attempt to achieve, or appear to achieve, the coordination of services. Once the crisis disappears, so does the apparent need for coordination.
• The budget process itself is a significant means of coordination. The allocation of funds is a most effective way to ensure coordination or anything else.

Yet, finally, a concerted effort by federal, state, and local governments to coordinate programs is conspicuously absent and much needed.

Little effective coordination is taking place in the Midwest. Coordination must be implemented selectively for clearly defined purposes. The indiscriminate support of coordination is as irresponsible as its indiscriminate rejection.

In this review, I have deliberately neglected the coordination of specific services for children and the elderly, since it rarely exists except on paper.

There are numerous reasons for the limited extent of effective coordination: narrow funding sources and systems; organizational alignments; parochialism; and the lack of assurance of a better way. Yet these reasons really boil down to one: Our society has grown so large and complex that simple solutions do not exist.

To improve coordination, many governmental units have been united into umbrella agencies or linked by cabinets, coordinating committees, and task forces. All have been useful. Yet the process of assembling units, staffs, programs, and budgets has had a curious countervailing effect. As the small units are coordinated by umbrella departments or cabinet committees, the perception of advocates for children or the aged is that less attention is being paid to their interests.

This perception can lead to a movement to disassemble a department and create separate agencies dealing with children or the elderly. In Michigan, such an effort occurred in 1978 and succeeded in part. Several legislators introduced legislation to establish an Office of Children and Youth Services as an autonomous state unit. I opposed autonomy, and the office is now an integral part of the Department of Social Services; however, I was bitterly attacked for "not caring about kids." In Rhode Island, in 1979, children's services were removed from the Department of Social and Rehabilitative Services and placed in a new separate department. The same occurred in Massachusetts in 1979. In Ohio, a legislative commission for children has recommended a similar change.

And so the pendulum swings back. In the 1960s and early 1970s, program unification was ascendant. Now, program separation is coming to the fore. Everywhere, the arguments are the same: The larger agency "doesn't care" about children, old folks, the mentally ill or handicapped; as resources grow scarcer, the interests of each group are "being overlooked"; "clearer and stronger advocacy" are needed; and so on.

I believe that, on the whole, governments do a fairly good job, which is too seldom recognized. Our successes are rarely applauded; our failures are widely publicized. I have experienced several strong attacks from the media and/or the legislature because "kids get lost in foster care," foster care placements fail, or because of other such problems.

My department is concerned about all the children of Michigan. Hundreds of thousands are in families receiving public assistance; at any given time, about three hundred thousand are in foster care or in departmental institutions; perhaps there are five

hundred to a thousand children whom we fail to help. And it is our failures which are heralded.

Several basic questions are posed.

Do state governments accept responsibility for the health and welfare of children and the frail elderly? For me the answer is clearly yes.

Does the current balance of mental health, public health, and social service programs match the balance of public needs? Recognizing that resources are never fully adequate, my answer is, again, yes.

What changes in the existing mix of services appear desirable in the 1980s? What barriers do governments erect to, and what incentives can they offer to promote, the better integration of services? The answers to these questions are not clear or simple.

Governments may not "erect" barriers, yet clearly they exist. Six should be mentioned:

• The sheer difficulty of determining "better" ways to administer and provide service. Present programs do accomplish much good. Poor people are given cash assistance; the hungry receive food; the sick get medical care; the elderly are taken care of. Despite all the limitations, problems, and failings, vital or significant help is provided to many. The natural tendency is to assume that more cash, food, and medical care will do even more good. Attempts to do different things, or to do things differently, may not be better; in fact, they may be worse.

• The dangerous consequences of failure. If we try integration, coordination, or a different mix of services, and it fails, there will be less service for the needy. We are not experimenting with mice; we are working with real people, and total failure cannot be tolerated.

• The need to believe in what we do. We need to believe in what we do: that our agency, our programs, our jobs are important, if not truly essential. To tinker with them can be to tinker with that belief and engender resistance to change, realignment, even reassignment.

• Turf. Institutions tend to protect themselves and resist intrusion from without. Accordingly, small public or private agencies especially will resist union with larger agencies, lest they be overwhelmed or even swallowed up.

• The problem of the leader. Leaders are expected by those who serve them to protect an organization and its programs. This integration of services and/or programs often also means the integration of organizations, which can lead to organizational change or

eclipse. The threat to individual careers and jobs produces natural resentment.

• Funding and reporting restraints. Every program and service must be funded, and those who provide the funds usually mandate the reporting of expenditures. The commingling of funds which occurs when services are integrated or coordinated hampers this reporting.

Solutions can be found only if discretion and flexibility are allowed. However, legislatures limit such discretion lest funds be used for purposes for which they have not been appropriated.

The key to improved coordination lies with the mayor, governor, or president. Each chief executive is responsible for everything in his jurisdiction. When he decides that change is required, he must personally and institutionally participate in achieving it. He can do this by designating a czar for children's or aging services, by reorganization, or by personal participation in cabinets or coordinating committees. But unless he makes a personal and continuing commitment to improvement, little will happen.

Several promising opportunities exist for the coordination of human services in the 1980s, such as common intake forms and systems, common needs assessment studies and systems, and common assessment centers for deinstitutionalized clients returning to the community.

In order to take advantage of such opportunities, each agency must change its focus from what it can do for a client to what the community can do regardless of which agency or network provides the service. The real challenge in coordination is to focus on the needs of the client and the community rather than on those of the agency.

SERVICES INTEGRATION AND COORDINATION IN THE WEST: THE WASHINGTON STATE EXPERIENCE

Scott Briar

To begin with a conclusion: In the West—and this conclusion may hold for the rest of the country as well—many persons with a professional interest in social services regard services integration as a dead issue. They also believe that services integration was tried—mainly in the Services Integration-Targets of Opportunity (SITO) projects—and that the evaluations of these experimental projects found that it was not effective. Those who accept this conclusion also argue that we should forget about services integration and look elsewhere for ways to improve the delivery of social services.

The problem is that the SITO projects did *not* show that services integration is ineffective. On the contrary, they generated little information about its effectiveness, because full administrative integration was never implemented and therefore not tested.[1]

The SITO projects did, however, identify and weigh some of the political, fiscal, and administrative obstacles to services integration. In fact, so formidable were these obstacles that most of the projects were unable even to implement the particular service integration model they were designed to test and, further, none was able to implement an administratively integrated service delivery system, with the possible exception of Florida, and the complete results of that effort are still not in. In other words, despite the substantial investment in SITO projects, we do not know what the effects—positive and negative—of a fully integrated service-delivery system would be in comparison to nonintegrated systems.

What is Services Integration?

That is a sweeping generalization. It is more or less true depending on how service integration is defined. Services integration means different things to different people. The SITO projects helped to identify some widely differing definitions of services integration, ranging from periodic case conferences among staff from several different agencies to a system that is fully integrated fiscally, administratively, and at the service-delivery level. The research process has a way of clarifying previously vague concepts. It is not surprising that whatever consensus had developed about the desirability of services integration started to evaporate when the persons involved began to realize that often they were not talking about the same thing at all. Case conferences to achieve *voluntary* cooperation among staff from different agencies are, at most, only mildly threatening, but each incremental step toward full administrative and fiscal integration of services heightens the concern of those who are strongly identified with categorical problems.

For example, collocation would appear to be relatively noncontroversial when the programs retain their separate identity and autonomy. But it raises such sensitive issues as the relative size of offices and the quality of furnishings for different programs, and whether different client groups can mingle in the same waiting rooms. Such mundane issues can generate deep and heated divisions.

The Roots of Services Integration

The idea of services integration has two principal sources. One was the community organization society (COS) movement at the beginning of this century. Its main objective was to avoid the waste that would be associated with the duplication of services—especially cash and in-kind relief—in the same case. There were other objectives, but they were secondary. This concern was rekindled in the 1950s by the work of Bradley Buell and his associates showing that a relatively few cases consumed a substantial proportion of community services.[2] This work identified what were called "multiproblem families" and the need to coordinate services for them. Parenthetically, other analyses suggested that these families were viewed as multiproblem because of the fragmentation of the service delivery system.[3] Subsequently, with the rapid growth and proliferation of categorical programs, each with

its own separate delivery system, concern developed over the extreme difficulties which clients experienced in obtaining service from more than one program.

Responses to these utilization problems evolved in two directions. One was to integrate services administratively into a single delivery system. The other was to expand the range of services provided by each categorical program which threatened to create parallel, comprehensive social service systems. A good example was afforded by the proposals offered a few years ago for the development of comprehensive social and human service programs within both the public welfare and the mental health systems. If these proposals had been implemented, we would have had two overlapping comprehensive personal social service systems serving the same target populations. Similar aspirations emerged in a number of categorical areas, including aging and developmental disabilities. If these aspirations are realized, we can expect the rediscovery of multiproblem families lost in two or more comprehensive social service systems.

As our brief historical review may suggest, the services integration movement has two primary roots, one concerned with efficiency, reduction of duplication, and administrative flexibility, and the other reflecting a desire to maximize the ease and effectiveness with which multiple services can be delivered to the same client.

It is perhaps not surprising that, over the past decade, the bulk of the attention given to services integration has approached the subject almost exclusively from an administrative perspective. After all, most of the decisions about how services integration is to be implemented, analyzed, and evaluated are made by administrators. It is natural for them to approach program issues and problems from their own vantage point and to assume that their perspective is critical for the viability of the program.

In any event, from SITO and other efforts we have learned much about the administrative aspects of services integration, but little about integration at the case level or from a client perspective. For those who think that the vital objective of services integration is to improve services to individual clients, the lack of information about the specific effects of different administrative arrangements at the case level is frustrating.

Developments in the West

To get a sense of the directions in which services integration and coordination are moving in the West, and of the current political issues associated with these trends, I interviewed some key persons who are exceptionally well informed about the developments.

Surprisingly, they said that Washington was the most significant state examined, because it has the most integrated state department in the region, and other states such as California and Oregon have not made a major commitment to social services coordination and integration. These are, perhaps, not so much factual conclusions as the perceptions of some well-informed observers. Nonetheless, I shall present a case study of developments in Washington. Of course, Washington is not "typical" of the West, but what is happening there is instructive.

Services Integration in Washington: Background

In 1970, responding to the recommendations of a task force appointed by the governor, the Washington State Legislature passed a bill creating the Department of Social and Health Services (DSHS), bringing under one umbrella five previously separate agencies: the Departments of Institutions, Public Assistance, Health, and Vocational Rehabilitation, and the Veterans Rehabilitation Council. The legislature gave remarkably extensive authority to the DSHS secretary; he was delegated all the powers and authority previously assigned to the separate agencies and was accountable only to the governor. Only two limitations were placed on the secretary's authority to organize the new department: Vocational rehabilitation would have divisional status, and the governor must approve the secretary's reorganization plans. As provided in the legislation, the new department came into existence on July 1, 1970. The purpose of the statute which, to date, has not been changed, was "to create a single department that will unify the related social and health services of state government. The department is designed to integrate and coordinate all those activities involving provision of care for individuals who as a result of their economic, social, or health condition require financial assistance, institutional care, rehabilitation, or other social and health services."[4]

In the short period before the new department announced operations, its first secretary, who formerly headed the Department of

Financial Assistance, did not have time to develop an organizational plan. Six months of extensive consultation followed before the secretary delivered his plan to the governor in January 1971. The plan called for six divisions: four for program development, under a deputy secretary; one for management services; and one for service delivery, with a regionalized delivery system. The governor approved the plan and, in April 1981, the new division directors were named.

However, another three to four months were devoted to enlisting the participation of more than three thousand citizens, including clients, staff, legislators, local officials, and special interest groups, in a planning process to determine regional boundaries, the services to be provided, and how they were to be delivered. One of the interesting legacies of this remarkable process was a large core of interested citizens who are exceptionally well informed about the organization and operation of the department and remarkably sophisticated about services coordination and integration.

Finally, on July 1, 1971, the new organizational structure was implemented, one year after the department was legally established. However, the regional structure, vital to the organizational plan for services integration, was not implemented until February 1972, when the ten regional administrators were appointed.

At this early stage in its development, the department already was seriously compromised in attempting to achieve its statutory goals. The long period of internal discussion and consultation before formulating the organization plan provided ample opportunity for opponents of integration to develop counter-strategies. And the ambiguity in the plan about the relationship between the program and service delivery divisions left unclear which set of interests would prevail. The underlying concept was that the program development divisions would set policies to ensure adequate standards in all programs, but that nearly all programs would be decentralized to the regional administrators. But the lack of clarity about the relationship between the service delivery and program divisions left open the strong possibility that the categorical program divisions would prevail on disputed issues.

An even greater problem arose later in 1972. The incumbent governor was engaged in a reelection campaign in which one of the major issues was the new umbrella agency. The governor defended the agency, but the attacks on it blunted and slowed the movement toward integration. After the governor's reelection, the first secretary of the department resigned. Interest in the new de-

partment's aspirations had crested and receded. The second secretary was interested in initiatives that could show results and regarded services integration as a long-range objective. He expressed the view that the department should be the agency of last resort for human and social problems. Some critics were later to say that his primary objective was to maximize the flow of federal dollars into the department.

In any event, for the next few years there was little activity related to services integration or coordination except for pressure from some citizens who had participated in the planning process and believed that the secretary still should pursue the purposes defined by the legislature. The department moved on to other things including strengthened centralized management systems and a SITO project, which was developed as part of its mission and ended for lack of state support.

A New Beginning: 1977

During the 1976 gubernatorial campaign, Democratic candidate Dixy Lee Ray promised that one of her first acts would be to appoint a panel, which she would chair, to determine to what extent the department's goals had been realized.

As promised, and even before her inauguration, she appointed fifteen persons to a Select Panel on DSHS which she chaired. Although the press suggested that the governor's intent was to break up the umbrella agency, she maintained that she wanted the panel's best advice, whatever that might be. The panel, of which I was a member, submitted its report in August 1977. On the purpose of the department, the report said:

> the Panel has concluded that the integration of services intended when DSHS was established in 1970 has neither been accomplished nor really ever been pursued. Similarly, the umbrella concept has remained more a concept than an operating principle; the separate programs which were brought together under the umbrella continue to resist coordination and even cooperation in many areas. The shortcomings of DSHS, in summary, seem not to result from trying too much or going too far, but from trying too little, with too little commitment and support from the Department's top leadership over the past five years.[5]

The panel called for a renewed and strengthened commitment by the governor and the secretary to the original purposes of the department. It recommended further regional decentralization as

essential to the achievement of services integration and coordination. Recognizing that it would be politically impossible to implement integration in the whole state at once, the panel recommended that an integrated system, including all categorical programs which still had their own, separate delivery systems, be tested on a pilot basis in two regions. Governor Ray praised the panel and assured the members that the report would be used and not left to gather dust on a shelf.

The secretary she appointed had served *ex officio* on the panel and, while not agreeing with all of its recommendations, indicated his intent to implement as many as possible. However, in 1978, after little more than a year, the governor found it necessary to remove the secretary. He was followed by two acting secretaries selected from inside the agency. In addition, the governor established a task force, drawn primarily from the business community, to advise her on the management of the department but not, she emphasized, to duplicate or replace the work of the Select Panel.

The new secretary subsequently selected from the Management Task Force brought with him into top positions several other persons who had also served on that body.

Current Status

In 1978–79, some movement occurred in directions recommended by the Select Panel, although the secretary did not express interest in services integration and coordination as department objectives.

Strong emphasis was placed on regionalization, which included three principal components. The discretion and authority delegated to the regional administrators significantly increased. In each region, a committee chaired by the regional administrator was established to improve management and coordination. It included representatives of categorical programs still centrally administered by DSHS as well as managers of local service offices and other regionally administered programs. The centralized program representatives were given limited authority to take some actions to facilitate coordination with other regional units.

In 1979, the secretary placed in the regions the first stage of the biennial budget planning process. This deserves a brief description since it was intended as a step toward integrated planning. Planning committees of representatives from the regional management and citizens' advisory committees developed written agreements with other planning bodies, such as the Area Agencies on

Aging, and local officials to obtain their participation in the planning process. These planning committees and subcommittees received staff support from the agency.

The parameters for budget proposals were clearly and tightly drawn by the secretary, so that the planning committees were severely limited both in the number and magnitude of initiatives they could propose. Committees were also required to consider budget reductions as well as increases; in fact, it sometimes seemed to participants that the agency was most interested in the committees' serving as the first line of action on budget controls and reductions. Theoretically, they could consider reallocations across categorical programs, where allowed by statute. However, the process started too late for such functional budget planning.

In addition, the department showed some limited interest in the use of case managers, although probably without the authority that elsewhere has been found necessary for their effectiveness.

Implications

What can be said about the implications of the Washington experience for service integration and coordination in the West? I emphasize "implications," since clearly one can generalize only if, at least in some respects, Washington has advanced further toward these goals than other Western states.

The Washington experience provides one more example of a principal conclusion of the SITO projects: that a strong, consistent commitment by the agency director and the governor and a willingness to pay its inevitable political costs are essential. Understandably, many governors and secretaries are unwilling or unable to pay the cost of pursuing an objective that will take a long time to achieve, especially when the benefits have not yet been fully demonstrated.

If the services integration and coordination movement is to be sustained, it will be important to show some tangible successes in the near future—not just in implementation (although that would be significant), but in the quality, economy, efficiency, effectiveness, or comprehensiveness of services. Eventually, Florida may be viewed as a case of services integration with such tangible success.

In contrast, Washington is a good state to observe on the issue of whether services integration and coordination can be implemented gradually and incrementally. The SITO experience and

my own conclusions are pessimistic. Nevertheless, some progress continues even in the absence of a clear, strong commitment from the top.

The widespread and growing reliance on case managers to achieve coordination and even integration deserves close attention and study. Some advocates point to the use of case managers in vocational rehabilitation as a model, but they can, if necessary, buy services for clients. Few other case managers have such authority or resources. This may be another instance of expecting one valuable but limited linkage mechanism to carry excessive weight in promoting coordination. If so, we can expect to hear about the "failure" of the case manager concept within a few years. Can case managers—typically, persons without professional training and with little authority—achieve what many SITO projects could not? Precisely what should they accomplish?

The trend toward reducing the educational and professional qualifications of direct service staff and the increasing reliance on purchase of specialized services could well make services integration even more difficult to implement. An integrated service system would require knowledgeable, skilled professionals to identify clients' problems accurately, to determine in which order these problems should be addressed, and to select the combination of interventions and services most likely to be effective. And the purchase of service from private providers obviously complicates coordination unless case managers with authority, knowledge, and skill can ensure that they are responsive to client needs.

What will the service delivery system look like in ten years if no further progress is made on integration and coordination? For example, in Washington, one sees a trend toward the atomization and routinization of the tasks assigned to line workers so that, in theory, they can be performed without prior experience or training. Not only can this be expected further to dehumanize the agency as clients experience it, but it will lead to a further reduction in effectiveness. Without increased coordination and with increased reliance on nonprofessional staff who lack expert knowledge and skill, referrals will become more frequent and less effective because those receiving them will be unable to solve the client's problems.

Conclusion

I have suggested that concern about services coordination and integration—at least at a level of intensity sufficient to general action—is on the decline, pushed aside in part by the kind of managerial approach that has dominated thought and practice in social services in recent years. In the State of Washington, managers have bypassed services coordination and integration despite strong and persistent citizen pressure for it.

If an emphasis on coordination and integration is to be revived, it must be shown to be feasible, and the differences it would make and the benefits that would follow must be demonstrated specifically and dramatically. These are very difficult tasks.

Notes

1. John Dewitt, "Managing the Human Service 'System': What Have We Learned from Services Integration?" Project Share, *Human Services Monograph Series,* No. 1, August 1977.
2. Bradley Buell *et. al., Community Planning for Human Services,* Columbia University Press, New York, 1952.
3. Scott Briar, "Family Services," in Henry S. Maas, ed., *Five Fields of Social Service: Review of Research,* National Association of Social Workers, New York, 1966, pp. 9–50.
4. Senate Bill 52, Washington State Legislature, 1970.
5. Governor's Select Panel on the Department of Social and Health Services, *Report to the Governor on the Department of Social and Health Services,* Olympia, Washington, August, 1977.

Glossary

AFDC—Aid to Families with Dependent Children, a program, authorized by Title IV-A of the Social Security Act, providing federal funds to the states for payments to low-income families and children

CETA—Comprehensive Employment and Training Act, a Department of Labor program, administered by state and local agencies, which provides on-the-job training, job development, and vocational counseling

collocation—the location of different services in the same facility

coterminality—common geographic boundaries for different services

EPSDT—Early and Periodic Screening, Diagnosis, and Treatment Program, authorized under Title II of the Social Security Act, provides medical examination and treatment of children eligible for Medicaid

GAO—U.S. General Accounting Office, the investigatory arm of Congress

Head Start—a federal program providing educational, health, and other services to preschool disadvantaged children and their families

HEW—Department of Health, Education, and Welfare

HHS—Department of Health and Human Services, formed in October 1979 from the former Department of Health, Education, and Welfare upon the creation of a separate Department of Education

HUD—Department of Housing and Urban Development

human services—an ill-defined range of services; the Academy panel used the term for health, mental health, social services, and public welfare; others may exclude health or include educational, vocational and employment training, housing, correctional, and other services

I&R—information and referral

Medicaid—a program authorized under Title XIX of the Social Security Act, which provides federal reimbursement to the states for medical costs of low-income persons

Medicare—a program authorized under Title XVIII of the Social Security Act, which covers the hospital costs of persons on Social Security pensions

Older Americans Act—a 1975 act authorizing federal assistance to state and area organizations for programs for older persons

OMB—Office of Management and Budget, an agency in the Executive Office of the President established in 1970 as successor to the Bureau of the Budget

Project Share—a service of the Department of Health, Education, and Welfare and its successor, the Department of Health and Human Services, providing

information and publications on the coordination and/or integration of human services

services coordination—the voluntary concerting of two or more services provided by autonomous agencies

services integration—the concerting of two or more services provided by an agency headed by an official with administrative authority over the services

SITO—Services Integration Targets of Opportunity, a series of state and local demonstration projects financed by the Department of Health, Education, and Welfare in the early 1970s

SSA—Social Security Administration

SSI—Supplemental Security Income, a federal program providing monthly benefits to needy blind, aged, and disabled persons

Title I—Elementary and Secondary Education Act, authorizes federal funds to local education agencies for the education of children of low-income families

Title IV-B—a section of the Social Security Act authorizing child welfare programs

Title V—a section of the Social Security Act authorizing maternal and child health programs

Title XX—a section of the Social Security Act authorizing grants to the states for a broad range of social services

WIN—the Department of Labor Work Incentive Program, authorized under the Social Security Act, which provides child care and supportive social services to help AFDC family members obtain employment

Contributors

David M. Austin, Professor, School of Social Work, University of Texas, Austin

Barbara B. Blum, President, Manpower Demonstration Research Corporation; former Commissioner, New York State Department of Social Services

Scott Briar, Dean, School of Social Work, University of Washington

John T. Dempsey, Director, Michigan Department of Social Services

Robert Morris, Emeritus Professor, Heller School, Brandeis University

John Mudd, Deputy Director, Children's Defense Fund, Washington, D.C.

Harold Orlans, Senior Research Associate, National Academy of Public Administration

T. M. Jim Parham, Professor, School of Social Work, University of Georgia

DATE DUE

AUG 12 1987			

DEMCO 38-297

THE LITTLE BOOK OF
FAST CARS

Written by Philip Raby

THE LITTLE BOOK OF
FAST CARS

This edition first published in the UK in 2006
by Green Umbrella

www.greenumbrella.co.uk

© Green Umbrella Publishing 2007

Publishers Jules Gammond and Vanessa Gardner

Printed and bound by J. H. Haynes & Co. Ltd., Sparkford

ISBN 1-905009-40-2

Contents

Introduction

MIDDLE This 1903
60bhp Mercedes had its
engine at the front
driving the rear wheels.
It set the tone for fast
cars for years to come

WHAT IS THE DEFINITION OF A fast car? These days, when even a modest family saloon can drive at over 100mph, you could argue that all cars are fast. But family saloons are also rather dull. So I like to think of fast cars as those that have been designed with the sole purpose of going fast and being fun to drive.

This thinking is nothing new. When the first motorcars were preceded by a bloke with a red flag, people were already getting excited by the prospect of driving fast.

Those first rear-engined machines only chugged along at speeds of around 10mph, but by 1901, Daimler had produced a 60bhp Mercedes that was capable of 60mph and is now considered to have been the world's first sports car.

And things just got better from then onwards, with more and more manufacturers jumping on the power bandwagon.

By the 1980s, the race was on to produce a 200mph sportscar, and in 1987 Ferrari's F40 hit 201mph and the magical figure was finally broken.

As the 1990s went on, the 200mph-

plus supercar became almost the norm, so McLaren had to pull out all the stops to come up with something special. And it did just that with the F1 of 1993. Not only could this reach a previously unheard of 240mph, it was also smaller, lighter and more nimble than most other supercars.

However, to reach such heady speeds cost a lot of money. Sensibly, perhaps, other manufacturers contented themselves with cars that had a top speed of close to 200mph, and concentrated

But that is missing the point. The human race has always strived to improve itself. If it hadn't, we'd still be sitting in caves wondering how to make fire. And if the motorcar hadn't been allowed to develop, it would still be chugging along behind a man waving a red flag.

So, what's next? Will there ever be a road car better than the Veyron? A car capable of even greater speeds? I sincerely hope so, because it will be a sad day, indeed, when mankind stops pushing the boundaries yet further. And, remember, the benefits of producing ultra-fast cars have always filtered down into more mainstream machinery. Which is why the humble family saloon can now drive at over 100mph.

So, fast cars are an important part of our lives. Over the following pages are sixty of some of the most interesting, influential and exciting cars which were built for the sole purpose of going at high speed. It's very much a personal choice – I could easily have included twice the number – and I'm sorry if your personal favourite isn't there. Enjoy!

instead on making machines that drove and handled superbly at rather more realistic speeds.

Until, that is, the Bugatti Veyron came along. With 1000bhp on tap, this had a top speed of no less than 253mph and a 0-60mph time of just 2.9 seconds – less than the time it took you to read this sentence! Of course, the critics shook their heads, asking what was the use of producing a car capable of such speeds, when most countries don't even allow you to drive at 100mph.

Philip Raby

Aston Martin DB5
1964 United Kingdom

HOW TO SPOT

Smooth two-door coupe with headlamps behind streamlined plastic cowls. Long rear overhang, and traditional Aston Martin grille and side strakes.

THE ASTON MARTIN DB5 IS ONE OF the most famous cars of all time – for the simple reason Sean Connery, as James Bond, drove one in the films Goldfinger and Thunderball, in the early 1960s.

Author Ian Fleming had Bond driving an earlier DB MkIII in the novel of Goldfinger, but when the film makers approached Aston Martin for a car, they were offered the prototype of the about-

BELOW The DB5 in rare drophead form was a seriously good-looking car

to-be-released DB5, and so a legend was born.

The DB5 was an evolution of the essentially similar DB4, but with covered headlamps (although these did appear briefly on the DB4 Vantage), a more powerful 4.0-litre engine and – on all but the very early examples – a five-speed gearbox.

The straight-six engine was endowed

with three SU carburettors and produced 282bhp – enough to propel the car to a top speed of 148mph. However, a rare and more powerful Vantage version was fed by triple Webers and pumped out no less than 314bhp. Also rare was a soft-top version which, unlike some Astons, was not badged Volante. The rarest DB5 of all, though, was a shooting brake version built for company boss David Brown to carry his dogs in!

The James Bond car came with many unique extras, including front and rear rams, machine guns, tyre slashers, bullet-proof screen, radar and telephone, smoke screen, revolving numberplates and – not least – a passenger ejector seat.

SPECIFICATION

Capacity: 3995cc
Cylinders: straight-six
Compression ratio: 8.0:1
Maximum power: 282bhp at 5500rpm
Maximum torque: 390Nm at 3850rpm
Gearbox: Five-speed manual
Length: 4572mm
Width: 1676mm
Weight: 1564kg
0-60mph: 8.6 seconds
Maximum speed: 142mph

The films gave Aston Martin excellent publicity and made the DB5 the car that young boys and grown men alike aspired to own. Bond was cool, so Astons were cool. Indeed, the effects of those early films remains to this day; surely anyone who buys an Aston Martin, if they're honest, must have been influenced by the James Bond connection.

Of course, 'real' DB5s didn't have such exotic accessories and, even putting aside the Bond connection, it was a seriously good-looking car with breathtaking performance for its time.

However, even though it's the most famous of all Aston Martins, the DB5 was in production for only two years, during which time around 1000 examples were built, with just 65 of them being the more powerful Vantage variant. Its replacement was the DB6 of 1966, which had a number of improvements, the most noticeable being a squared-off tail to improve the aerodynamics. The DB6 was built until 1971.

Aston Martin Lagonda
1978 United Kingdom

IN THE 1970S, IF YOU WANTED A large, luxury car you bought a staid and regal Rolls Royce. But then Aston Martin came up with a radical alternative – the Lagonda was like nothing else on the road.

Designed by William Towns, the Lagonda had razor-sharp lines, with Towns' trademark wedge shape led by a rather incongruous radiator grille. At over 17 feet long, the Lagonda was an imposing machine that turned heads wherever it went.

Just as futuristic as the exterior styling was the interior, which was way ahead of its time. Instead of conventional dials, Aston Martin chose to endow the Lagonda with an ultra modern electronic dashboard with LED displays and touch-sensitive switches. More traditional were the plush leather seats and walnut trim.

BELOW The Lagonda's angular lines are like nothing else on the road

Large, low, four-door saloon with very angular, thrust-back, wedge-shaped styling and small radiator grille on nose. Pop-up headlamps on early cars; six fixed lights on later models.

Under the pointed bonnet of the Lagonda lay a rather less than hi-tech engine. The 5.3-litre V8 was Aston's own unit and was linked to a relatively simple three-speed automatic transmission driving the rear wheels.

Unfortunately, the Lagonda's electronics were to prove troublesome and, over the years, Aston Martin made changes. The original LED instruments were replaced in 1984 with three mini cathode ray tubes (essentially tiny television screens) which displayed speed, revs and other information. This was backed up with voice messages in a choice of languages (the Lagonda was popular in Arabic countries). In 1987 these screens gave way to vacuum fluorescent read-outs.

The car's appearance was updated over the years, too. In 1987, the original sharp lines were softened – under the watchful eye of William Towns, the original designer – to drag the car some way out of the 1970s. At the same time, the pop-up headlamps – also very much of their time – were replaced by an impressive array of six fixed headlamps in the snout.

The Aston Martin Lagonda was one of the most striking cars ever made, and a tribute to 1970s design. It was, though, very expensive, sometimes unreliable and somewhat quirky. When production ended in 1989, just 645 examples were built, with about a quarter of those remaining in the UK; making the Lagonda a very rare car today.

ABOVE In 1978 this all-black dash with touch-sensitive switches was positively space age!

SPECIFICATION (1987)

Capacity: 5340cc
Cylinders: V8
Compression ratio: 9.5:1
Maximum power: 280bhp at 5000rpm
Maximum torque: 434Nm at 4000rpm
Gearbox: Automatic three-speed
Length: 5283mm
Width: 1791mm
Weight: 2023kg
0-60mph: 8.9 seconds
Maximum speed: 145mph

Aston Martin DB9
2004 United Kingdom

HOW TO SPOT

Large, sleek coupe with projector head-lamps under big, sweptback covers. Distinctive Aston Martin grille and side strakes. Slim LED rear lights.

AFTER FORD TOOK OVER ASTON Martin in the 1987, it produced the achingly beautiful DB7 of 1993. And when that car was due for replacement, the company did the impossible and made an even better-looking car – the DB9. Why not DB8? Because Aston's marketing department felt that name would suggest an eight-cylinder car and the DB9 had no less than 12 cylinders under the bonnet (they also argued that

BELOW Inside, the DB9 is a blend of British luxury and high technology

skipping a number would show what a great leap forward the new car was...).

The engine was essentially the same as that found in the Vanquish S, which made the DB9 remarkable value, at around £50,000 less expensive.

In the DB9 the V12 developed 450bhp with a healthy 570Nm of torque at just 5000rpm, so buyers didn't feel at all short-changed. There was a choice of transmissions – a Touchtronic automatic or a conventional six-speed manual, for those who liked to be in full control

The bodywork was arguably better-looking than that of the rather aggressive-looking Vanquish, too, with a purity of line that was hard to match. The panelwork was mainly aluminium and composites, bonded together using aerospace technology to give a combination of light weight and high strength. The Volante version had a fully automatic folding roof, for luxury open-air motoring. In the event of an accident, rollbars automatically popped-up on the Volante to protect passengers.

Inside, as you'd expect of an Aston

Martin, the finish was exemplary, with hand-finished leather and wood everywhere you looked. The instruments and

SPECIFICATION

Capacity: 5935cc

Cylinders: V12

Compression ratio: 10.3:1

Maximum power: 450bhp at 6000rpm

Maximum torque: 570Nm at 5000rpm

Gearbox: Automatic or six-speed manual

Length: 4710mm

Width: 1875mm

Weight: 1800kg

0-60mph: 4.9 seconds

Maximum speed: 186mph

door handles were aluminium, while the starter button was made from crystal-clear glass. The DB7 was criticised for its Ford-sourced switchgear, but you could find nothing of the sort in the DB9.

If you should ever get bored of the sound of that V12 engine, you could enjoy music from the built-in Linn hi-fi system, while letting the cruise control help waft you to your destination.

There was very little to fault with the DB9; it's a luxury, high-performance sports car to match the best from Germany and Italy. And it encapsulated true British values of quality and craftsmanship. What more could you want?

Aston Martin Vanquish S
2004 United Kingdom

ABOVE The Vanquish S is an aggressive but elegant machine

THE ASTON MARTIN VANQUISH arrived in 2001 and was undoubtedly a great car. With the advent of the S version three years later, things got even better.

Under that oh-so-long bonnet lay a V12 engine that looked as beautiful as the car. In S form it produced no less than 520bhp – 60bhp more than in the standard Vanquish. And 577Nm torque made the power very accessible and easy to use. It's hard to believe that this won-derful engine was, essentially, two Ford Mondeo units end to end, developed with the help of Cosworth.

The drive was taken to the rear wheels via a high-tech six-speed transmission unit that gave a choice of manual gearchanges via finger-operated paddles on the steering column, or automatic changes. In both modes there was an optional Sports setting which held lower gears for longer to make more use of the engine's power.

Large, curvaceous coupe with long, flowing bonnet and subtly bulging wings. Trademark Aston front grille and side strakes.

The Vanquish's bodyshell was lovingly hand-built from aluminium and carbonfibre, and each car took 385 man-hours to create – compared with 202 hours for its little brother, the DB9. However, there was nothing quaint or old-fashioned about the car's construction methods. Each car started as a heat-cured aluminium bonded monocoque, which was formed from a combination of extruded and folded aluminium panels that were bonded and then riveted together. The monocoque was bonded to a nine-layer carbonfibre tunnel, which gave the Vanquish S an extremely rigid yet lightweight backbone. Onto this were then affixed hand-finished aluminium body panels.

Inside, passengers were treated to an opulent cockpit. Dominating the cabin was a leather-clad centre console that arched from the top of the facia down to the transmission tunnel. Grab handles and gearshift paddles were finished in matching cast aluminium, while the rest of the cabin was trimmed in high-quality leather, Alcantara, and Wilton carpet. The instruments were a slightly retro black-on-cream and changed to a soothing blue at night.

As Ford-owned Aston Martin moved into more mainstream cars, such as the DB9 and V8 Vantage, the handcrafted Vanquish was a reminder of how Astons used to be made. And that was something to savour; especially when it was also such a gorgeous-looking and powerful beast.

ABOVE The Vanquish's cockpit is stunning. Note the paddle-shifters by the steering wheel

SPECIFICATION

Capacity: 5925cc
Cylinders: V12
Compression ratio: 10.8:1
Maximum power: 520bhp at 7000rpm
Maximum torque: 577Nm at 5800rpm
Gearbox: Manual/automatic, six-speed
Length: 4665mm
Width: 1923mm
Weight: 1875kg
0-60mph: 4.7 seconds
Maximum speed: 202mph

Audi quattro
1980 Germany

HOW TO SPOT

Angular two-door hatchback with prominent wheelarch extensions front and rear, thick rear pillars, and trademark Audi 'rings' in front grille.

THE AUDI QUATTRO WAS revolutionary in more ways than one. First, it was the first production car with four-wheel-drive since the Jenson FF of 1966. Second, it began the transformation of Audi from a somewhat staid brand into the sporty, prestige marque it is today.

While the Jenson's transmission system was heavy and troublesome, the Audi's was lightweight and reliable, thus showing to the world that production cars could, indeed, have four-wheel-drive. The quattro may not have been the first road car so-equipped, but it was certainly the first truly successful one, and other car manufacturers were soon jumping on the bandwagon.

The key to the success was the way the drive system worked. Instead of the usual

BELOW The original Audi quattro, with its rally heritage, looks at home in a forest

transfer box and driveshaft, the quattro had a conventional gearbox behind the front-mounted engine. However, behind this gearbox was a small differential from which one driveshaft went to the rear wheels, and a second ran forward to the fronts. It was simple but effective, and endowed the Audi with exception traction in slippery conditions, enhanced the handling in the dry and helped put down the power without the wheels spinning.

SPECIFICATION

Capacity: 2144cc
Cylinders: straight-five
Compression ratio: 7.0:1
Maximum power: 200bhp at 5500rpm
Maximum torque: 285Nm at 3500rpm
Gearbox: Five-speed manual
Length: 4404mm
Width: 1722mm
Weight: 1290kg
0-60mph: 7.1 seconds
Maximum speed: 137mph

That power, incidentally, came from a five-cylinder engine (an unusual configuration that Audi favoured for its smoothness over a four) which was turbocharged to enable it to produce 200bhp. This was to be a fast as well as an innovative car.

The quattro went onto storm rallying events around the world through the early 1980s, with its drive system offering astonishing levels of grip and traction. A short wheelbase version of the quattro, called the Sport, evolved from the rally cars and went on sale in 1984, with 396bhp on tap. This stripped down coupe could reach 60mph in just 4.5 seconds and had a top speed of 155mph. It remains the ultimate road-going quattro.

The Audi quattro continued in production, albeit with many updates, until 1991. However, the name – and the technology – has lived on. Audi has become well-known for its four-wheel-drive systems and so today quattro versions of most Audi road cars are offered.

ABOVE From the side, the quattro's angular lines are apparent

Audi TT 1.8T quattro Sport
2005 Germany

THE AUDI TT WAS SURELY THE most stylish car of the 1990s, with its Bauhaus-inspired lines and neat, squat appearance. It first appeared as a show-car in 1995 and created such a stir that Audi put it into production, with surprisingly few changes, just three years later.

In the years that followed, the TT became a style icon with fashion-con-scious drivers around the world. It was offered with a choice of engines, from 180bhp and 225bhp four-cylinders to a 250bhp V6, with four-wheel-drive standard on all but the entry-level car.

The TT's lines stood the test of time remarkably well, but ten years after it first appeared it had become relatively commonplace and was not such a fashion statement. What's more, there was com-

BELOW Any TT is a great-looking car. The Sport with its black roof especially so

HOW TO SPOT

Small two-door coupe with distinctive
styling and small curved cabin top.
Wraparound front and rear lights and
black-painted roof.

petition from the likes of Nissan's 350Z
and Porsche's Cayman, so Audi fought
back with the TT 1.8T quattro Sport.

This was essentially a more extreme
version of the car; lighter and sportier
than the standard TT. Power came from
the standard 1.8-litre turbocharged
engine, albeit tweaked to produce
240bhp rather than 225bhp. However,
the extra power was helped by a worthwhile 49kg weight reduction. This was
achieved by ditching the spare wheel and
the rather limited rear seats and parcel
shelf, and by fitting lightweight Recaro
seats in the front, with a aluminium
strut-brace behind.

Furthermore, the suspension was
firmed up to give sharper handling, and
the brakes were the larger items from the
V6 version of the TT.

Externally, the Sport was identified by
18-inch, 15-spoke alloy wheels, the larger
front and rear spoilers from the V6 and –
most noticeably – the roof and door mir-
rors were painted black, which gave the
car a visual transformation.

The four-cylinder Sport was more
expensive and (slightly) faster than the
contemporary 3.2 V6 quattro, and
offered a quite different driving style;
being more of a stripped out sports car,
while the V6 was more refined and digni-
fied. It did, though, freshen up the TT
while the world eagerly awaited an all-
new version.

ABOVE The Sport's
superb interior is
further enhanced with
racing seats and
steering wheel

SPECIFICATION

Capacity: 1781cc
Cylinders: Straight four
Compression ratio: 9.5:1
Maximum power: 240bhp at 5700rpm
Maximum torque: 320Nm at 2300-5000rpm
Gearbox: Manual, six-speed
Length: 4041mm
Width: 1764mm
Weight: 1416kg
0-60mph: 5.9 seconds
Maximum speed: 155mph

Bentley R Continental
1952 United Kingdom

WHEN IT WAS LAUNCHED IN 1952, the Bentley R Continental was hailed as the fastest production four-seater car in the world. And, at the time, a top speed of 115mph was quite something, when most family saloons struggled to exceed 70mph.

Much of the Bentley's performance excellence was down to its shape; it was designed, with the aid of a wind-tunnel, to be aerodynamically efficient. Downforce was not a consideration in those days, so the car was shaped to slip through the air as smoothly as possible. This led to the distinctive long, flowing tail. The rear wings were finned to help high-speed stability, while on the first cars the back wheels were covered with spats for extra efficiency. The Continental was an elegant and stately

Large and elegant coupe with tall Bentley grille, long bonnet, sweeping wings and smooth fastback tail between finned rear wings.

ABOVE The streamlined rear with finned wings to aid stability

car but, at the same time, one that looked fast, even when it was standing still.

Under the smooth and lightweight skin was a Rolls Royce R-Type chassis with independent front suspension with wishbones and coil springs, and a fixed rear axle with half-elliptic springs.

The engine was an inline, 4.6-litre, six-cylinder unit with twin SU carburettors. It was based on a Rolls Royce unit, but was given a higher compression ratio and a more efficient exhaust system. The power went through a manual four-speed gearbox to the rear wheels.

Priced at £6929 in 1952, the Continental was a very expensive motorcar, but lucky buyers were treated to more than just high-speed performance. The interior was, as you'd expect of a Bentley, of the highest quality, with plenty of beautifully finished leather and walnut.

In 1954, buyers were given the option of a four-speed automatic transmission, while the engine capacity was increased to 4.9-litres. A year later, the car was lengthened slightly to accommodate a new chassis. In this form, the Continental remained in production until 1959. It was to be the last purpose-designed Bentley until the Continental R of 1991; this was then followed by the all-new Continental GT of 2003, which draws inspiration from this original Continental.

SPECIFICATION

Capacity: 4566cc
Cylinders: Straight-six
Compression ratio: 7.25:1
Maximum power: 178bhp at 4500rpm
Maximum torque: n/a
Gearbox: Manual, four-speed
Length: 5232mm
Width: 1778mm
Weight: 1882kg
0-60mph: 13.5 seconds
Maximum speed: 115mph

Bentley Continental GT
2003 United Kingdom

FOR 70 YEARS, BENTLEY AND ROLLS Royce were produced side by side and, latterly, Bentleys were little more than rebadged Rollers. However, in 2003 Bentley was taken over by Volkswagen and finally separated from its stablemate. This led to the all-new Continental GT which harked back to the glory days of the Bentley R Continental of the early 1950s which, in its time, was the fastest four-seater car in the world. Now,

Bentley could once again boast that same accolade; this time with an utterly modern car that tops 198mph.

Most cars that can get to that sort of speed are uncompromising supercars with two seats and little in the way of creature comforts. Not so the Continental GT. This was a true four-seater car with all the luxury you'd expect of a Bentley. The interior was lined with acres of leather and walnut, combined

BELOW The Continental GT doing what it's best at travelling fast

HOW TO SPOT

Large four-seater coupe with front wings
sweeping down to meet four headlamps
between smoothed-out traditional
Bentley grille. Prominent rear wings and
high back end.

with modern essentials such as climate
control, satellite navigation, hi-fi and
fully electric massaging seats. The rear
passengers didn't want for anything,
either, with plush, cosseting seats and
their own climate control.

Comfort was further enhanced by
computer-controlled air springs with
adjustable dampers which could be set to
Sport or Comfort mode to suit the driver's style of driving.

But the GT was about more than luxury – it was also an extremely powerful
motorcar. The engine was a 6.0-litre W12
unit that produced 552bhp and 650Nm
torque; the latter from as little as
1600rpm. The power was fed to all four
wheels via a six-speed automatic gearbox
(with fingertip manual override), and
was enough to make the car hit 60mph in
4.7 seconds; which is particularly
impressive when you consider that the
large GT weighed a hefty 2385kg.

From the outside, the Continental GT
wore its heritage in pride, but without
being overly retro. Its elegant lines
harked back to the glory days of the

1950s, yet the car looked muscular and
purposeful. Like any Bentley, it por-
trayed a perfect mix of exclusivity and
sporty rawness. It was a motorcar for
people with class but a hint of wildness
about them.

ABOVE The Continental
GT's cockpit is opulent
in only the way a
Bentley can be

SPECIFICATION

Capacity: 5998cc
Cylinders: W12
Compression ratio: 9.0:1
Maximum power: 552bhp at 6100rpm
Maximum torque: 650Nm at 1600rpm
Gearbox: Automatic, six-speed
Length: 4803mm
Width: 2100mm
Weight: 2385kg
0-60mph: 4.7 seconds
Maximum speed: 198mph

BMW M1
1978 Germany

HOW TO SPOT

Sleek mid-engined coupe. Low front end features pop-up headlamps and tiny stylised BMW grille in bumper. High rear deck with louvres over.

WHEN BMW MOTORSPORT WANTED a car that could compete in Group 5 racing, against the likes of Porsche, it turned to Lamborghini for help. The project, designated E-26, was initiated in 1976 and involved building a 850bhp Group 5 car, a similar Group 4 version with 470bhp, plus a production run of 400 de-powered road-going cars for homologation purposes.

Lamborghini and Ital Design developed a sleek, ultra-modern glassfibre body over a tubular steel chassis. Power for the road-going version came from a BMW six-cylinder engine from the then-current 635 CSi coupe. Enhanced with twin overhead camshafts and four valves per cylinder, this engine produced 277bhp; 66bhp more than in the 635. Racing versions were turbocharged to produce more power. In true supercar fashion, the engine was mid-mounted to give optimum weight distribution and thus enhance the handling. The gearbox, meanwhile, was a five-speed unit driving the rear wheels.

Unfortunately, problems at Lamborghini led to delays and, eventually, BMW moved assembly to Baur in Germany, with its own Motorsport division finishing the cars. The M1 was finally launched in 1978,

BELOW The M1 had a louvred rear deck, but still gave reasonable rear-view visibility

ABOVE The M1
supercar was like no
BMW before – or since

however, this was later than planned and, by this time, Group 5 rules had changed so the car was no longer viable and, besides, BMW had not sold enough road-going examples for homologation. Instead, then, the M1 raced with some success in the new Procar series until production ceased in 1981.

As a road car, the M1 excelled. It offered excellent performance and handling combined with BMW's usual reliability and build quality, plus relatively low running costs. The two-seater cockpit was very BMW-like and, as such, was functional and comfortable, with full carpets, leather and air-conditioning.

The M1 was undoubtedly a great car, and a worthy competitor to often less-reliable supercars from other manufacturers. Sadly, though, in total, just 455 examples were built, of which 399 were road-worthy, making it an extremely rare collector's item today. Famously, artist Andy Warhol hand-painted a racing M1 in 1979, as part of BMW's 'Art Cars' programme.

SPECIFICATION

Capacity: 3453cc
Cylinders: Straight-six
Compression ratio: 9.1:1
Maximum power: 277bhp at 6500rpm
Maximum torque: 329Nm at 5000rpm
Gearbox: Manual, five-speed
Length: 4346mm
Width: 1823mm
Weight: 1440kg
0-60mph: 5.6 seconds
Maximum speed: 162mph

Bugatti Veyron 16.4
2005 France

THERE ARE SUPERCARS AND THERE is the Bugatti Veyron 16.4. When Volkswagen decided, in 1998, to resurrect the famous Bugatti name it didn't hold anything back. The Veyron redefined the term supercar with power and torque figures unlike anything that has come before it.

Let's cut straight to the chase. The Veyron mid-mounted engine produced over 1000bhp. Actually, the official VW figure was 'only' 987bhp, but in reality the output was believed to be closer to 1035bhp. Indeed, an indicator on the dash let you know when the power reached the magic four-figure number (if you dared look because you were likely to be travelling at over 200mph when this happened…). But perhaps even more impressive was the engine's torque figure of 922lb ft or 1250Nm; that's almost double the figure of the McLaren F1.

Those impressive figures came courtesy of an impressive engine, with no less than 16 cylinders arranged in a 'W' configuration (essentially, two V8s joined at the crankshaft). The capacity was a hearty 8.3-litres and the cylinders were fed by no less than four turbochargers. And to keep it all cool, there were ten – yes, ten – radiators and two independent cooling circuits.

The power was fed to all four wheels through a seven-speed gearbox with the option of automatic or manual shifts, the latter courtesy of steering wheel-mounted paddles. And the power was then harnessed back by a set of massive ceramic disc brakes.

All this technology was clothed in an astonishingly beautiful body hand-made from carbonfibre and aluminium. It was undoubtedly a modern car, yet the designers managed to incorporate some of the old Bugatti charm into its lines;

BELOW The Veyron has a retractable rear spoiler to give extra downforce at high speed

not least with the evocative radiator grille and badge. And, of course, the shape was defined by aerodynamic requirements to ensure that the car remained firmly on the roads at speeds up to over 250mph.

Inside, the Veyron was pure luxury, with no plastic to be seen anywhere.

SPECIFICATION

Capacity: 8.3-litre
Cylinders: W16
Compression ratio: 9.0:1
Maximum power: 987bhp at 6000rpm
Maximum torque: 1250Nm at 2200-5500rpm
Gearbox: Semi-automatic, six-speed
Length: 4380mm
Width: 1994mm
Weight: 1888kg
0-60mph: 2.9 seconds
Maximum speed: 253mph

Instead, you found leather and aluminium, all lovingly hand-crafted. Even the hi-fi unit had bespoke aluminium controls.

Incidentally, the Veyron was named after the French racing driver, Pierre Veyron, who won the 1939 Le Mans race in a 57C Bugatti.

The top speed of the Veyron was limited – if that's the right word – to 253mph because the tyres were not considered capable of faster speeds. No one knows what the car was truly capable of. Combined with a price tag in 2005 of $1-million (around £840,000), these are yet more figures that help to define the Bugatti Veyron as the supercar to beat all supercars. Surely, in these politically correct days, no one will ever have the tenacity to produce a more outrageous machine.

ABOVE The fastest car on the planet. And it looks it!

Caterham Seven CSR260
2006 United Kingdom

WAY BACK IN 1957, A NEW SPORTS car was unveiled that was to become an enduring legend. It was the Lotus Seven; a simple two-seater car for track and road use, that you built yourself from a kit of parts.

Over the years, the little Lotus became a firm favourite with drivers looking for an affordable and fun car, and the model was refined with more power and sophistication, while retaining the classic appearance. It gathered a cult following

after it was featured heavily in the introduction of the 1960s television series, The Prisoner.

However, by 1973 Lotus was more interested in its upcoming and upmarket Esprit and Elite models, so it passed the rights to build the Seven on to Caterham Cars, which was previously an agent for Lotus.

The car was renamed the Caterham Seven and continued to go from strength to strength, with a number of redesigns

BELOW The CSR260 gives ultimate driving thrills

over the years to keep it competitive.

The Caterham CSR260 appeared in 2006, and was claimed to be 85 percent new and the fastest production Seven to date. Under the tiny bonnet was shoehorned a 2.3-litre Cosworth-developed all-alloy, 16-valve Ford engine that produces 260bhp. In the small and lightweight aluminium and glassfibre Seven, this gave crazy performance, with a top speed of 155mph and a 0-60mph time of just 3.1 seconds. This made it one of the world's fastest accelerating cars – beating even the McLaren F1 and only a fraction behind the Bugatti Veyron, which cost more than 20 times the price of the little Caterham!

An all-new, Formula 1 style fully independent suspension system, front and rear, combined with 10-inch wide rear wheels, ensured that the CSR260 handled as well as it accelerates. And a six-speed gearbox let you make the best use of the power.

No Caterham is luxurious, but the CSR made some concessions to passenger comfort in the form of a new curved dash with novel exposed steel tubing, carpets and even some storage space.

The CSR260 was a frighteningly fast car – there are few that could beat it from A to B on the public roads – and not one for the faint-hearted. However, Caterham still produces a range of less-extreme Sevens, including some you can still build yourself; which really is in the spirit of the original Lotus all those years ago.

ABOVE The CSR260 has a small but perfectly formed cockpit. Note the exposed tubework

SPECIFICATION

Capacity: 2261cc
Cylinders: Straight-four
Compression ratio: 12:1
Maximum power: 260bhp at 7500rpm
Maximum torque: 271Nm at 6200rpm
Gearbox: Six-speed manual
Length: 3300mm
Width: 1685mm
Weight: n/a
0-60mph: 3.1 seconds
Maximum speed: 155mph

Chevrolet Corvette Sting Ray
1963 USA

IN THE EARLY 1950S, AMERICANS were increasingly buying open-top British sports cars, so in 1953 General Motors hit back with the Chevrolet Corvette.

However, it was the Corvette Sting Ray a decade later that really made the model a legend. Here was a car which looked quite stunning with its long bonnet, flowing wings and fast-back rear with a distinctive split back window. Like earlier (and all subsequent) Corvettes, the body was made of glassfibre, which afforded the designers the freedom to be extra adventurous with the car's lines.

Inspired by Britain's E-type Jaguar, the Sting Ray looked fast from every angle, and is still remembered as the definitive Corvette that all later ones try

BELOW The Corvette Stingray was a true American supercar. This is a 1967 drophead

HOW TO SPOT

Distinctive coupe with 'Coke bottle' lines, long bonnet with concealed headlamps, split rear window (on early cars) and four round rear lamps.

to emulate. An open-top roadster version looked pretty but lacked the ultimate outrageousness of the coupe.

Under that long, sleek bonnet lurked a 5.4-litre (or 327cid in US-speak) V8 engine that initially produced 250bhp – a very respectable figure in 1963. However, over the years the engine was upgraded to as much as 435bhp.

The power was fed through a relatively simple two-speed automatic or a three-speed manual transmission. Luckily, the torquey engine almost negated the need for more gear ratios, although a four-speed manual was an option.

The Sting Ray was a fast car, even in 250bhp form, with 60mph coming up in just 5.9 seconds and the top speed was 142mph. However, the soft leaf-sprung independent suspension and all-round drum brakes on the first examples (thankfully, discs arrived in 1965) meant that the car didn't have the handling or stopping capabilities to match its power!

A year after the car's introduction, the split rear window was replaced by a single-piece item to improve visibility. However, to this day, the early Sting Rays are the most sought after for the simple reason that the split window looks so good.

Now known as a second-generation or C2 Corvette, this Sting Ray was discontinued in 1967, to be replaced by a larger, more powerful car. However, these early Sting Ray remain the most striking and memorable of all Corvettes. They really are the true American supercar.

ABOVE Under the bonnet lay a small-block V8 engine

SPECIFICATION

Capacity: 5300cc

Cylinders: V8

Compression ratio: 10.5:1

Maximum power: 250bhp at 4400rpm

Maximum torque: 474Nm at 2800rpm

Gearbox: Two-speed automatic or three-speed manual

Length: 4450mm

Width: 1758mm

Weight: 1424kg

0-60mph: 5.9 seconds

Maximum speed: 142mph

Chevrolet Corvette Z06
2006 USA

THE AMERICANS HAVE ALWAYS lagged behind Europe when it comes to supercars, but the Corvette Z06 was designed to give Porsche and Ferrari a run for their money. Indeed, in 2006 it was the fastest car Chevrolet had ever built, with a top speed of 190mph.

In 2004 the company had a successful year with the Corvette C5-R race-car, so it decided to apply some of that car's technology to a road vehicle. And the Z06 was the result.

Based on the standard Corvette, the Z06 had a massive 7.0-litre V8 engine that produced 505bhp and a serious 637Nm of torque. The engine covers were painted bright red to distinguish it from lesser powerplants.

Unlike other Corvettes, which could be bought with an automatic transmis-

HOW TO SPOT

Sleek, low coupe with scalloped sides, air
intakes in wings and high rear end.
Distinctive slanted headlamps and trademark Corvette round rear lights.

sion, the Z06 was only available with a
six-speed manual gearbox, driving the
rear wheels.

Visually, the Z06 was similar to the
rest of the Corvette family, but with the
addition of vents in the front and rear
wings, a deeper front spoiler and a
small bonnet scoop to feed air to the
engine. The wings were slightly wider
front and rear, too, and there was a
small ducktail spoiler to aid aerodynamics. Unlike the other models, the
Z06's roof panel was fixed in place to
save weight and increase body stiffness.

The body, by the way, was made of
glassfibre and carbonfibre and mounted
on a lightweight aluminium chassis.

Despite its racecar heritage, the Z06
had a highly specced interior with supportive, two-tone leather-clad sports
seats (with 'Z06' logos on the head-
rests), and even included cupholders.
An interesting feature was a head-up
display that projected your speed,
engine revs and G-force up in front of
your face. It was similar to the technology used in modern fighter jets.

The Corvette Z06 was an odd mix of

traditional Yank muscle car (the engine
used old-fashioned pushrods) and
high-technology (the chassis and body
construction. It may not have had the
finesse or quality of a European supercar, but it sure made up for it in terms
of sheer grunt and road presence.

ABOVE From behind,
the Z06 has the
trademark Corvette
round lights – there's
no mistaking what it is

SPECIFICATION

Capacity: 6998cc

Cylinders: V8

Compression ratio: 11.1:1

Maximum power: 505bhp at 6300rpm

Maximum torque: 637Nm at 4800rpm

Gearbox: Six-speed manual

Length: 4460mm

Width: 1928mm

Weight: 1421kg

0-60mph: 3.7 seconds

Maximum speed: 190mph

Dare DZ
1998 United Kingdom

HOW TO SPOT

Tiny, two-seater with low, pointed snout with small fins on each side and separate front 'cycle wings'. Retractable headlamps below windscreen. Bulbous rear with side air intakes. Gullwing doors on coupe.

THE BRITISH HAVE ALWAYS BEEN good at building small, fun sports cars and the Dare DZ was no exception. The distinctive car was the brainchild of the Walklett brothers who previously produced the Ginetta range of cars from the 1950s to the 1980s.

The little mid-engined DZ first appeared in 1998 and immediately appealed to enthusiasts who wanted a lightweight, mid-engined car that would, above everything else, be a lot of fun to drive.

And the DZ was certainly that. Power came from a transverse-mounted Ford Zetec 2.0-litre engine that produced 130bhp in conventional form, or a heady 210bhp when supercharged. In a car that weighed just 680kg, that made for very lively performance, with 60mph coming up in 4.7 seconds in the supercharged car, followed by a top speed of 145mph.

The mid-mounted engine ensured a 50:50 weight distribution which, combined with all-round fully independent wishbone suspension, meant that the DZ handled like a racecar, with no need for any form of driver aids; not even power steering.

The wasp-like body was available in both open and closed forms. The open car had a tiny removable hood, while the coupe had a very curved roof with gullwing doors. A clever feature were the headlamps, which were neat retractable units that popped out from each side of the body, just below the curved windscreen. The bodyshell was glassfibre and mounted on a light but strong tubular-steel chassis.

BELOW The DZ's interior is small but surprisingly well-equipped

SPECIFICATION

Capacity: 1996cc

Cylinders: Straight-four

Compression ratio: 10:1

Maximum power: 210bhp at 5750rpm

Maximum torque: 254Nm at 4250rpm

Gearbox: Five-speed manual

Length: 3470mm

Width: 1650mm

Weight: 680kg

0-60mph: 4.7 seconds

Maximum speed: 145mph

The DZ's interior was small but surprisingly well-appointed, with leather seats, race harnesses and a comprehensive range of instruments in a leather-clad dash. It had carpets and a full heating and ventilation system, and there was even a small but useful boot space behind the engine.

The Dare DZ was built in very small numbers but proved popular with people looking for a mid-mounted and modern alternative to, say, a Caterham.

ABOVE The Dare DZ is an intriguing mix of old and modern. It's like nothing else on the road

De Tomaso Pantera
1970 Italy

BORN IN ARGENTINA, ALEJANDRO DE Tomaso founded his automobile company in Modena, Italy, in 1959. At first, it built racing cars and limited-production sports cars but then, in 1970, it unveiled its first real production car – the Pantera (which is Italian for panther). And what a car it was!

The Pantera was developed in co-operation with Ford, USA, which wanted an affordable mid-engined supercar. To this end, the car was powered by a 5.7-litre Ford V8 engine. This developed 310bhp and, following the example set by the Lamborghini Muira, it was mounted amidships, to ensure a perfect weight distribution front and rear. Unlike the Muira, though, the V8 was mounted longitudinally, with a five-speed gearbox driving the rear wheels.

BELOW This 1974 Pantera looks wilder than ever in bright yellow

Performance was good, with 60mph coming up in just 5.5 seconds, and the top speed hitting 159mph.

The bodywork was styled by Ghia and was an all-steel monocoque which gave a relatively light and strong structure for a reasonably low cost. Interestingly, though, in 1989 the car was redesigned with a separate tubular chassis.

The first Panteras were sold in the USA through Ford's Lincoln and Mercury dealers and were competitively priced at 'around $10,000', to quote the advertising of the day. However, these early cars suffered reliability problems and, for this and other reasons, Ford withdrew from its partnership with De Tomaso in 1973,

SPECIFICATION (1971)

Capacity: 5763cc

Cylinders: V8

Compression ratio: 11.0:1

Maximum power: 310bhp at 5400rpm

Maximum torque: 481Nm at 4000rpm

Gearbox: Manual, five-speed

Length: 4242mm

Width: 1701mm

Weight: 1416g

0-60mph: 5.5 seconds

Maximum speed: 159mph

after 6128 cars had been sold. However, that was not the end of the Pantera – far from it.

De Tomaso moved to smaller premises and continued to build the Pantera, albeit in much smaller quantities and at a higher price. Indeed, over the next 17 years only about another 1000 examples were built, and it was no longer sold in the USA.

The Pantera was, though, developed over the years. The GTS model of 1973 had a 350bhp engine, while GT4 version had a 500bhp 5.7-litre and was, essentially, a racecar for the road. Indeed, in the 1970s the Pantera proved itself as a successful racer at events such as Le Mans.

The final incarnation came in 1989 when the body was redesigned with the aforementioned tubular chassis and updated, more aggressive, lines. The last Pantera was built in 1993, to be replaced by the Guara.

De Lorean DMC-12
1981 United Kingdom

WHEN AMERICAN ENGINEER AND automobile executive, John De Lorean, decided to build his own sports car he ended up creating a scandal and a motoring legend at the same time. De Lorean had a vision of an 'ethical sports car' and began planning it in the mid-1970s, using some radical engineering solutions.

However, these turned out to be impractical and the car had to be redesigned with the help of Lotus, which meant it ended up with much the same chassis and suspension as the Lotus Esprit.

However, the Giugiaro-designed body with its distinctive gullwing doors remained. The most striking aspect of

HOW TO SPOT

Low and wide coupe with angular lines, four square headlamps, gullwing doors and unique stainless-steel finish.

the body was its unpainted stainless-steel cladding, which meant that minor scratches could easily be removed.

Underneath this was a Renault-built 2.8-litre V6 engine that produced 130bhp (it was heavily restricted for the USA market). This was a good unit, but not powerful enough to enable the De Lorean to compete with similarly priced offerings from the likes of Porsche. The handling, too, was compromised from Lotus's original configuration, because the ride height had to be raised for US regulations.

To try and keep costs down, De Lorean chose to build his car in Northern Ireland, which at the time had high unemployment so the British Government gave him a large grant to get the factory established, despite warnings from industry experts that the project was unlikely to succeed.

However, even government help wasn't enough to make the De Lorean succeed. The cars were plagued with problems, due to poor development and an inexperienced workforce, and production was intermittent. And then, in 1982, John De Lorean was arrested for selling cocaine and the company finally went into liquidation shortly afterwards. Less than 9000 cars were built.

The De Lorean story is one of countless mistakes, but it's also a story of one man's vision to build an all-new sports car. And the De Lorean could have been so much more, if only things had turned out differently. As it was, the De Lorean was guaranteed immortality after appearing in the Back to the Future films of the 1980s. Let's face it, what other car travels in time once it reaches 88mph?

ABOVE The interior was less radical, and you could have been in any car of the period

SPECIFICATION

Capacity: 2849cc

Cylinders: V6

Compression ratio: 8.8:1

Maximum power: 130bhp at 5500rpm

Maximum torque: 208Nm at 2750rpm

Gearbox: Five-speed manual or three-speed automatic

Length: 4267mm

Width: 1988mm

Weight: 1233kg

0-60mph: 10.1 seconds

Maximum speed: 110mph

Dodge Viper SRT10
2003 USA

WHEN DODGE SHOWED THE original Viper concept car in 1989, it created a storm. In 1992, the production roadster went on sale, followed a year later by a coupe version. Americans were delighted – here was a true Yank muscle car with power and handling to match its looks.

The first Vipers were powered by a Lamborghini-developed 8.0-litre V10 engine that developed 400bhp and, in true American fashion, was front-mounted and drove the rear wheels. Interestingly, the engine was based on an iron truck unit that was revamped in aluminium; yet it still retained its anti-quated pushrod, two valves per cylinder design. This was an engine that relied on capacity, not sophistication, for its power! The simple approach continued

HOW TO SPOT

Aggressive-looking two seater. Long bonnet with air intake and slanted headlamp units with large driving lights below. Massive vents behind front wheels. Exhausts exit from side sills.

with the glassfibre body on a steel tubular frame, while there were no driver aids such as ABS or traction control.

The Viper was a great success and was followed by more powerful versions, including the lightweight GTS-R racecar which had a 700bhp engine and finished first and second in class at Le Mans in 1998.

In 2003, a new Viper was introduced. Called the SRT-10, this had a heavily restyled body which was more angular and even more aggressive than the original. The engine was enlarged to 8.3-litre, which increased power to 500bhp and torque to 711Nm. In fact, in American-speak, this equated to 500ci capacity, 500bhp of power, and 500lb ft of torque – three 500s!

The new Viper had more sophisticated suspension and brakes (with ABS this time) and was a competent performer on road and track. Performance was better than ever, with a top speed of 190mph and a 0-60mph time of just 3.9 seconds. Not bad for a truck engine!

In fact, the same engine has been installed into a Dodge Ram SRT-10 truck and – bizarrely – into a motorcycle! That's right, the Dodge Tomahawk was little more than an engine with a wheel at each end. Although ten examples were sold as 'rolling sculptures' to show off the V10 engine it could, in theory, be ridden; with an estimated 0-60mph time of just 2.5 seconds and a top speed of over 300mph! And you thought the Viper was mad!

ABOVE Under the Viper's long bonnet lurks a powerful V10 engine

SPECIFICATION

Capacity: 8300cc
Cylinders: V10
Compression ratio: 9.6:1
Maximum power: 500bhp at 5600rpm
Maximum torque: 711Nm at 4100rpm
Gearbox: Six-speed manual
Length: 4445mm
Width: 1911mm
Weight: 1533kg
0-60mph: 3.9 seconds
Maximum speed: 190mph

Ferrari 250 GTO
1962 Italy

HOW TO SPOT

Curvaceous coupe with long, low bonnet and cockpit thrust back. Twin vertical 'gills' in each front wing. Three half-round intakes in the nose, with an oval intake below. Large air vents behind the rear wheels.

THE LEGENDARY 250 GTO IS ONE OF the most sought-after sports cars, not to mention Ferraris, of all time. And for good reason, too. Just 39 are believed to have been built, essentially for use in sport car racing events – GTO stands for 'Grand Turismo Omologato' or 'Grand Touring Homologated'. Homologated essentially means approved for racing. Actually, racing rules stipulated that 100 examples of a model be built for it to qualify, but Enzo Ferrari somehow overcame that technicality, arguing that it was based on an older model.

It was, in fact, developed from the 250 GT, and the GTO's flowing lines were developed with the help of a wind tunnel, and was one of the first road cars to have a rear spoiler to aid aerodynamics. Of course, it also had more than a dash of Italian flair drawn into its styling, and the GTO must surely be one of the best-looking cars of all time.

Under that long bonnet sat a 3-litre, V12 engine that developed 295bhp – an astonishing amount in the early 1960s. A handful of cars were fitted with even more powerful 4-litre engines. Even the standard engine, though, was enough to propel the GTO to a top speed of 185mph. A dry-sump lubrication system enabled the engine to sit low in the car to reduce the centre of gravity. The engine was fed by a mouth-watering array of six Weber 38DCN twin carburettors, and had just two valves per cylinders. The block and cylinder heads were made of alloy.

Unfortunately, the car's suspension didn't really do the immense power justice. For homologation purposes, it had to have the live rear axle and leaf springs of the older GT. At the front, though, there was a more sophisticated

BELOW The 250 GTO is surely one of the most beautiful cars ever

independent wishbone system.

That said, the 250 GTO was a formidable machine on the racetrack and with it Ferrari won the 3-litre GT World Championship in 1962, 1963 and 1964. One also came second at Le Mans in 1962. In addition, GTOs triumphed at a range of other races around the world.

This race history, the prancing horse badge, the car's rarity and its drop-dead-gorgeous lines, all combined to make the 250 GTO the coveted machine it is today, with the few examples there are changing

SPECIFICATION

Capacity: 2953cc

Cylinders: V12

Compression ratio: 9.8:1

Maximum power: 290bhp at 7400rpm

Maximum torque: 339Nm at 8000rpm

Gearbox: Manual, five-speed

Length: 4325mm

Width: 1600mm

Weight: 1060kg

0-60mph: 5.8 seconds

Maximum speed: 185mph

ABOVE A GTO where it's most at home – on a racetrack

Ferrari Testarossa
1984 Italy

HOW TO SPOT

Wide, low car with distinctive fined side-intakes, with the waistline curving up into the rear wings. Back lights hidden behind full-width grille.

WHEN THE TESTAROSSA APPEARED in 1984 it was the world's fastest production car, with a top speed of 180mph, making it a fitting replacement for the Berlinetta Boxer.

It was planned to be, not only supremely fast, but also luxurious and comfortable for long-distance cruising. This was no stripped out racer.

Like the Boxer, the Testarossa had a horizontally opposed 12-cylinder engine, although this was an all-new 4942cc unit that had little in common with its predecessor. Producing 390bhp, it didn't use any form of forced induction, relying instead on good old-fashioned capacity for its power, that pushed the car to 60mph in 5.6 seconds. The engine's red-painted cam covers gave the car its evocative name – 'red head'.

The engine was cooled by twin radiators mounted on each side of the car, in front of the rear wheels. And this led to the Testarossa's most distinctive features

BELOW The Testarossa's side profile, with those massive strakes, was unmistakeable

ABOVE One of the most evocative badges in motoring

– its immense width and those air intakes. The car had to be wide at the back to accommodate the big engine, and sticking a radiator on each side, meant it ended up being the widest car of its time, at no less than 1976mm from flank to flank.

The finned air intakes were unmistakeable and helped direct air to the radiators, but their main purpose was surely to give the Testarossa an aggressive and purposeful side view. Whatever way you looked at it, this was one mean-looking car, with its oh-so-wide flanks, low bonnet, pop-up headlamps and rear lamps concealed menacingly behind a full-width grille.

SPECIFICATION

Capacity: 4942cc
Cylinders: flat-12
Compression ratio: 9.0:1
Maximum power: 390bhp at 6300rpm
Maximum torque: 480Nm at 4500pm
Gearbox: Manual, five-speed
Length: 4486mm
Width: 1976mm
Weight: 1506kg
0-60mph: 5.6 seconds
Maximum speed: 180mph

Inside, occupants were treated to a pair of electrically-adjustable, leather-trimmed seats, with some handy luggage space behind (special leather bags were offered that made the best use of this, and the front boot, area). Many of the controls were positioned between the seats in the centre console, alongside the slender gearstick in its traditional Ferrari 'gate'.

In 1991, the Testarossa evolved into the 512TR and then, in 1995, into the F512M. With each evolution, the car's styling and performance were enhanced to keep it up to date.

To some, the Testarossa looks dated these days, but to others it is the epitome of supercar cool, and the subject of many a schoolboy's poster.

ABOVE One of the most evocative badges in motoring

Ferrari F40
1987 Italy

THE F40 WAS PRODUCED IN 1987 TO celebrate 40 years of Ferrari car production; hence the name. It was also a response to Porsche's world-beating 959.

Ferrari wanted a car that would eclipse Porsche's glory, and the F40 did just that. With a top speed of 201mph it was, at the time, the world's fastest production car.

BELOW The F40 has a no-nonsense shape designed for speed. Count those air intakes!

It was, though, quite different to the hi-tech and complex 959. The F40 was very much a no-frills racecar for the road with none of the Porsche's sophisticated drivetrain and electronics.

Instead, the F40 gained its advantages by being lightweight and simple. Extensive use of Kevlar and carbonfibre

in the bodyshell, and the elimination of any unnecessary 'luxuries', helped ensure that the Ferrari weighed just 1100kg (the 959, in comparison, was a portly 1650kg).

This, combined with a 478bhp engine, ensured the Italian car's dominance. The alloy V8, which was derived from the GTO's unit, had a capacity of just 3-litres but careful design, combined with four valves per cylinder and twin turbochargers, gave the incredible output. And if that wasn't enough, buyers could opt for power upgrades of up to 200bhp!

The F40's styling was derived from that of the GTO, but designed with aerodynamic stability in mind, with a low front, smooth undertray and a large rear spoiler. NACA-style ducts on each side of the car fed the turbochargers and cooling system, while louvres on the plastic rear window further helped the engine to dissipate heat.

Inside, there was little in the way of luxuries, with no carpet, no provision for a stereo (not that you'd hear one), while the door releases were simple cords, and the windows sliding plastic panels. Occupants were held in place by lightweight Kevlar racing seats and harnesses. This was very much a car for use on the track, not for long road journeys; although there was a surprisingly spacious luggage compartment at the front.

Not only was the F40's top-speed world-beating, the car could also get there quickly; with 60mph coming up in 4.8 seconds, and 124mph in just 12 seconds. This was a pure driver's car; but only for those drivers with the skill and confidence to tame such a phenomenal beast.

ABOVE Lift the F40's lightweight rear end for access to the engine, suspension and exhaust system

SPECIFICATION

Capacity: 2936cc
Cylinders: V8
Compression ratio: 7.7:1
Maximum power: 478bhp at 7000rpm
Maximum torque: 577Nm at 4000rpm
Gearbox: Manual, five-speed
Length: 4430mm
Width: 1980mm
Weight: 1100kg
0-60mph: 4.8 seconds
Maximum speed: 201mph

Ferrari F50
1995 Italy

HOW TO SPOT

Low and wide with cab thrust forward. Distinctive black 'gap' down each side of the bodywork, deep scoops in the front engine, and large, integral rear wing.

THE F40 ARRIVED IN 1987 TO celebrate Ferrari's 40th birthday that year, but its successor, the F50, came two years early, in 1995, and is an even faster car.

Like the F40, the F50 was essentially a lightweight racer for the road, with a carbonfibre bodyshell. Under this was a chassis – also carbonfibre – which, unusually, was integral with the mid-mounted engine. In other words, the front part of the chassis was attached to the front of the engine, and the rear part to the back of the engine, so that the engine actually formed part of the chassis. This saved weight, but did mean that more engine noise was transmitted into the cockpit, because there were no isolating engine mounts.

The engine itself, unlike the F40's, was not turbocharged. Instead, it was a natu-

BELOW The F50's beautifully sleek lines look especially good in red

rally aspired V12 unit with a capacity of 4.7-litres and a power output of 513bhp, which made it the most powerful non-turbo engine of its day. Interestingly, this arrangement followed Formula 1 thinking because, in the days of the F40, Formula 1 cars were turbocharged, but in 1995 turbos were banned by F1 in favour of larger capacity normally aspired engines.

The power went to the rear wheels via a six-speed gearbox utilising a conventional floor-mounted shift with a traditional Ferrari 'gate'. In this area, the F50 broke with Formula 1 technology, where gear changes are made electronically with finger-operated paddles.

The F50's interior was a no-nonsense place to be, trimmed with lightweight carbonfibre and aluminium. The two dials – a speedometer and tachometer – were hi-tech liquid-crystal displays, while occupants benefit from air-conditioning (although you could argue that was a necessity in such a cramped cockpit with a V12 engine behind your head!) but very little else. For instance, there was no provision for a stereo system, which reflected the serious nature of the car as a pure driving machine (not to mention the fact the very high noise levels would render one useless). The leather-covered, lightweight racing seats were available in two sizes – large or small and had simple manual adjustment. The pedals, too, were adjustable.

The Ferrari F50 was offered in both coupe and open-top forms, and just 349 examples were built between 1995 and 1997, making it rare and sought-after car.

ABOVE Much of the F50's bodywork was made of lightweight carbonfibre

SPECIFICATION

Capacity: 4698cc
Cylinders: V12
Compression ratio: 11.3:1
Maximum power: 513bhp at 8000rpm
Maximum torque: 470Nm at 6500rpm
Gearbox: Manual, six-speed
Length: 4480mm
Width: 1986mm
Weight: 1230kg
0-60mph: 3.7 seconds
Maximum speed: 202mph

Ferrari Enzo
2002 Italy

BELOW The Enzo may not be the prettiest Ferrari, but its Formula One inspired lines leave no doubt as to the car's potential

WITH THE HELP OF MICHAEL Schumacher, Ferrari dominated Formula 1 in recent years, so what better way to celebrate than to produce what was essentially a racing car for the road?

The Enzo even looked a bit like a Formula 1 car, with its pointed nose and forward cab position. It may not have been the prettiest Ferrari, but this car's styling was all about function. The carbon-fibre-clad shape drew on Formula 1 aerodynamics to give ground-hugging downforce at speed, to the extent that the Enzo didn't need a large rear wing, as often found on supercars.

And good aerodynamics are essential

for a car with 660bhp on tap. The power came from a lightweight, normally aspirated, 6.0-litre V12 engine, mounted amidships. This hi-tech engine produced 519Nm of torque from as low as 3000rpm to ensure that – unlike an Formula 1 car – the Enzo was relatively easy to drive on the public roads.

The power was fed to the rear wheels only (as with a Formula 1 machine) via a six-speed sequential gearbox operated via paddle-shifters on the steering column.

With these shifters was a race-style 350mm diameter steering wheel, with a flat-top containing a row of LEDs that indicated the engine revs – yet another feature borrowed from Formula 1.

SPECIFICATION

Capacity: 5998cc
Cylinders: V12
Compression ratio: 660bhp at 7800rpm
Maximum power: 657Nm at 5500rpm
Maximum torque: 657Nm at 5500rpm
Gearbox: Six-speed sequential
Length: 4702mm
Width: 2035mm
Weight: 1365kg
0-60mph: 3.6 seconds
Maximum speed: 217mph

And another was the fact that each Enzo was custom-built to suit its owner. After you placed an order for one of the ultra-rare cars (only 399 were produced), you were invited to the Ferrari factory for a 'fitting'. The leather-trimmed Sparco seats were then made to suit your body size, while the accelerator and brake pedals were positioned to suit your height and driving technique.

The Enzo was named after the company's founder, Enzo Ferrari, who died in 1988 and, to date, was the fastest road car the company has ever built, with a top speed of 217mph and a 0-60mph time of just 3.65 seconds. It was car that does justice to its name, carrying on Ferrari's original tradition of building cars that are, first and foremost, exhilarating and pure to drive. The Enzo shunned unnecessary luxuries in favour of an experience which was as near as a few, very lucky people, would ever get to piloting a Formula 1 car.

ABOVE The Enzo's 6.0-litre V12 engine develops no less than 660bhp

Ferrari F430
2004 Italy

HOW TO SPOT

Two seater bodyshell with high front bumper containing two large, curved air intakes. Projector headlamps under elongated covers. Round rear lamps protrude from the back wings.

THE F430 WAS LAUNCHED IN 2004 as the replacement for the 360 Modena. Although based on the outgoing car, Ferrari said the F430 is 70 percent new, including the larger and more powerful engine.

That engine was a mid-mounted V8 of 4.3-litre capacity. Normally aspirated, it

BELOW The F430 in open-top Spyder form with its cool transparent engine cover

produced 490bhp and the power was fed to the rear wheels via an all-new six-speed sequential gearbox. Called 'Impulse', in race mode this could make changes in as little as 150 milliseconds. The transmission had another innovation called 'E-Diff', which allowed the driver to adjust the differential to suit the conditions, choosing from snow, slippy, sport, race and disengage; the latter being a conventional limited-slip differential setting.

This and other settings were made by a knob called 'Manettino', which also adjusted the suspension and traction control, plus the change speed of the transmission.

Behind the 19-inch wheels were optional massive carbon-ceramic brake discs that provided stopping capabilities to match the power and speed of the F430 – yet another example of the high technology built into this Ferrari.

The F430's distinctive lines were designed to be aerodynamically efficient, with a flat undertray. The drag co-efficient was 0.33, while at 186mph the car generated 280kg downforce to help pin it

to the road. It perhaps was not the prettiest or the most outrageous-looking Ferrari, preferring instead to appear functional and understated.

Inside, as well as the aforementioned Manettino, the steering wheel also held the bright-red starter button, and gearchanges were made via Formula 1-style

paddles on the steering column. The driver was treated to a view of a bright-yellow tachometer, while the rest of the cockpit was typically Ferrari-functional, albeit clad in high-quality leather.

The F430 was also available in open-top Spyder form. This was arguably the better-looking car, with an electrically operated hood and a transparent engine cover, so onlookers could see the pulsing heart of the car.

Although this was the entry-level Ferrari of the early 21st century, it's interesting to note that it had more power than the wild F40 of 1987, and outperformed that car to 60mph, although the F430 just failed to hit the magic 200mph mark. But for real-world use, it had all the performance you could ever want, and was infinitely more user-friendly and practical than the F40, great as that car was.

ABOVE The F430's cockpit. Note the Manettino and starter buttons on the steering wheels

SPECIFICATION

Capacity: 4308cc

Cylinders: V8

Compression ratio: 11.3:1

Maximum power: 490bhp at 8500rpm

Maximum torque: 465Nm at 5250rpm

Gearbox: Six-speed sequential

Length: 4512mm

Width: 1923mm

Weight: 1450kg

0-60mph: 3.9 seconds

Maximum speed: 197mph

Ford GT40
1964 United Kingdom

HOW TO SPOT

Low and taut mid-engined sports coupe with very curved windscreen, cowled head-lamps, triangular air intakes in bonnet, and further intakes in the rear wings.

THE FORD GT40 WAS DEVELOPED solely because Henry Ford II wanted a car that would win the Le Mans 24-hour race. The company had tried to do this by buying Ferrari but, when that plan failed, it decided to built its own racecar, using a new facility in Slough, England and with input from racecar specialist Lola.

The resulting car had a mid-mounted 4.2-litre Ford V8 engine which, in the early 1960s, was a radical solution when most other Le Mans racers were front-

BELOW The GT40 from the rear, showing the mid-engine configuration

engined. Indeed, the design was based on the Lola GT which ran at Le Mans in 1963. The Ford was named GT40 because it stood just 40-inches high.

Three GT40s ran at Le Mans in 1964 and were fast but ultimately troublesome and they all retired from the event. However, Ford learned from the experience and returned the following year with an improved 'MkII' version that boasted a 7.0-litre Shelby engine. . Again, though, the cars were unable to complete the demanding race. In 1966, however, Ford finally got it right and the modified MkII cars took Le Mans by storm, finishing in first, second and third places. The GT40's place in motoring history was guaranteed.

Ford continued to develop the GT40 for racing until 1968, by which time its competitors had moved on to such an extent that the GT40 was no longer competitive.

Around seven examples of a road-going GT40, the MkIII, were built between 1965 and 1969. This had a detuned 4.7-litre engine and radically restyled bodywork with four head-

SPECIFICATION (MK1)

Capacity: 4942cc

Cylinders: V8

Compression ratio: n/a

Maximum power: 425bhp at 6000rpm

Maximum torque: 540Nm at 4750rpm

Gearbox: Manual, five-speed

Length: 4343mm

Width: 1753mm

Weight: 950kg

0-60mph: 4.1 seconds

Maximum speed: 211mph

lamps and a higher rear end to create some luggage space. However, it was not such an attractive-looking car, so most customers opted to have race versions converted for road use.

Only a very small number of genuine GT40s were built in total, but it has become one the great motoring legends and countless replicas have been produced over the years, ranging from cheap glassfibre kit cars, to very high quality hand-crafted aluminium replicas.

ABOVE The GT40 is low, at just 40 inches high.

Ford GT
2003 USA

HOW TO SPOT

Retro-styled mid-engined coupe closely based on the 1960s' Ford GT40, but slightly larger and more angular. 'Ford GT' side decals and optional over-body stripes.

THE FORD GT40 WAS A LEGENDARY Le Mans winner from the golden age of motorsport. So when Ford unveiled a concept car in 2002 that was a modern take on the classic, it caused enough of a frenzy for the company to put the car into limited production in 2003.

The new car was badged simply 'GT' because Ford did not have the rights to the 'GT40' name. Although it was styled after the classic racecar, the GT was very much a supercar for the road and, as such, was larger than the original.

Stunning performance – with a top speed of over 200mph and a 0-60mph time of just 3.3 seconds – came courtesy of a supercharged, all-aluminium, 5.4-litre V8 engine that produced 550bhp and generated a monumental 678Nm of torque. As before, the engine was mid-

BELOW The GT is very obviously styled after the classic GT40, but is larger all round

mounted, but this time it drove the rear wheels through a modern six-speed gearbox. Under the gorgeous aluminium body lay a spaceframe chassis, also made from lightweight aluminium. Behind the 18-inch wheels were hugely powerful Brembo brakes with four-piston calipers.

Wealthy buyers in the 21st century demand much more than racing drivers in the 1960s, which was one reason the GT was larger than its inspiration. The more spacious interior was fully equipped with leather seats, climate control, electric windows, hi-fi, airbags, central locking and more. With its stylish perforated seats and alloy trim, the GT's cockpit was an inspiring place to be, even if some of the trim looked a bit cheap.

ABOVE The GT's two-seater cockpit is modern but has been critisised for the quality of its fittings

There was nothing particularly high-tech about the GT's execution. It was rear-wheel-drive with no traction control, other than ABS, and the suspension featured simple double-wishbones. Yet it worked surprisingly well, being very competent at high speed while, at the same time, remaining easy to drive. It was also relatively comfortable for a supercar, with acceptable ride quality for long-distance touring (although there was precious little luggage space).

The GT was a strictly limited-production car, with Ford building around 1500 a year over three years. That makes it less rare than a genuine GT40 but it nonetheless looks set to be a future classic, just like its predecessor.

SPECIFICATION

Capacity: 5409cc
Cylinders: V8
Compression ratio: 8.4:1
Maximum power: 550bhp at 6500rpm
Maximum torque: 678Nm at 3750rpm
Gearbox: Manual, six-speed
Length: 4643mm
Width: 1953mm
Weight: 1580kg
0-60mph: 3.3 seconds
Maximum speed: 205mph

Honda NSX
1990 Japan

HOW TO SPOT

Two-door coupe with low front with pop-up headlamps (up to 2002), rising to a high rear with integral spoiler. Angular side air intakes. Black-painted roof panel.

SUPERCARS WERE, FOR MANY years, the preserve of the Europeans, with manufacturers such as Ferrari and Porsche dominating the market. On the other hand, Japanese car manufacturers were best known for producing reliable and well-engineered saloon cars.

BELOW The NSX has neat and understated lines, yet is nonetheless a true supercar

So when Honda, which had an envious background with motorcycles and Formula 1 cars, unveiled its own supercar,

Europe sat up and took notice. And for good reason, too. The NSX had taken six years to develop, and it showed. Here was a car that combined high performance with comfort and usability.

Mounted transversely in the centre of the NSX was a 3.0-litre V6 engine that produced 270bhp. Made entirely of alloy and with four valves per cylinder, VTEC variable valve timing, and titanium con-

necting rods, this could rev to 8300rpm – Honda's motorcycle influence, perhaps. Linked to the engine was a five-speed manual gearbox (or an optional automatic) driving the rear wheels.

The NSX's sleek and understated body may not have had the 'wow factor' of a European sports car, but it was nonetheless made from lightweight aluminium and – unusually for a car of this type – offered good all-round visibility.

And this ease of use extended throughout the NSX. You could get in it as easily as a saloon car, and the interior was practical and well laid-out, if a trifle ordinary. Passengers benefited from air-conditioning, decent stereo system, and remarkably

SPECIFICATION

Capacity: 2977cc
Cylinders: V6
Compression ratio: 9.6:1
Maximum power: 270bhp at 7100rpm
Maximum torque: 284Nm at 5300rpm
Gearbox: Manual, five-speed
Length: 4425mm
Width: 1810mm
Weight: 1610g
0-60mph: 5.9 seconds
Maximum speed: 161mph

civilised noise levels and ride quality. There was even a decent-sized luggage area behind the engine.

Even better, though, was that you got all this plus a car that was great fun to drive both in town and on the open road. At slow speeds, the NSX behaved impeccably, but get the revs up and it revealed another side to its character. The spirited engine propelled the car to 60mph in just 5.9 seconds and on to a top speed of 161mph, while the handling was hard to beat.

The NSX remained in production with minor changes until 2005. It may not have had the badge, but it was still a supercar; and one which you could happily use every day.

ABOVE The NSX's interior is businesslike and practical

Jaguar E-Type
1961 United Kingdom

ABOVE The E-Type with its oh-so-long bonnet is, for many, the ultimate sports car

THE JAGUAR E-TYPE IS SURELY THE quintessential British sports car of the 1960s. When it was unveiled in 1961 it took the world by storm. That long, long bonnet suggested speed and power, while the sleek, near-perfect looks were hard to beat in those days of boxy saloon cars.

The E-Type was available in hardtop form – with a novel (for the time) 'hatch-back' rear window for luggage – and as an open-top roadster. Both versions were equally good-looking.

The huge one-piece bonnet tipped forward to give superb access to the engine. In the early cars was found a 3.8-litre straight-six, triple-carburettor engine from the XK150. This developed 265bhp and was capable of pushing the E-Type to speeds as high as 150mph. The six-cylinder engine was enlarged to 4.2-litre in

1966, then in 1971 a 5.3-litre V12 powerplant was installed.

By then, the E-Type had grown from a relatively light sports car into a two-plus-two grand-tourer. In order to fit two small seats in the back, the wheelbase was stretched and the roofline raised. While these later cars were undoubtedly roomier and more practical, they were not quite as elegant as the first E-Types.

The early cars had simple polished aluminium dashboards and small bucket seats. However, the equipment and comfort levels rose over the years, with better seats and more luxurious fittings.

SPECIFICATION

Capacity: 3781cc
Cylinders: straight-six
Compression ratio: 9.0:1
Maximum power: 265bhp at 5500rpm
Maximum torque: 349Nm at 4000rpm
Gearbox: Four-speed manual
Length: 2438mm
Width: 1656mm
Weight: 1206kg
0-60mph: 7.0 seconds
Maximum speed: 150mph

The first E-Types had race-style cowls over the headlamps which looked wonderful but didn't conform to US regulations, so were deleted in 1968. The USA, incidentally, was the car's largest market, although emissions regulations stifled the power output. In North America the car was known as the Jaguar XK-E and around 80 percent of production went there.

The Jaguar E-Type remained in production until 1975 when it was replaced by the XJS, a car that failed to have the same long-term appeal as its predecessor. Yes, the E-Type is one of the world's great motoring legends; a car that defined a generation and has an ever-lasting appeal.

ABOVE Under the bonnet of this 1964 example is a 3.8-litre straight-six

Jaguar XJ220
1991 United Kingdom

HOW TO SPOT

Large, low and wide coupe with short bonnet and concealed headlamps. Long rear deck with integral spoiler. Scalloped sides with air intakes in rear wings.

WHEN IT WAS LAUNCHED IN 1991, the Jaguar XJ220 was the world's fastest car, with an incredible top speed of 213mph. A remarkable achievement when you consider that the car which made it into production was nothing like as sophisticated as the original concept.

The supercar which was unveiled to the public at the Birmingham motor show in 1988 was clearly inspired by the highly advanced Porsche 959. It was a huge but beautiful beast with a 6.2-litre V12 engine mounted amidships and powering all four wheels. The 200mph Jaguar also boasted forward-tilting doors and adaptive suspension – it promised to be a stunning machine.

A year later Ford took over Jaguar but, thankfully, agreed to progress the supercar project and build 350 production XJ220s. However, for economic reasons, the car's specification was much-reduced. Even though, it was said that each one would still cost a cool £361,000 –

BELOW A true big cat! The XJ220 is a large and powerful beast

twice the price of a Ferrari F40!

The production car retained the concept's sleek looks, but was slightly shorter and had conventional doors. The main changes, though, were hidden from sight. Gone was the 48-valve V12 engine and, in its place, came a 3.5-litre V6.

Still, buyers were not to be short-changed – the new engine boasted twin turbochargers and produced an impressive 542bhp, now driving the back wheels only. Also deleted was the trick suspension, in favour of conventional wishbones and coil springs.

A lot of time was spent developing the car's aerodynamics, to ensure a high top speed, but perhaps the main reason

– after the engine – for the XJ220's impressive performance was its light weight; 1372kg was not a lot for a car of this size. The secret behind this was a bonded aluminium honeycomb body construction that was very light but at the same time strong.

Tests proved that the Jaguar could reach 213mph and its 0-60mph time was four seconds, while 100mph could be reached in just eight seconds. There was no doubt that the XJ220 was fast but it wasn't perfect. It was, quite simply, too big to be practical on most roads, and visibility was poor. It was also very expensive; by the time the car reached production in 1991 it cost no less than £403,000. In the end just 275 examples were built 1994.

Still, the Jaguar XJ220 is still one of the world's fastest cars, and one of Britain's few true supercars.

SPECIFICATION

Capacity: 3498cc

Cylinders: V6

Compression ratio: 8.3:1

Maximum power: 542bhp at 7200rpm

Maximum torque: 644Nm at 4500rpm

Gearbox: Five-speed manual

Length: 4930mm

Width: 2007mm

Weight: 1372kg

0-60mph: 4.0 seconds

Maximum speed: 213mph

Jaguar XK
2005 United Kingdom

THE FIRST JAGUAR XK DEBUTED IN 1996 to replace the XJS, and its svelte styling harked back to the glory days of the E-Type. It was an immediate success and helped Jaguar to regain its reputation as a manufacturer of high-quality, luxury performance cars.

In 2005 an all-new XK appeared which raises the ante in all respects. Like the contemporary XJ saloon, the new car had an all-aluminium bodyshell developed using aerospace technology to ensure it was immensely strong, rigid and – above all – light. Jaguar claimed that the new convertible XK was 48 percent more rigid and 140kg lighter than its predecessor. The design was very clearly a Jaguar, but more angular and aggressive-looking than the outgoing model.

Under the bonnet was a 4.2-litre V8 which was a development of that in the old XK. New fuel injection and variable valve timing helped ensure an output of 300bhp, while being more responsive and efficient than before.

The transmission was a six-speed automatic with manual shifts possible through fingertip controls on the steering wheel. The engine management system would even will blip the throttle for you during rapid downshifts.

More driver aids came in the form of active suspension that automatically adjusted to suit the road and the driving style, plus stability control that intervened when required to apply the brakes to individual wheels or reduce engine torque to help in critical handling situations.

As you'd expect of a Jaguar, the new

BELOW The XK's interior is a pleasant mix of British luxury and modern features

XK's interior was plush and luxurious, with plenty of leather and wood on offer. A large screen in the centre console allowed you to control the climate con-

SPECIFICATION

Capacity: 4196cc

Cylinders: V8

Compression ratio: n/a

Maximum power: 300bhp at 6000rpm

Maximum torque: 310Nm at 4100rpm

Gearbox: Six-speed sequential

Length: 4791mm

Width: 2070mm

Weight: 1595kg

0-60mph: 5.9 seconds

Maximum speed: 155mph

trol, satellite navigation, audio system and even linked with your Bluetooth mobile phone.

A neat feature was the optional Jaguar Smart Key System. Instead of a conventional ignition key, the XK had a keyfob that you keptp in your pocket or briefcase. When the car detected the proximity of this device, the engine could be started by means of the large red starter button. What's more, as you approached the Jaguar with the keyfob on your person, the car automatically unlocked itself for you. How cool is that?

The Jaguar XK offered a perfect blend of good looks, performance, luxury and practicality. It was a worthy successor to the original XK.

ABOVE The 2006 XK's styling draws on Jaguar's rich heritage without looking retro

Jensen FF
1966 United Kingdom

HOW TO SPOT

Large coupe with long bonnet and roofline. Twin slats in sides of front wings, curved glass rear hatch. Four headlamps in angular front grille.

THE JENSEN FF WAS BILLED AS 'The World's most advanced car' for good reason. It was the four-wheel-drive version of the Jenson Interceptor and, as such, it was a revolutionary car. FF stood for 'Ferguson Four' after the tractor company that developed the transmission system. Driving all four wheels was, up until then, the preserve of off-road vehicles; this was the first time that any-

BELOW The stylish FF was the first sportscar with four-wheel-drive

one had applied the principle to a sports car. And, indeed, it would be another 11 years before it would be done again; this time with the rather more successful Audi Quatro.

Four-wheel-drive was claimed to help get the power – and the FF had 325bhp – to the road without spinning the wheels, improve the handling, and make the car safer on slippery surfaces. On the down-

side, though, the complex transmissions was heavy, expensive and sapped power.

As well as the novel transmission, the FF also boasted a Dunlop anti-lock braking system – many years before such devices became the norm. This car really was ahead of its time!

It was a large car, too, transporting two adults and two children in comfort and style. The interior was well-appointed with wood and leather, while the large opening tailgate allowed a useful amount of luggage to be carried. This really was a grand tourer.

Under that long and elegant bonnet lay a Chrysler V8 engine with a capacity of 6.2-litres. Linked to a three-speed auto-

ABOVE The FF, with its massive rear window, held four people and luggage in comfort

matic gearbox, it offered lazy power with plenty of torque. Despite the all-wheel transmission absorbing some of the power, it was still enough to waft the FF to 60mph in 8.5 seconds and on to a top speed of 130mph.

The FF was sold alongside the Interceptor, which was essentially the same car but with conventional rear-wheel-drive and, therefore, better performance at a lower price. Whereas the FF was not a sales success and went out of production in 1971, the Interceptor was sold until 1976. It then went back into production in very limited numbers between 1983 and 1992.

Only 224 examples of the Jensen FF were ever built and it's often forgotten about when people talk about the history of four-wheel-drive sports cars. The FF does, however, mark the start of an exciting new era; even if it was many years ahead of its time.

SPECIFICATION

Capacity: 6276cc
Cylinders: V8
Compression ratio: 10.0:1
Maximum power: 325bhp at 4600rpm
Maximum torque: 576Nm at 2800rpm
Gearbox: Three-speed automatic
Length: 4572mm
Width: 1778mm
Weight: 1564kg
0-60mph: 8.5 seconds
Maximum speed: 130mph

Lamborghini Miura
1966 Italy

ITALIAN FERRUCCIO LAMBORGHINI made his fortune building tractors and enjoyed driving fast cars; namely Ferraris. However, he was disappointed by the build quality of these cars and, when he complained, Enzo Ferrari told Lamborghini to stick to building tractors and leave him to worry about cars." That's the legend anyway.

Whatever the truth, the fact is that Lamborghini decided to build his own supercar and the result was the 350 GTV of 1963. That front-engined car was good, but not remarkable. It's replacement, the Miura, was both these things and much more.

The Miura of 1966 shocked the supercar world and changed it forever. Why? Because its engine was not mounted at the front, but in the middle. This gave

Very low mid-engine coupe with pop-up headlamps with 'lashes'. Air intakes in centre of bonnet, and further ones behind each side window. Louvres above engine.

near-perfect weight distribution which, in turn, helped give superb handling. It's a configuration that most supercars – and some lesser sports cars – use to this day.

Unusually, though, the 4.0-litre V12 was mounted transversely, which meant it could fit behind the seats and in front of the rear axle without the car being overly long. It's an idea that debuted in – of all things – the Mini, which had a transverse engine at the front.

The mid-engined layout meant that the Bertone-designed body could be low and sleek. The nose, in particular, is very low and is distinguished by pop-up headlamps with, on early examples, were framed by air intakes for the front brakes that looked a bit like eyelashes. At the rear, meanwhile, a set of louvres helped engine cooling and gave some rear visibility.

The Miura was gradually developed over the years, with improvements to the chassis and engine. The SV version of 1971 boasted 385bhp, a wider track, improved suspension and a stiffer bodyshell. A one-off open-top Miura was produced for the 1968 Brussels motor show, but this never went into production.

The Miura was not perfect – it had a tendency for the front-end to lift at high speed – but it set the tone for supercars to follow; not least its own successor, the Lamborghini Countach of 1974. It does, though, remain one of the most beautiful cars of all time.

ABOVE A distinctive feature of the Miura were its headlamps with vents top and bottom that looked like eyelashes

SPECIFICATION

Capacity: 3929cc

Cylinders: V12

Compression ratio: 9.8:1

Maximum power: 350bhp at 7000rpm

Maximum torque: 369Nm at 3850rpm

Gearbox: Five-speed manual

Length: 4255mm

Width: 1803mm

Weight: 1292kg

0-60mph: 6.0 seconds

Maximum speed: 171mph

Lotus Esprit V8
1996 United Kingdom

THE LOTUS ESPRIT DATES RIGHT back to 1975. The original car was extremely angular and powered by a mid-mounted four-cylinder engine that developed 156bhp, or 210bhp in turbocharged form. Over the years, the square lines were rounded off as fashion changed, and the twin-cam engine was refined with more power.

However, the Esprit's biggest leap forward came in 1996 when, for the top models, the four-pot engine was thrown out in favour of an all-new V8. This 3.5-litre unit was cleverly designed by Lotus to be compact, light and – above all – powerful. Twin Garrett turbochargers assured an output of 349bhp which put the Esprit, at last, into true supercar league, with a 0-60mph time of 4.7 seconds and a top speed of 175mph. The

BELOW The Esprit V8 retained the original car's wedge shape, but with softer lines

power was controlled by a manual five-speed gearbox driving the rear wheels.

Yet there was more to the Esprit than sheer performance. Right from the start, the mid-engined, glassfibre, car was renowned for its handling; Lotus's chassis engineers did a superb job of creating a perfectly balanced sports car that was a joy to drive.

SPECIFICATION

Capacity: 3506cc
Cylinders: V8
Compression ratio: 8.0:1
Maximum power: 349bhp at 6500rpm
Maximum torque: 400Nm at 4250rpm
Gearbox: Five-speed manual
Length: 4369mm
Width: 1883mm
Weight: 1380kg
0-60mph: 4.7 seconds
Maximum speed: 75mph

In 1998, the Esprit V8 was treated to a smart new interior that eliminated the old car's rather dated dash layout. Strictly a two-seater, you sat low with a wide centre console between you and your passenger. However, the interior didn't have the air of quality expected of a supercar at the end of the 20th century.

An extreme lightweight V8 appeared in 1999 and was badged Sport 350. A limited edition of just 50 cars, each was finished in silver with a blue interior and massive rear wing. By reducing the weight by 80kg and remapping the engine to give more torque at low revs (the overall power remained unchanged), Lotus created the fastest and most exciting Esprit ever.

Sadly, though, the model was really showing its age by now, and the Esprit finally went out of production in 2004, after 29 years. Flawed it may have been, but it was still a great British supercar and a fantastic-looking one at that.

ABOVE Despite dating back to the 1970s, the Esprit's shape still looks stunning today

Lotus Exige Cup 240
2006 United Kingdom

THE LOTUS ELISE OF 1995 MARKED a return to basics for Lotus; the tiny roadster was the spiritual successor of the Lotus Seven (now the Caterham Seven). It was fun, fast and affordable.

In 2000, Lotus produced a Sport Elise for racing, which had 200bhp and a fixed roof. Such was the interest in this pocket racer that Lotus went on to build a production version of

the road. This was the Exige.

The original Exige had a mid-mounted four-cylinder K-series engine that produced 190bhp – a lot of power in a car that weighed less than 1000kg. The low weight was thanks to a high-tech epoxy-bonded aluminium chassis and glassfibre body panels. The Exige was a pure driving machine, with lively performance and superb handling, all unhindered by

BELOW The tiny Exige Cup in its home environment – a racetrack

HOW TO SPOT

Tiny mid-engined two-seater with slanted headlamps, two large intakes in top of bonnet, air scoop in roof and large rear wing.

weight or complex electronics found on most other modern sports cars.

Adding a fixed roof in place of the Elise's soft-top allowed Lotus to place a distinctive air scoop on the top of the car, which fed air into the engine. Black grilles over the engine aided cooling, but didn't do anything for rear visibility.

As great as the original Exige was, it couldn't be sold in the all-important US market because the K-series engine didn't comply with local emissions regulations, so in 2004, Lotus announced the Exige S2 with a Toyota engine, which offered similar performance.

SPECIFICATION

Capacity: 1796cc

Cylinders: Straight-four

Compression ratio: 10.9:1

Maximum power: 243bhp at 8000rpm

Maximum torque: 236Nm at 8000rpm

Gearbox: Six-speed manual

Length: 3797mm

Width: 1850mm

Weight: 875kg

0-60mph: 4.5 seconds

Maximum speed: 150mph

This new engine had the potential for further tuning, though, which made possible the Exige Cup 240. This had essentially the same engine but enhanced with a Rootes supercharger that boosts power to 243bhp. In the same lightweight body, this gave astonishing performance, with 60mph being reached in 5 seconds and a top speed of 150mph – not bad for a 1.8-litre engine! The engine was linked to a six-speed gearbox and limited-slip differential driving the rear wheels.

Designed as a track car that can also be used on the road, the Cup 240 came complete with roll-cage, harnesses, fire extinguisher system and ignition kill-switch. What you didn't get, of course, were any luxuries – not even a radio.

At almost £50,000, the Exige Cup 240 was not a cheap car, but it did give a mouth-watering blend of power and lightness which was hard to beat at any price.

ABOVE The Cup's interior is very much that of a racecar, with full rollcage and fire extinguishing system

Marcos TSO-GT2
2005 United Kingdom

THE TSO-GT2 FOLLOWED A LONG tradition of Marcos sports cars. The company was founded in Luton in 1959 by Frank Costin and Jem Marsh. Their first vehicles were kit cars that, unusually, used plywood in their construction. The company went through mixed fortunes and produced a range of dif-

ferent models over the years, before turning its back on kit cars in 1992 to concentrate on the fully-built Mantura sports car, which was powered by a Rover V8 engine.

After going out of business (not for the first time) in 2000, the company was bought by an American investor and a

BELOW The TSO is a surprisingly small car, but a very capable one, nonetheless

new range of cars was launched, including the exciting TSO-GT2 in 2005.

The surprisingly small TSO-GT2 had obvious Marcos styling cues, including headlamps under plastic cowls and a distinctive rear end that harked back to Marcos designs from the 1960s. It was, however, a very modern car under the skin. The high-quality glassfibre bodyshell was attached to a light but stiff tubular steel spaceframe chassis.

Under that long bonnet lay a 5.7-litre Chevrolet V8 that was tuned to produce a hefty 475bhp together with 535Nm of torque. Driving the rear wheels, this gave explosive performance with a top speed of 185mph and a 0-60mph time

ABOVE The TSO's interior is small but well-appointed

of just 4 seconds. To help keep this power in check, the car's suspension was developed in conjunction with rally experts Prodrive.

Inside the TSO-GT2 was a compact but very distinctive two-seater cockpit. A concave aluminium dashboard housed a cluster of centrally-mounted instruments with retro-style cream faces. The rest of the interior was hand-trimmed in high-quality leather, while the steering wheel was surprisingly upright. It was undoubtedly a unique place to be.

The Marcos TSO-GT2 may not have been the most sophisticated sports car ever built, but it was exciting and full of character at a time when mass-produced cars were becoming more and more similar and soulless.

SPECIFICATION

Capacity: 5665cc

Cylinders: V8

Compression ratio: 10.1:1

Maximum power: 475bhp at 6500rpm

Maximum torque: 535Nm at 5500rpm

Gearbox: Manual, six-speed

Length: 4020mm

Width: 1680mm

Weight: 1170kg

0-60mph: 4.0 seconds

Maximum speed: 185mph

Maserati Bora

1971 Italy

IN THE LATE 1960S AND EARLY 1970S, the Italian Maserati company was owned by Citroën and it was during this time that the stunning-looking Bora – the first mid-engined production Maserati – was conceived. Here was a car that was undoubtedly a high-power supercar but, at the same time, looked modest and understated.

BELOW The Bora was an elegant and understated supercar. Note the stainless-steel roof

Perhaps the most extraordinary thing about the Giugiaro design was its roof and windscreen pillars. Those were made from unpainted satin-finish stainless-steel which, from a distance, made it look as if the car had a glass roof. Behind that was an almost horizontal glass panel which lifted to gain access to the engine bay.

The engine was a 4.7-litre V8 driving the rear wheels. With 310bhp on tap, it gave very respectable levels of performance for the time, with a top speed in excess of 160mph. To rein in this power, the Bora had a very unusual braking system, thanks to its Citroën parentage. Instead of a conventional arrangement, the car had a high-pressure hydraulic system, driven from the engine. Similar hydraulics were used for powering the lift-up headlamps, the adjustable driver's seat, pedals and even the steering column.

The reason for the adjustable pedals was because the driver's seat didn't actually move fore and aft – the pedals moved instead, to adjust for different heights of driver. It is claimed that when cars were ordered new, the seats were adapted to suit the owner's build.

In 1976, fuel prices escalated and Citroën parted company with Maserati. The Bora remained in production, latterly with a 4.9-litre engine, until 1978; by which time 571 examples had been built. Meanwhile, though, Maserati was also selling its 'baby Bora'; the more popular Merak, which had the same body but was powered by a more economical 2.0-litre V6 engine, and didn't have the complex Citroën hydraulic systems. Around 1500 Meraks were built by the time production ceased in 1983.

The Bora remains one of the most elegant Maseratis of all time, and the unusual technology it embraces continues to fascinate enthusiasts.

ABOVE The Bora's cockpit was comfortable and well-equipped for its time

SPECIFICATION

Capacity: 4719cc
Cylinders: V8
Compression ratio: 8.5:1
Maximum power: 310bhp at 7500rpm
Maximum torque: 440Nm at 4200rpm
Gearbox: Manual, five-speed
Length: 4335mm
Width: 1768mm
Weight: 1520g
0-60mph: 6.5 seconds
Maximum speed: 162mph

Maserati MC12
2004 Italy

HOW TO SPOT

Very long race-style coupe with 'bubble' cockpit, air intake on roof, sweeping wings, finned intakes in top of bonnet and large rear spoiler.

AFTER A 37-YEAR BREAK IN motorsport, Maserati wanted to enter a car into the GT category of the Le Mans 24-hour race, and to do so the company had to produce a minimum of 25 road-going examples of the car for customers.

That car was the MC12 – essentially a road-going Le Mans racer and, as such, it wa very long and low, with classic

BELOW It looks more like a Le Mans racer, but the MC12 is actually road-legal

Le Mans lines. Developed in a wind-tunnel, the body was made from lightweight but strong carbonfibre honeycomb and it had a removable roof panel for open-air motoring.

Power came courtesy of a mid-mounted, Ferrari-developed V12 engine that produced 623bhp – very useful in a car that weighed just 1335kg. Indeed, it was enough to

propel the MC12 to 60mph in 3.8 seconds and onto a top speed of 205mph. The rear-mounted gearbox was controlled by fingertip paddles on the steering column, as has become the norm for racing cars, and the power went straight to the back wheels.

Despite its racing heritage, the MC12 was a surprisingly civilised car to travel in, with tolerable levels of noise and comfort. The cockpit was well appointed with leather and carbonfibre, and benefited from climate control and there was even the trademark oval Maserati clock on the centre console. It was everything you'd expect of a grand tourer.

ABOVE The MC12's cockpit is surprisingly luxurious. It even has the trademark Maserati clock!

SPECIFICATION

Capacity: 5998cc
Cylinders: V12
Compression ratio: 11.2:1
Maximum power: 623bhp at 7500rpm
Maximum torque: 652Nm at 5500rpm
Gearbox: Manual, six-speed
Length: 5143mm
Width: 2096mm
Weight: 1335kg
0-60mph: 3.8 seconds
Maximum speed: 205mph

The only problem, though, was that the MC12 was enormous – no less than two feet longer than a Ferrari Enzo, and a foot wider. Which meant that it wasn't an easy machine to manoeuvre; especially when you consider that there was no rear window whatsoever! But then supercars are not meant to be practical, are they? This, however, was surely one of the most impractical ever built!

Never mind, get on the open road and put your foot down to get the full effect of those 623 horses and any worries about practicality soon vanished as you experienced the sheer performance of this Italian supercar. And with only 25 examples worldwide, you could be assured of exclusivity wherever you went.

Maserati GranSport
2005 Italy

MASERATI AND FERRARI USED TO BE competitors but are now part of the same Fiat organisation. To avoid the two marques clashing, therefore, Ferrari is the hardcore sports brand, while Maseratis are more luxurious grand tourers. This was demonstrated perfectly by the GranSport, a powerful machine that could transport two adults and two children in extreme comfort and speed over long distances. It was a development of the 3200GT – which dates back to 1998 – and the more recent Coupe, but was substantially updated and improved.

Under that elegant bonnet lay a V8 engine that produced 400bhp and could propel the Maserati at speeds of up to 180mph. It was linked to a six-speed transmission with fingertip changers; this was a car that was designed for the enthu-

Large two-plus-two coupe with low waist-line and distinctive grille with Maserati 'trident' badge. Downward curve to each side of boot.

siastic family driver. Maserati called its gearshift system Cambiocorsa, and it was electronically controlled with a choice of four settings – Normal, Sport, Automatic and Low Grip.

The handling, too, would please the sporty pilot, but excellent road-holding does not come at the expense of comfort; unlike some extreme coupes, this one did not offer a rock-hard ride. Yes, it was firm, but remained compliant enough to be comfortable on all but the bumpiest roads. An option was Skyhook adaptive damping which automatically adjusted to suit the driving style and road conditions.

Inside, you found even more comfort, but was not just the traditional leather that you might expect. Yes, there was plenty of high-quality hide on the seats and dash, but you also found something quite unusual. It was a 'technical' fabric developed for the nautical industry and almost resembled carbonfibre but was flexible, non-slip and extremely hard-wearing, making it ideal for trimming the central area of the seats, the lower rim of the steering wheel and the central part of the dash. It looked refreshingly different.

A Maserati of any sort is a quirky purchase and you'd think twice about choosing one over, say, a Porsche 911 for similar money. But it is a car with class and luxury, and is just that little bit different to the norm.

ABOVE Unlike most supercars, the GranSport has room in the back for two passengers

SPECIFICATION

Capacity: 4244cc
Cylinders: V8
Compression ratio: 11.2:1
Maximum power: 400bhp at 7500rpm
Maximum torque: 451Nm at 4500rpm
Gearbox: Manual, six-speed
Length: 4523mm
Width: 1822mm
Weight: 1580kg
0-60mph: 4.8 seconds
Maximum speed: 180mph

McLaren F1
1993 United Kingdom

WHEN GORDON MURRAY, OF Formula 1 manufacturer McLaren, decided to build a supercar, the world knew it would be something special. As it turned out, the McLaren F1 was more than just special – it was out of this world.

BELOW The F1's neat and taut lines were designed for aerodynamic efficiency above all else

Unlike some other supercars, the F1 was relatively small, making it easier to drive on public roads. Styled by Peter Stevens, it looked purposeful but restrained – as you'd expect of a true British car – the only concession to outrageousness being a pair of forward-opening doors.

But there was nothing restrained underneath that rear engine cover. The mid-mounted 627bhp powerplant was a purpose-built BMW V12 with a 6-litre capacity. In a nod to McLaren's racing heritage, drive was to the rear wheels only, via a manual six-speed gearbox.

The bodywork was extremely light in weight because it borrowed from Formula 1 technology. It consisted of a carbonfibre monocoque reinforced by aluminium honeycomb panels, which combined to give a very light but strong structure. With a weight of just 1137kg, the powerful engine propelled the car to 60mph in just 3.2 seconds, 100mph in a mere 6.5 seconds, and on to a blistering top speed of 240mph. No other road car had ever come near such figures, and the McLaren was by far the fastest car in the

world – a title it held onto until the launch of the even wilder Bugatti Veyron in 2005.

Inside, the F1 had a novel arrangement; the driver sat in the centre of the car, surrounded by a passenger seat on each side. The driver's seat was forward of the passengers', to ensure good visibility. This set-up made it awkward to get in and out, but once in place, you had a near-perfect driving position, and it was suitable for driving on the left or the right. The F1 also had the advantage of being able to seat three people, whereas most supercars were strictly two-seaters.

The F1 had a price tag as astonishing as

SPECIFICATION

Capacity: 6064cc
Cylinders: V12
Compression ratio: 10.5:1
Maximum power: 627bhp at 7400rpm
Maximum torque: 1250Nm at 2200-5500rpm
Gearbox: Manual, six-speed
Length: 4290mm
Width: 1820mm
Weight: 1137kg
0-60mph: 3.2 seconds
Maximum speed: 240mph

its performance – over half a million Pounds – and only 100 examples were built by the time production ended at the end of 1997.

The McLaren remains one of the world's ultimate supercars. Its sensible size, modest appearance, light weight, high performance, phenomenal handling and exquisite build quality remain unbeaten to this day. Indeed, it's unlikely there will ever be another car like it.

ABOVE Massive Brembo brakes help tame the F1's power

Mercedes-Benz SLR McLaren

2005 Germany/United Kingdom

IN 1995, MERCEDES-BENZ AND McLaren joined forces to create a formidable Formula 1 team. And just four years later, the partnership revealed the SLR Vision concept car. This stunning road-going machine finally went into production, with just some changes (and minus the 'Vision' name), in 2005.

The SLR's styling drew inspiration from the classic Mercedes SL coupe of the 1950s, as well as the recent McLaren-Mercedes Formula 1 cars. The forward-pivoting doors hinted at the SL's gullwing doors, while the pointed nose was a shameless nod to Formula 1 design. The long bonnet and the cabin pushed right back gave the range-topping Mercedes a traditionally aggressive and powerful appearance, which was refreshingly different to that of most mid-engined supercars.

The SLR monocoque was of strong but light carbonfibre, just like a Formula 1 car, and was built by McLaren in the UK. This material was about half the weight of steel for the same strength.

BELOW The SLR is an imposing car with its long bonnet and distinctive lines

HOW TO SPOT

Two-door coupe with very long bonnet with bulge narrowing towards nose. Forward-hinging doors and distinctive vents and strakes in front wings.

Under the long bonnet was an AMG-built V8 engine set well back in the car to give an almost 50:50 weight distribution front to rear – called a 'front mid-engine' configuration. The all-alloy power unit was supercharged and develops 626bhp, together with a hefty 780Nm of torque from as low as 3250rpm. In such a light-weight body, this was enough to give the SLR true supercar performance – the top speed was 207mph, and 0-60mph took a mere 3.8 seconds.

Yet the SLR was very different to most supercars. Being front-engined meant that it was much more practical than a mid-engined car. You got good all-round visibility, for starters; while the boot was large enough for two sets of golf clubs or enough luggage for two people to take a touring holiday.

The SLR was more of a super grand tourer than a racecar for the road. Inside, passengers were cosseted in high-quality leather seats and there were all the luxuries you'd expect of a top-class sports saloon. A neat feature was the engine-start button hidden under a flip-up lid on the gear selector knob. The transmission,

incidentally, was automatic.

The Mercedes-Benz SLR McLaren was an eye-catching car with its Batmobile-like styling, and performance to match. You wouldn't expect anything less from the pairing of two great companies.

ABOVE This cutout shows how far back the SLR's engine sits. You can also see the unusual doors

SPECIFICATION

Capacity: 5496cc

Cylinders: V8

Compression ratio: 8.8:1

Maximum power: 626bhp at 6500rpm

Maximum torque: 780Nm at 3250rpm

Gearbox: Five-speed automatic

Length: 4655mm

Width: 1907mm

Weight: 1692kg

0-60mph: 3.8 seconds

Maximum speed: 207mph

MG Metro 6R4
1984 United Kingdom

HOW TO SPOT

Metro body shape with massive, boxy front and rear wheel-arch extensions, deep sill extensions with large side air intakes above. Massive front and rear spoilers.

SOME CARS ARE SO SILLY YOU JUST have to love them. And the MG Metro 6R4 is right up there with the best. Surely only a British company could have the audacity to turn a mundane town car into an outrageous rally beast.

In the early 1980s, Group B rally cars were able to have very high levels of power, and in order to compete on the world stage, Austin-Rover had to come up with something very special.

The standard Austin Metro was as dull as they came, but there was very little of the standard car in the 6R4 (the name, incidentally, means six-cylinders; rear engine; four-wheel-drive). Out went the front-mounted A-series engine and in came a purpose-built V6 unit mounted amidships, where you'd normally find the back seats.

The 3-litre, all-alloy engine was developed with the help of Cosworth and had twin camshafts per cylinder head and four valves per cylinder. Unlike many of its competitors, it was not turbocharged, but even so it could be tuned to produce as much as 410bhp, although most pumped out between 250bhp and 380bhp. The power was fed to all four wheels via a five-speed gearbox and Ferguson-developed transmission system.

As impressive as the drivetrain was, it was the bodywork that really caught people's attention. Here was a car that was certainly not designed for its looks. The basic shape of the Metro remained – albeit largely formed from plastic – but was mostly hidden under huge plastic

BELOW A 6R4 doing what it does best at the 1985 RAC rally

wheel arch and sill extensions, needed to accommodate the wider track. Big front and rear spoilers helped to push the car onto the road at high speed.

Inside, the rear was completely given over to the engine, while the front seats were supportive race items with four-point harnesses. As you'd expect, there was no carpeting although, bizarrely, the standard Metro dash and door panels remained, while the steering wheel was from the Maestro.

SPECIFICATION

Capacity: 2991cc
Cylinders: V6
Compression ratio: 12.0:1
Maximum power: 410bhp at 6500rpm
Maximum torque: 362Nm at 6500rpm
Gearbox: Manual, five-speed
Length: 3350mm
Width: 1880mm
Weight: 1040kg
0-60mph: 4.3 seconds
Maximum speed: 155mph

It may have looked ridiculous, but the 6R4's performance was nothing to laugh about. Figures depended on engine specification and gearing, but the car could rocket to 60mph in as little as 4.3-seconds. Top speed could be as much as 155mph.

Sadly, the 6R4 never got a chance to prove itself on the rally circuit because, after a series of high-profile crashes, Group B competition was banned, and the age of wild rally cars came to an end. However, 6R4s have continued to compete in other events over the years and the engine went on to form the basis of the Jaguar XJ220, after the rights were bought by Tom Walkinshaws Racing.

ABOVE Coping with the mud at the 1986 RAC Rally

MG X-Power SV-R
2004 United Kingdom

HOW TO SPOT

Long, louvred bonnet, and further large louvres in each front wing. Large wheel-arch extensions, deep front spoiler and optional rear wing

IT WAS AN ODD THING FOR A struggling UK car company to do; buy a struggling Italian sports car design that was sold in the US and revamp it as a high-power supercar that wouldn't be sold in the USA.

Yet that is just what MG Rover did. The MG X-Power SV was based on the Qvale Mangusta, but heavily restyled and re-engineered as a pure sports car.

BELOW The SV-R is an MG like no other – wild to look at and wild to drive

It was an imposing car, the SV; long, low and wide, with air intakes and spoilers everywhere you looked. Pretty, it was not, but it certainly looked as if it meant business. The bodyshell was made of lightweight carbonfibre and enveloped a steel box-frame chassis. The shape was honed in a wind tunnel, while the traditional long bonnet gave away the fact that the engine was mounted at the front.

Actually, to be precise, the SV was 'front mid-engined'. In other words, the engine was set right back in the chassis to give a well-balanced weight distribution.

Two versions were produced; the standard 320bhp SV and the more powerful SV-R you see here, which developed a heady 385bhp.

The relatively simple American V8 engine had a capacity of 5-litres and relied on sheer size to develop its power, instead of bolt-on turbo- or superchargers. And with 510Nm of torque on-tap, it was a lazy, easy-to-live-with sort of power.

But floor the throttle, and all that power going through just the rear wheels was a far from lazy experience. Surprisingly, though, the SV-R was a well-balanced and light car to drive, with superb handling characteristics.

ABOVE The rear of the SV-R with the optional rear spoiler

The two-seater interior was fully finished in leather and Alcantara, with aluminium trim hinting at MG's heritage. Each car was hand-built to order, so customers could choose their own interior and exterior colours and finishes.

Sadly, as good as the SV-R was, it was not a sales success – at over £80,000 it was a lot of money for an MG – and it could be argued that the company made a mistake investing in such a niche-market product.

MG Rover went out of business in 2005, after producing only a handful of SVs. Those few cars that were built are testimony to an enthusiastic group of designers and engineers who let their hearts lead their heads to develop an exciting British supercar. And in that they certainly succeeded!

SPECIFICATION

Capacity: 4996cc

Cylinders: V8

Compression ratio: 11.4:1

Maximum power: 385bhp at 6000rpm

Maximum torque: 510Nm at 4750rpm

Gearbox: Manual, five-speed

Length: 4480mm

Width: 2670mm

Weight: 1500kg

0-60mph: 4.9 seconds

Maximum speed: 175mph

MINI Cooper S Works
2003 United Kingdom

THE COOPER NAME HAS BEEN inextricably linked with MINI since the original MINI Cooper was launched in 1961. In those early days, John Cooper uprated standard MINIs to make them even more fun to drive, and had some success racing his modified MINIs in the 1960s.

Before long, BMC realised the appeal of the Cooper name and began producing its own 'official' MINI Coopers, paying royal-ties for the use of the name. John Cooper, however, continued to develop his own tuning kits and, after the production MINI Cooper was discontinued in 1971, he kept producing his own upgrades for loyal enthusiasts.

When the new MINI was launched in 2001, parent company BMW again pro-duced a sporting version with the revered Cooper badge on the back. A more

powerful incarnation, the Cooper S, boasted a supercharged engine.

Sadly, John Cooper died before he could see this exciting new generation of MINIs, but his son Mike kept the company going, under the name John Cooper Works, and soon developed his own upgrades for the factory Cooper and Cooper S.

The Works tuning kit for the Cooper S produced a heady 210bhp, which was a worthwhile 40bhp more than standard. The extra power came courtesy of an uprated supercharger, tuned cylinder head, sports air intake and exhaust, and the ubiquitous engine-management upgrades.

In addition, John Cooper Works offered uprated brakes and suspension, 18-inch alloy wheels, and sports seats, not to mention tasteful body and interior upgrades.

The extra power transformed an already superb car. With 60mph coming up in just 6.6 seconds and a top speed of 143mph, the Cooper S Works was a seriously fast MINI and not a car to be taken lightly.

In 2005, BMW began to offer the Works kit as a factory option on brand-new MINIs and as a retrofit upgrade through its dealers, thus endorsing it as a fully approved performance package.

Any new MINI is great fun, the Cooper S especially so. Add the Works magic into the equation and you had one very special car, indeed. With sparkling performance, leach-like handling, cheeky looks and a well-appointed, comfortable interior; all at a sensible price. What more could you want? The MINI Cooper S Works really was an affordable supercar.

SPECIFICATION

Capacity: 1598cc

Cylinders: straight four

Compression ratio: 8.3:1

Maximum power: 210bhp at 6950rpm

Maximum torque: 245Nm at 4500rpm

Gearbox: Manual, six-speed. Optional Steptronic

Length: 3655mm

Width: 1688mm

Weight: 1140kg

0-60mph: 6.6 seconds

Maximum speed: 143mph

Mitsubishi Lancer Evolution IX

2006 Japan

THE 'EVO' AS WAS COMMONLY known, first appeared in 1992. It was initially an homologation special to enable Mitsubishi to enter the World Rally Championship's Group A class and the SCCA Pro Rally Championship. Based on the Lancer saloon car, the first Evos were only officially sold in Japan but some entered Europe as grey-market imports, until official imports to the UK started in 1998.

The first Evolution had a 2.0-litre engine that produced 244bhp and drove all four wheels through a five-speed gearbox. It was to set the trend for all future Evos – and there have been plenty! Over the years, the model was developed in tandem with the standard Lancer saloon and the power and handling improved as time went on;

BELOW The Evo may not be much to look at, but it knows how to perform!

HOW TO SPOT

Mid-sized four-door saloon with angular nose, offset front numberplate and bonnet scoop. Massive rear spoiler.

although the car's weight also increased. The name Evolution turned out to be very apt – this was a car that gradually evolved over time.

The Evolution IX of 2006 was the last of the line before an all-new model replaced it. By this time, the Evo boasted a six-speed gearbox, Super Active Yaw Control, an aluminium roof to save weight and a larger carbonfibre rear wing. The engine remained a 2.0-litre turbocharged unit but by now it produced 345bhp and 435Nm of torque, thanks to a number of improvements including – for the first time – variable valve control. In standard form this was enough to record the car to 60mph in 4.3 seconds and on to a top speed of 157mph.

However, the Evo was known for more than just its power: it was one of the best-handling saloon cars ever. This was thanks to its four-wheel-drive low centre of gravity, Bilstein dampers and yaw control There wasn't much that could beat an Evo from A to B on winding roads or track.

In 2005 Mitsubishi unveiled the Concept-X show car that hinted what the next-generation Evolution X may be like. While still obviously an Evo, it had a sleeker more modern body and was, once again, very much an evolution of the previous cars.

ABOVE The Evo's interior is typical of a Japanese saloon car

SPECIFICATION

Capacity: 1997cc
Cylinders: Straight four
Compression ratio: 8.8:1
Maximum power: 345bhp at 6800rpm
Maximum torque: 435Nm at 4600rpm
Gearbox: Manual, six-speed
Length: 4490mm
Width: 1770mm
Weight: 1400kg
0-60mph: 4.3 seconds
Maximum speed: 157mph

Morgan Aero Eight
2000 United Kingdom

HOW TO SPOT

Two-seater roadster with unusual mix of traditional and modern styling. External front and rear wings sweep back. Headlamps appear to point inwards towards streamlined Morgan grille.

MORGAN IS A TRADITIONAL BRITISH car manufacturer, based in the Malvern Hills. It's been producing its 4/4 model since 1936, so it was quite a shock when the company announced a brand-new model in 2000. And it was even more of a shock when the new car was unveiled!

The Aero 8 looked like no other Morgan; or, indeed, like any other car.

BELOW The Aero 8 is an odd but strangely elegant car

Designed with the aid of a wind tunnel, it had essentially the traditional Morgan shape, but smoothed and updated to ensure a better drag co-efficient. Perhaps the strangest thing about the Aero 8's appearance were its headlamps, which were swept back but also appeared to point inwards,

giving the car a cross-eyed look.

Morgans have traditionally been built on an ash frame, and the Aero 8 was no exception. However, the aluminium bodywork rode on a high-tech bonded aluminium chassis and the ash-work visible inside the cockpit was more for show.

The suspension, too, was a leap away from traditional Morgan technology, which relied on an antiquated sliding pillar system. The Aero 8 had, instead, a fully independent double wishbone set-up with race-quality joints. This, at last, was a Morgan that handled well.

And it needed to handle well, too, with 325bhp on tap. The power came, not from a Rover V8 like previous Morgans,

ABOVE The Aero 8's cockpit is an attractive mix of retro and modern. Note the exposed ashwork

but from a modern BMW 4.4-litre engine from the 5-series. This was linked to a modern six-speed Getrag gearbox driving the rear wheels. In a relatively lightweight car, the engine ensured good performance, with 60mph coming up in 4.7 seconds and on a top speed of 160mph.

Inside, occupants enjoyed a mix of traditional and modern. There was plenty of wood, aluminium and leather on show, of course, but you also benefited from electrically heated windows all round, a CD player, plus optional air-conditioning and satellite navigation. The luggage area, meanwhile, had room for a set of golf clubs.

The Morgan Aero 8 was a car people either loved or hated. But if you ignored its bizarre appearance, you had a truly great and unique motorcar.

SPECIFICATION

Capacity: 4398cc
Cylinders: V8
Compression ratio: 10.0:1
Maximum power: 325bhp at 6100rpm
Maximum torque: 330Nm at 360rpm
Gearbox: Six-speed manual
Length: 4120mm
Width: 1770mm
Weight: 1132kg
0-60mph: 4.7 seconds
Maximum speed: 160mph

Nissan 350Z
2003 Japan

HOW TO SPOT

Taut two-door coupe with small, curving side windows. Distinctively shaped front and rear lights with narrow vertical indicators on front quarters. Large rectangular front intake.

BELOW The 350Z draws inspiration from the 240Z of the 1960s, but updated for the 21st century

IN 1969 NISSAN – OR DATSUN AS IT was then known – introduced a fantastic sports coupe. Called the 240Z, it combined muscle-car looks and lively performance with Japanese affordability and reliability. It was the poor man's E-Type but, at the same time, a great car in its own right. Sadly, though, it didn't last. Sure, the Z range continued over the years with the 260Z, 280Z and 300Z, but these were bloated compared with the original and, in 1996, the Z range was dropped.

And then, in 2003, Nissan brought out the brand-new 350Z which returned to the original concept of the 240Z. The car's squat and compact looks were inspired by the 240Z (and, if we're honest, by Audi's TT)

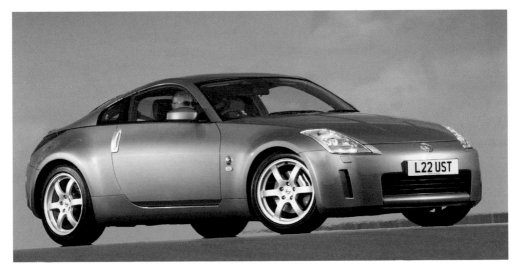

but brought bang up to date.

Like the original, the 350Z was front-engined, although Nissan preferred to call it 'front mid-ship'. In other words, the engine was located well-back under the bonnet to give near-perfect 53/47 weight distribution. The engine itself was an all-alloy 3.5-litre V8 unit that produced a useful 280bhp, going through a six-speed manual transmission to the back wheels. Performance figures were impressive, with a top speed of 155mph and a 0-60mph time of 5.9 seconds.

The suspension was race-car inspired, being an advanced multilink, fully independent system, with many

SPECIFICATION

Capacity: 3498cc
Cylinders: V6
Compression ratio: 10.3:1
Maximum power: 280bhp at 6200rpm
Maximum torque: 362Nm at 4800rpm
Gearbox: Manual, six-speed
Length: 4310mm
Width: 1815mm
Weight: 1547kg
0-60mph: 5.9 seconds
Maximum speed: 155mph

of the components made of aluminium to reduce unsprung weight. Braking, meanwhile, was courtesy of Brembo ABS- and EBD-equipped vented discs at each corner. Nissan's Vehicle Dynamic Control (VDC) stability control system was an option.

However, the 350Z was also a comfortable cruiser for two people, with a well-specified interior that included, unusually, a driver's seat which was shaped differently to the passenger's. and an instrument pod that moved in conjunction with the adjustable steering wheel.

The Nissan 350Z brought the legendary Z concept back to form and introduced it to a whole new generation of car enthusiasts.

ABOVE The 350Z's cockpit is a modern, comfortable place to be

Noble M14
2006 United Kingdom

NOT CONTENT WITH PRODUCING some of the world's best-handling cars for track enthusiasts, Lee Noble went on to take on the likes of the Porsche 911 Turbo and Ferrari F430, with his M14 supercar. This was a car for people who demand luxury and performance.

The M14 used a new steel spaceframe chassis that drew upon the success of the Noble M400 to ensure unsurpassed handling capabilities. It was shod in a distinctive glassfibre body (a carbonfibre version could follow) that had hints of Porsche and Ferrari about it, and boasted an

BELOW From behind, the M14 looks menacing and powerful

aggressiveness and presence that the M400 lacked.

Behind the seats sat a Ford-soured V6 engine with a capacity of 3.0-litres and this was fed by a pair of turbochargers to help create 400bhp of power that went, via a six-speed manual gearbox, to the back wheels. It was enough to give true supercar performance, with a top speed of 190mph and a 0-60mph time of 4.3 seconds, while at the same giving enough tractability to be easy to drive in traffic.

Previous Nobles were criticised by the quality of their interiors – something that was of no real consequence to track enthusiasts. For the M14 market, though, a luxurious cockpit was demanded, so Noble went all out to create just that. The seats were specially made with carbonfibre frames and covered with high-quality Italian leather (as used by Ferrari). The same leather could also be found on the door panels and dashboard. All the instruments and controls

SPECIFICATION

Capacity: 2968cc

Cylinders: V6

Compression ratio: 8.5:1

Maximum power: 400bhp at 6100rpm

Maximum torque: 522Nm at 4750rpm

Gearbox: Six-speed manual

Length: 4267mm

Width: 1935mm

Weight: 1100kg

0-60mph: 4.3 seconds

Maximum speed: 190mph

were easy to use, with some of the most frequently required buttons being located on the steering wheel itself.

The M14 was also practical, with plenty of room for two people to sit in comfort, and a decent amount of luggage space in compartments at the front and rear of the car.

Noble, with its stunning M14, is single-handedly reinventing the British supercar industry. And that can only be a good thing. This is a company with a very exciting future ahead of it.

ABOVE The M14 takes Noble into true supercar territory

Pagani Zonda C12 F
2005 Italy

THE PAGANI ZONDA C12 FIRST appeared in 1999 and was the brain-child of Argentinean-born Horacio Pagani, who had previously worked at Lamborghini in Italy before setting up his own engineering company in that country.

The Zonda was a striking car with lines inspired – we're told – by the curves of Mrs Pagani's body! The beautifully

shaped car, with its taut lines, simply oozes power and is hand-built from light-weight carbonfibre. The shape is designed – not only to look good – but also to push the car down onto the road at high speeds to ensure stability.

The Zonda C12 F first appeared in 2005, and the suffix stood for Fangio – Pagani was close friends with the leg-endary racing driver, who helped with the

Stunning two-seater coupe with thrust-forward cabin. Very curvaceous front wings with six protruding projector headlamps. Long rear deck with separate spoiler. Four exhaust tailpipes grouped together in central outlet.

ABOVE Inside, the Pagani appears to have come from the past, with a bizarre but endearing retro look

design of the car. The F was a development of the original C12 and was lighter in weight and had a more powerful engine – in short, it was an even faster car.

Hidden under that long rear deck was a 7.3-litre V12 Mercedes-Benz engine that was a work of art in itself to look at. The engine produced 620bhp – 70bhp more than the standard Zonda C12 – which gave the supercar a top speed of 214mph, while it could reach 60mph in just 3.6 seconds.

Inside, the Zonda F was even more striking. There was hardly any plastic to be seen; just leather, aluminium, wood and carbonfibre, all lovingly hand-crafted to create one of the most incredible cockpits ever. Especially wonderful were the alloy dials which hada retro look about them.

The Zonda C12 F was also available in Clubsport form, which was even lighter and faster, with a 650bhp engine. This version of the car had an incredible power-to-weight ratio of 521bhp/ton.

Pagani invested in a new factory in the early 21st Century to increase production of the Zonda from around 25 cars a year to 250. It will be on sale in the USA for the first time from 2007. Even these figures are tiny on a worldwide scale, though, so ownership of a Pagani Zonda will remain very exclusive.

SPECIFICATION

Capacity: 7291cc
Cylinders: V12
Compression ratio: n/a
Maximum power: 620bhp at 6150rpm
Maximum torque: 400Nm at 4000rpm
Gearbox: Six-speed manual
Length: 4435mm
Width: 2055mm
Weight: 1234kg
0-60mph: 3.6 seconds
Maximum speed: 214mph

Panoz Esperante
2001 United States

HOW TO SPOT

Sleek open-topped two seater with long bulging bonnet, swept-back headlamps and straked vents in front wings.

AT FIRST SIGHT, YOU'D BE MISTAKEN for thinking that the Esperante was a traditional, low-volume British sports car, with its long bonnet and understated looks. However, it was designed and built in the USA, by one of the country's only low-volume car manufacturers – Panoz.

BELOW The Esperante looks more European than American

The Esperante was the brainchild of Daniel Panez, who started his company in 1989 and went on to become well-known for his involvement in US motorsport, in particular ALMS.

The Panez Esperante first appeared in 2001 and was more hi-tech than its looks

suggested, with a bonded aluminium chassis under aluminium and carbonfibre body panels to keep the weight down. Although the Esperante had a folding roof, there was also a GT version with a sleek fixed lid.

The engine was front-mounted, but positioned well back to give a good front to rear weight distribution. It was a 4.6-litre Ford V8 all-alloy unit with four valves per cylinder that produced 320bhp, which led through a five-speed gearbox to the rear wheels.

Inside, the Esperante had a luxurious feel, with plenty of hand-finished leather and wood covering the seats and dash

SPECIFICATION

Capacity: 4601cc
Cylinders: V8
Compression ratio: 9.8:1
Maximum power: 320bhp at 6000rpm
Maximum torque: 430Nm at 4750rpm
Gearbox: Manual, five-speed
Length: 4478mm
Width: 1859mm
Weight: 1451kg
0-60mph: 5.1 seconds
Maximum speed: 155mph

areas. Unusually, the instrument pod was mounted in the centre of the dashboard, instead of in front of the driver.

The Esperante offered lively performance, with a 0-60mph time of 5.1 seconds and a top speed of 155mph. However, Panoz developed a faster version in the form of the GTLM, which boasted a supercharged engine that developed 420bhp and rocketed the car to 60mph in 4.2 seconds and on to 180mph. Beyond that, there was also the GTS racecar which had lightweight plastic panels and a 5.8-litre, 430bhp engine. The GTS proved popular as an affordable racecar and was also adopted by some US racing schools.

The Panoz Esperante offered discerning American buyers a unique and exciting alternative to similarly priced sports cars from larger manufacturers on both sides of the Atlantic.

ABOVE The leather-trimmed cockpit is unusual in that the instruments are mounted centrally

Porsche 911 Carrera 2.7 RS
1973 Germany

TODAY, THE CARRERA 2.7 RS IS, quite simply, the most sought-after production 911 ever. It's reached almost legendary status among Porsche aficionados, and prices are sky-high.

Yet this oh-so-perfect sports car almost never happened. The RS was developed as a homologation special to allow Porsche to compete in GT racing – the company was required to build 500 road-going cars in order to qualify. However, the marketing department doubted whether they

could persuade people to pay a premium for a 911 with few creature comforts. Thankfully, they were overruled.

The car was developed from the 911S but was significantly modified to improve performance. The 2.4S engine was increased in capacity to 2681cc to push power to 210bhp at 6300rpm and torque to 255Nm at 5100rpm – a useful increase over the 911S's 190bhp.

However, the main performance gains were made by putting the car on a weight-

BELOW The 2.7RS is one of the most sought-after Porsches ever built

ABOVE The rear of the RS is defined by the classic ducktail spoiler

Classic 911 body-shape, often with bold 'Carrera' side decals and colour-coded wheels. 'Ducktail' rear spoiler with 'Carrera RS' and '2.7' badging.

saving programme. The roof, wings and bonnet were made of thinner (and so lighter) steel, while the windscreen and rear quarter windows used thinner glass.

The rear arches were flared to accommodate wider Fuchs alloy wheels, and there was the option (which most buyers took) of a distinctive 'ducktail' spoiler to give added downforce.

Also optional were large and distinctive 'Carrera' side stripes that ran from the front to rear arches. Offered in red, blue, black or green, you could have the Fuchs wheel centres colour-coded to match. Combined with distinctive Grand Prix White paintwork, this gave what is now recognised as the classic, and much imitated, RS look.

The Carrera RS was produced in two road-going versions. The RS Sport (often called Lightweight) had a very basic specification to keep the weight down to just 975kg. However, not everyone wanted to rough it, which is why Porsche also made the more popular RS Touring model, with a fully specced interior.

A total of 1580 RS cars were built. Of these, the majority were Tourings and 200

were Sports. There were also 17 in the very basic RSH homologation specification, and 55 were race-ready RSRs. The latter boasted a rollcage, even wider rear arches and a 2.8-litre engine that produced 300bhp.

Today the Carrera RS is the Holy Grail of Porsches, and good genuine ones are extremely sought-after, leading to a healthy business in replicas, based on contemporary 911s.

SPECIFICATION

Capacity: 2687cc
Cylinders: flat-six
Compression ratio: 8.5:1
Maximum power: 210bhp at 6300rpm
Maximum torque: 255Nm at 5100rpm
Gearbox: Manual, five-speed
Length: 4163mm
Width: 1610mm
Weight: 1975kg (Sport)
0-60mph: 5.6 seconds
Maximum speed: 153mph

THE LITTLE BOOK OF FAST CARS | 105

Porsche 911 Turbo
1975 Germany

HOW TO SPOT

Distinctive 911 body shape endowed with wide front and rear arches, massive 'teatray' rear spoiler, and full-width rear reflector announcing the word 'Porsche'

IN 1974, PORSCHE ANNOUNCED A car that would take the motoring world by storm and go on to become a legend in its own right.

That car was the 911 Turbo and, bizarre as it seems today, was originally planned as a limited-edition run of 500 cars with a stripped out, race-inspired interior. Thankfully, though, interest was so great that Porsche decided to built the car as an

BELOW The Turbo had wider front and rear wings than the standard 911. This is a 1975 car

on-going, luxury model at the top of the 911 range.

Mounted at the back of the new Porsche was a 2994cc flat-six engine with a secret weapon – a single KKK turbocharger which was powered by the exhaust gases from both cylinder banks. Spinning at up to 100,000rpm, the turbo helped create a maximum power output of 260bhp at 5500rpm – an astonishing

amount in the mid-1970s when turbocharged road-going cars were still a novelty. By comparison, the standard 911 Carrera 3.0 of the day produced 200bhp.

The bodyshell was based on that of the contemporary 911 but fitted with much-extended wheel arches front and rear that gave the Turbo its distinctive aggressive appearance. The whaletail rear spoiler may have debuted on the earlier 911 3.0 RS, but it soon became inextricably linked to the 911 Turbo.

Surprisingly, perhaps, the 911 Turbo was equipped with a four-speed gearbox – Porsche claimed that the five-gear 915 unit used in the standard 911 wouldn't cope with the extra power

and, besides, the engine's power and torque were such that four gears were all that were required.

To fill those massive arches, the Turbo was equipped with 15-inch Fuchs alloy wheels, which were 7-inches wide at the front and 8-inches wide at the rear.

The 911 Turbo developed steadily over the years, gaining more power as it went along. In 1993 it gained four-wheel-drive and a twin-turbocharged 3.6-litre engine that produced a healthy 408bhp. In 2000 it was replaced by an all-new version with a watercooled engine.

It may have seemed mad producing a gas-guzzling supercar in the middle of the 1970s' fuel shortages, but it paid off and the 911 Turbo was a great success, and went on to become a motoring legend in its own right. It's become the definitive Porsche, its distinctive shape has graced many a poster and its always been the car that other manufacturers have used as a benchmark.

ABOVE The rear of the early Turbo had the trademark whaletail spoiler

SPECIFICATION

Capacity: 2994cc
Cylinders: flat-six
Compression ratio: 6.5:1
Maximum power: 260bhp at 5500rpm
Maximum torque: 343Nm at 4000rpm
Gearbox: Four-speed manual
Length: 4491mm
Width: 1775mm
Weight: 1195kg
0-60mph: 6.4 sec
Maximum speed: 152mph

Porsche 924 Carrera GT
1980 Germany

THE 924 WAS PORSCHE'S ENTRY-level car, introduced in 1976. Its smooth lines and practical two-plus-two hatchback configuration made it a great sales success, but the lacklustre performance from the 2-litre, 125bhp engine was never going to set the world on fire.

That, though, was all to change in 1980 when Porsche put the 924 on steroids and unveiled the mad 924 Carrera GT. Designed as an homologation special for the FISA Group 3 production sports car

class, just 400 were built, with 75 right-hand-drive examples coming to the UK.

The 2-litre engine was developed from the 924 Turbo, and a larger turbocharger plus other enhancements pushed the power output to 210bhp – no one could accuse this 924 of being underpowered. The transmission, suspension and brakes were all uprated to cope with the increased power.

All this, though, was overshadowed by what Porsche did to the 924's delicate and

smooth lines. Polyurethane front and rear wheel arch extensions suddenly gave the petite 924 an aggressive and businesslike appearance. An impression that was enhanced by air intakes in the nose plus a massive bonnet scoop; the latter accommodating the turbo's intercooler. However you looked at it, there was no doubt that the 924 Carrera GT meant business.

The GT was available only in black, red or silver, while the interiors were all black with red-pinstripe fabric on the seat centres.

Driving the Carrera GT took some getting used to. The big turbocharger took time to spool up, so there was a distinct lag between pressing the accelerator and something happening. But when it finally happened, you knew about it!

Porsche went on to produce the Carrera GTS in 1981, which was even more extreme. Glassfibre body panels and a lack of sound insulation made it a full 60kg lighter than the GT. That, combined with a power output of 245bhp, made the GTS a seriously fast car, reaching 60mph

in 6.2 seconds and going on to a top speed of 155mph. It can be distinguished from the GT by its fixed, recessed headlamps.

The 924 Carrera GT is a rare car, but its styling went on to be the inspiration for the mainstream 944 which replaced the 924. This had the same bulging wheel arches, albeit better integrated with the surrounding bodywork.

ABOVE The GT's rear arches were stuck-on plastic items

SPECIFICATION

Capacity: 1984cc
Cylinders: straight-four
Compression ratio: 8.5:1
Maximum power: 210bhp at 6000rpm
Maximum torque: 280Nm at 3500rpm
Gearbox: Five-speed manual
Length: 4212mm
Width: 1755mm
Weight: 1180kg
0-60mph: 6.7 sec
Maximum speed: 150mph

Porsche 959
1986 Germany

HOW TO SPOT

Sleek two-plus-two bodyshell with swept-back headlamps, flared wheel-arches with air vents in the rears, and large rear spoiler.

DEVELOPED AS AN HOMOLOGATION special to enable Porsche to compete in Gruppe B motorsport, the 959 was one of the most technologically advanced – and fastest – cars ever built.

Based on a 911, the 959 had carbonfibre body panels, sophisticated four-wheel-drive, six-speed gearbox, active suspension, magnesium-alloy wheels with tyre-pressure sensors, run-flat tyres, and stunningly styled lines.

At the rear of the car was a twin turbocharged engine. This was a four-valve per cylinder, hybrid air- and water-cooled unit based on the 2.65-litre engine developed for the 956 and 962 race cars. For the 959, the capacity was increased to 2.85-litres.

The sequential twin-turbocharger system was developed to overcome, to a large extent, the marked turbo-lag that was a characteristic of the 911 Turbo of the day. At low revs all the exhaust gases powered the right-hand turbocharger to give a light boost. Once the revs started to climb the left-hand blower started to kick in, powered by that side's exhaust, to give the full 450bhp. So you still got a distinct turbo 'kick' but not at the expense of low-speed driveability.

But perhaps the greatest innovation of the 959 was its drivetrain. It was the first ever Porsche – not to mention the first true sports car – to feature four-wheel-drive. Power from the rear-mounted engine went through a six-speed gearbox with a transaxle driving the rear wheels, while a propshaft led forward to a second differential driving the front wheels. The power split between the front and rear axles was varied, either automatically or manually, to suit the driving conditions.

BELOW The 959 still looks modern today

ABOVE The 959's lines were positively space age compared to the standard 911

The suspension, too, could be adjusted in height and firmness, so that the car sat lower at high-speeds, or with increased ground clearance for negotiating rough surfaces.

SPECIFICATION

Capacity: 2847cc

Cylinders: flat-six

Compression ratio: 8.3:1

Maximum power: 450bhp at 6500rpm

Maximum torque: 500Nm at 5500rpm

Gearbox: Manual, six-speed

Length: 4260mm

Width: 1840mm

Weight: 1650kg

0-60mph: 3.6 seconds

Maximum speed: 197mph

All this technology was clad in a body based on the galvanised-steel shell of the contemporary 911 Turbo. However, the doors and front luggage-compartment lid were lightweight aluminium, while most of the remaining panels are made from Kevlar and carbonfibre.

Two specifications were offered, and the vast majority of cars were built to what Porsche called Confort (yes, that's the correct spelling) specification. A handful were Sport models that were stripped of variable ride height, central-locking, electric windows and seats, air-conditioning and a passenger-side door mirror, to save 100kg in weight.

It is believed that just 292 road-going 959s were built, making it a rare and sought-after machine.

Porsche 928 GTS
1992 Germany

HOW TO SPOT

Large, very rounded two-door coupe with extended wheel arches, exposed pop-up headlamps and full-width rear reflector.

THE PORSCHE 928 DATES RIGHT back to 1978 and it was developed to replace the legendary 911, but it never did. It was a quite different car, with a large, water-cooled V8 engine mounted at the front, driving the back wheels via a rear-mounted gearbox, to give an even weight distribution.

The 928 was a large car and boasted spaceship-like lines that seemed very futuristic in the mid-1970s, with exposed pop-up headlamps and lots of glass, including a lifting hatchback to give access to the luggage area.

It was the same story inside, with a luxurious and modern interior that boasted an instrument pod that moved in conjunction with the steering column. The back seats cocooned small children in comfort, while in the front there was

BELOW The GTS was the ultimate incarnation of the 928 and still looks modern today

plenty of space for two adults to stretch out and enjoy long journeys.

Over the years, the 928 evolved into the last and best version – the GTS of 1992. This had a 5.3-litre, 32-valve V8 engine that produced 350bhp (by contrast, the first 928 had 240bhp). With a 0-60mph time of 5.6 seconds and a top speed of 171mph, this truly was a supercar. Also, unlike most earlier 928s, the GTS had a five-speed manual gearbox, not an automatic, to make the best use of the power, while the suspension was firmer to improve the handling.

The GTS also had restyled bodywork that dragged the 928 into the 1990s and gave it a more aggressive appearance.

ABOVE The 928 had a front-mounted V8 engine linked to a gearbox at the rear for perfect weight distribution

SPECIFICATION

Capacity: 5397cc
Cylinders: V8
Compression ratio: 10.4:1
Maximum power: 350bhp at 5700rpm
Maximum torque: 491Nm at 4250rpm
Gearbox: Five-speed manual
Length: 4519mm
Width: 1849mm
Weight: 1600kg
0-60mph: 5.6 seconds
Maximum speed: 171mph

The wings bulged purposefully to accommodate wider wheels, the front and rear ends were updated with smoother lines and, at the rear was a large, body-coloured spoiler in place of the earlier cars' rubber item.

The interior was fundamentally unchanged from that of earlier 928s, but was treated to full leather trim and equipment updates to ensure it still looked modern. It was a wonderful place in which to be transported in speed and style across continents.

The 928 was quietly discontinued in 1995, while the 911 – which it was meant to replace – has gone from strength to strength. However, the 928 – especially in GTS guise – was a great car in its own right, and its space-age lines still look modern today. There aren't many cars from the 1970s you can say that about!

Porsche 911 Turbo S
2004 Germany

BY THE START OF THE 21ST CENTURY, the 911 Turbo had developed into what many regarded as the best sports car in the world. It's power, handling, practicality and durability were all hard to beat. Four-wheel-drive and electronic driver aids had tamed the older Turbo's sometimes wayward handling, while a twin-turbocharged, water-cooled engine – still mounted at the back – gave almost seamless power delivery, with only a hint of the old turbo lag.

However, in 2004, Porsche produced an even better version – the 911 Turbo S. This last of the 996-model Turbos had an output of 450bhp, thanks to a 30bhp power upgrade that had previously been offered as an option to buyers of the standard Turbo. The upgrade consisted of larger KKK turbochargers, uprated intercoolers and a revised engine management system. As well as the extra power (which peaked at just 5700rpm), the torque was increased from 560Nm to no less than 620Nm, which was available from 3500 to 4500rpm.

Wide rear arches with large air intakes in each side, three massive front air intakes, fixed rear spoiler with extendable section.

To keep this power in check, the Turbo S was fitted with Porsche's ceramic brake discs. Made from carbon-reinforced silicon carbide, these were gripped by six-piston calipers that had a distinctive yellow finish. The advantage of these brakes, said Porsche, was that they were lighter, more responsive, performed better in the wet and would last for over 150,000 miles.

Visually, the Turbo S was identical to the standard 911 Turbo, but the 18-inch alloys were finished in GT Metallic Silver – a shade that was used on the bodywork of the Carrera GT supercar – with coloured Porsche crests in the centres.

Inside, there were one or two more changes. The 'Turbo S' logo appeared on the door sills, centre console tachometer. The instruments themselves had a unique aluminium finish, while the leather of the seat centres, steering wheel rim, gearlever and handbrake lever have a special embossed finish. Standard equipment for the Turbo S included sat-nav, six-CD changer and cruise control.

In creating the Turbo S, Porsche proved that even it could make the best even better.

ABOVE From behind you can see the Turbo's wider rear arches and fixed rear spoiler

SPECIFICATION

Capacity: 3600cc

Cylinders: flat-six

Compression ratio: 9.4:1

Maximum power: 450bhp at 5000rpm

Maximum torque: 620Nm at 3500 to 4400rpm

Gearbox: Six-speed manual or optional Tiptronic

Length: 4435mm

Width: 1830mm

Weight: 1590kg (coupé)

0-60mph: 4.0 seconds

Maximum speed: 191mph

Porsche Carrera GT
2003 Germany

When Porsche decided to produce a range-topping supercar, it didn't hold back. The exciting Carrera GT was, in many ways, a road-going race car that utilised space-age technology.

For instance, it was the world's first production car to use a carbon-reinforced plastic chassis. This offered a substantial weight-saving over metal, while much of the car's bodywork was also lightweight carbonfibre and Kevlar; as were the seats. All this meant that the Carrera GT weighed in at just 1380kg.

Saving weight means better performance, which is extra-good news when you consider that the GT's mid-mounted V10 engine produced 610bhp – a fact which is even more impressive when you learn that it was a normally aspirated (in other words, not turbocharged or supercharged).

That power drove the rear wheels only (to enhance the race-car feel) via a six-speed gearbox and – another world first – a ceramic clutch. This remarkable innovation was lightweight and only 169mm in diameter, yet could more than cope with the phenomenal

HOW TO SPOT

Sleek two-seater, mid-engined roadster with projector headlamps, massive side air-intakes, twin humps behind the seats, with V10 engine visible under.

forces involved; and it would outlast a conventional clutch.

The massive 340mm brake discs were also ceramic, rather than steel, which meant they could better cope with high temperatures and, again, were lighter and longer-lasting than conventional discs.

The Carrera GT had a relatively simple, two-seat, carbonfibre-trimmed cockpit which reflected its racing pedigree. Indeed, the birch-wood gearknob harked back to the golden days of motorsport. The driving position was perfect, with the gearstick and other controls all close at hand, while the leather-clad bucket seats offered excellent support during high-speed cornering.

Although an open-top car, the Carrera GT came with a Targa-type roof system comprising of a pair of lightweight carbonfibre shells, which could be stored in the luggage compartment when not in use.

The shape of the Carrera GT was stunning, but it was also functional. Like a race car, it was designed to create downforce to hold the car onto the road at high speed. At its maximum speed of 205mph, the GT developed a downforce of 4000

Newtons, which was the equivalent of a load of 400kg pushing down on the rear axle. Furthermore, the car's carbonfibre undertrays created a suction effect that further helped to hold it onto the road.

ABOVE The mid-mounted engine sits under those twin humps

SPECIFICATION

Capacity: 5.7-litre
Cylinders: V10
Compression ratio: 12.0:1
Maximum power: 612bhp at 8000rpm
Maximum torque: 590Nm at 5750rpm
Gearbox: Manual, six-speed
Length: 4610mm
Width: 1920mm
Weight: 1380kg
0-60mph: 3.6 seconds
Maximum speed: 205mph

Subaru Impreza WRX STi

1993 Japan

THE SUBARU IMPREZA WRX BECAME the performance car of choice for a generation. And for good reason, too; it won the World Rally Championship three years running in 1996, 1996 and 1997; thanks in no small part to the driving abilities of Colin McRae and the late Richard Burns. Skills which millions have tried to emulate on exciting computer games featuring the Impreza.

It's this heritage that's made the Impreza, especially in WRX form, such an icon; plus its astonishing performance and value for money. Its success was

HOW TO SPOT

Mid-sized four-door saloon with prominent wheelarch extensions, large bonnet scoop and massive rear spoiler. Gold-finished alloy wheels.

certainly not down to its looks; a more unlikely-looking sports car there has never been. Essentially a boxy four-door saloon, the Impreza was endowed with big wheel arches, bonnet scoop and prominent rear wing, just like the rally car. And a trademark feature was gold-painted wheels. Subtle it was not.

The performance was far from subtle, either. Powered by a turbocharged, flat-four (essentially the same configuration as an old VW Beetle) 2.0-litre engine, the WRX (in 2005 form) had 265bhp on tap. The unusual engine configuration ensured a low centre of gravity which, in part, was responsible for the car's excellent handling; both on the road and on the rally track.

The power was fed to all four wheels to ensure optimum traction and handling, so 60mph was reached in a mere 5.5 seconds, and the WRX went on to a top speed of 152mph. Not bad for a four-seater saloon costing around £25,000, and coming from a company that was better known for its staid four-wheel-drive estate cars!

The Subaru rally cars were prepared by UK-based Prodrive and, over the years, this motorsport company has given its name to some limited-edition road-going Imprezas. These had more powerful engines, revised suspension and brakes, modified bodywork and interiors, and special badging.

The original Impreza was replaced by a revised model in 2000, but has remained essentially the same car throughout its life, retaining the original mechanical configuration and boy-racer looks. After all, that is the appeal of the WRX.

SPECIFICATION

Capacity: 1994cc

Cylinders: Flat-four

Compression ratio: 8.0:1

Maximum power: 265bhp at 6000rpm

Maximum torque: 343Nm at 4000rpm

Gearbox: Six-speed manual

Length: 4415mm

Width: 1740mm

Weight: 1475

0-60mph: 5.5 seconds

Maximum speed: 152mph

TVR Cerbera Speed 12

1999 United Kingdom

IT'S NOT OFTEN THAT A manufacturer develops a car and then decides not to sell it to the public because it's just too powerful. Yet that is what happened with the TVR Cerbera Speed 12. Company boss, Peter Wheeler, wanted to produce a car that would beat the McLaren F1. And, while the F1 relied on high-technology, the Speed 12 drew on good old-fashioned brute power.

And what power it was! The TVR-developed V12 engine (basically two V6 units joined together) had a capacity of 7.7-litres and produced no less than 800bhp without the aid of turbochargers or superchargers. The engine was linked to a six-speed manual gearbox

BELOW The Speed 12 looks outrageous from any angle. Look at those side-mounted exhausts

Low and wide curvaceous coupe with four angled projector headlamps, large sill extensions, jutting out rear bumper and large rear spoiler.

ABOVE The Speed 12's interior is not as slick as the outside, but is stripped right down to keep weight to a minimum

driving the rear wheels. Legend had it that the unit broke a dynometer during testing because it was so powerful.

Despite the stupendous power, TVR still ensured that the Speed 12 was extremely light in weight. A carbonfibre bodyshell sat atop tubular-steel and aluminium honeycomb chassis and the entire car weighed just over 1000kg.

In true TVR tradition, the body looked as outrageous as the car's specification, with long, low and wide lines, and a chopped roofline that gave the Speed 12 a mean and aggressive appearance. Inside was a different story, though, with the cockpit being simple and austere, like a racecar, in an effort to keep the weight down.

A handful of race-ready Speed 12s were built and tested on track. TVR claimed that the car could reach speeds of around 240mph and would hit 60mph in just 3.2 seconds. Figures that put the Blackpool beast on a par with the legendary McLaren F1.

Orders were taken for the £160,000 machine but, after Peter Wheeler drove it, he decided that 800bhp in such a light-weight car was simply too dangerous and the programme was cancelled. However, one lucky customer in the UK did, in fact, buy a road-going Speed 12, and this has made guest appearances at supercar events around the country.

As it is, though, the TVR Cerbera Speed 12 remains one of the greatest supercars never to be put into production.

SPECIFICATION

Capacity: 7736cc
Cylinders: V12
Compression ratio: 12.5:1
Maximum power: 800bhp at 7250rpm
Maximum torque: 881Nm at 5750rpm
Gearbox: Manual, six-speed
Length: n/a
Width: n/a
Weight: 1070kg
0-60mph: 3.2 seconds
Maximum speed: 240mph

Ultima GTR
1999 United Kingdom

HOW TO SPOT

Two-seater coupe with very low front end between bulging wings. Bulbous cabin with curved windscreen and roof-mounted air intake. Large rear spoiler.

BELOW The Ultima is one of the fastest cars around – and it looks it!

IN 2005, WHAT WAS ESSENTIALLY A kit car broke the world record for the fastest accelerating car, reaching 60mph in just 2.7 seconds. It also set a new record in reaching 100mph in an incredible 5.8 seconds. And then went on to break a third record by accelerating from standstill to 100mph and then braking back to standstill in 9.8 seconds. These figures were better than anything achieved by such exotica as the Ferrari Enzo and McLaren F1.

The Ultima story dates back to 1983 when Lee Noble (later to produce the Noble cars) built the Ultima MkI with a mid-mounted Ford V6 engine and looks based on a Le Mans racecar. Over the years, the component car developed and a Chevrolet V8 engine became a popular power source. Interestingly, in 1991 McLaren bought two Ultima MkII kits to use in the development of its F1 supercar. A year later, Lee Noble sold the company to one of his customers, but the Ultima continued to be developed, resulting in the GTR which first appeared in 1999.

The all-new GTR took build quality to new levels and featured a lightweight tubular-steel spaceframe chassis with

SPECIFICATION

Capacity: 6300cc
Cylinders: V8
Compression ratio: n/a
Maximum power: 534bhp
Maximum torque: 716Nm
Gearbox: Five-speed manual
Length: 4000mm
Width: 1850mm
Weight: 990kg
0-60mph: 2.7 seconds
Maximum speed: 231mph

integral rollcage. Over this went the unstressed glassfibre bodyshell with its compact and distinctive racecar styling.

The mid-mounted engine was a specially built Chevrolet V8 unit linked to a Porsche gearbox and transaxle, driving the rear wheels. Power depended on what you specified, but could be as much as 534bhp which, combined with a body that weighed less than 1000kg, accounted for the phenomenal acceleration. The fully independent suspension was racecar-developed, with double unequal-length wishbones and fully adjustable dampers.

As always, the Ultima was offered either as a complete, ready to drive car, or in component form for self-build. Fully built, it was about the same price as a standard Porsche 911; but with the performance of a car costing much more. Build it yourself and you ended up with the same performance for even less money. How satisfying would that be?

ABOVE The Ultima exposed! No wonder the car is so light – there's really not much to it

Vector WX-3
1992 United States

HOW TO SPOT

Wide and low mid-engined coupe with narrow nose, very deep sills, large side air intakes and long rear deck with louvres over.

BELOW The Vector WX-3 was a striking car which, sadly, was doomed to failure

THE VECTOR CAR COMPANY NEVER quite made it, despite the best efforts of company boss, Gerald Wiegart. The American built his first Vector, the W2, in 1978 as a concept car which late went into (very) limited production in the early 1980s. In 1991 the mid-engined supercar evolved into the W8, which was a 200mph-plus machine powered by a 600bhp V8 engine. Just 17 examples were sold.

This was replaced by the WX-3, which was Wiegert's dream car. Based on the W8, it was powered by the same Chevrolet V8 engine, driving the rear wheels through an automatic gearbox. The turbocharged unit produced 600bhp of power, and Weigert claimed

that his car was capable of 250mph.

The striking bodywork was made of lightweight Kevlar and carbonfibre, and was mounted on a tubular steel and aluminium chassis with integral rollcage.

Inside, the WX-3's cockpit was more like that of an aircraft than a car. The instrumentation was all electronic and the driver was faced with an impressive mass of controls. Unusually, the car seated three people in a row.

In 1993, Vector was bought out by an Indonesian company called Megatech which, at the time, also owned Lamborghini. Weigert was offered a position as a designer, but turned it down and retained the rights to the W8 and WX-3

ABOVE The WX-3 had a hi-tech dashboard and was very modern for its time

cars, which meant that the latter never went into production.

Under Megatech's control, Vector produced the M12, which was an evolution of the WX-3 but powered by a Lamborghini engine and developed in Europe. Only 14 cars were built before the company ran into financial difficulties. Later, a similar car was built and powered by an American Corvette engine. This was called the SRV8 but, again, never made it into production.

Gerald Weigert regained control of the Vector name but, to date, no more cars have been built. Which is a shame because the concept cars, although flawed, showed great potential and, if nothing else, were exciting machines to behold.

SPECIFICATION

Capacity: 5998cc

Cylinders: V8

Compression ratio: n/a

Maximum power: 600bhp at 5700rpm

Maximum torque: 813Nm at 4900rpm

Gearbox: Automatic, three-speed

Length: 4368mm

Width: 1930mm

Weight: 1620kg

0-60mph: 3.3 seconds

Maximum speed: 250mph

Also available

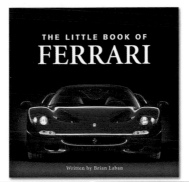

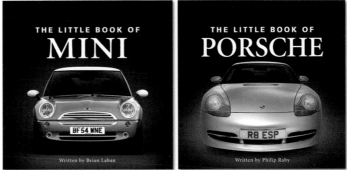

Available from all major stockists or online at:
www.greenumbrellashop.co.uk